Trauma in the Lives
of Children

ABOUT THE AUTHOR

Kendall Johnson was born in Pomona, California, in 1945, the son of a college professor and an elementary school teacher. After completing high school he worked as a firefighter for the U.S. Forest Service and served for a time with the U.S. Navy in Vietnam. Upon his return he started work as a psychiatric technician, married, and resumed college studies. Over the next ten years, he obtained master's degrees in philosophy, counseling, and education, and a doctoral degree in clinical psychology.

Dr. Johnson's publications include papers and books on trauma and crisis management. After receiving training in Critical Incident Stress Debriefing, he adapted the techniques for a school setting. This became the subject of a booklet published in 1987 titled *Classroom Crisis: A Readi-Reference Guide.* Later titles include this book, *School Crisis Management: A Hands-On Guide to Training Crisis Response Teams,* and *Turning Yourself Around: Self-Help Strategies for Troubled Teens.* Dr. Johnson's postcrisis workbook series for use by school psychologists is in preparation by Hunter House, Inc., and he is currently completing a book on using activities in the classroom following crisis and disaster.

Currently, Dr. Johnson is a mentor teacher in a school for troubled teens and maintains a private practice as a family therapist. He regularly delivers seminars on crisis management, the effects of trauma on children, and teacher trauma and self-care to school personnel, mental health professionals, and emergency care givers. He is an adjunct faculty member of the California Specialized Training Institute (Governor's Office of Emergency Services), a Professional Advisory Board member of the Center for Study of Psychological Trauma, Los Angeles, and trauma advisor to several other national and international organizations.

Kendall Johnson and his wife Wendy Losh live in Claremont, California. They have two children, a son Trevor and a daughter Whitney.

Trauma in the Lives of Children

Crisis and Stress Management
Techniques for Counselors, Teachers,
and Other Professionals

Kendall Johnson, Ph.D.

Library of Congress Cataloging-in-Publication Data:

Johnson, Kendall, 1945–
>   Trauma in the lives of children : crisis and stress management techniques for teachers, counselors, and student service professionals / Kendall Johnson. — 2nd U.S. ed.
>   p. cm.
>   Includes bibliographical references and index.
>   ISBN 0-89793-233-1. ISBN 0-89793-232-3 (pbk.)
>   1. Stress in children. 2. Post-traumatic stress disorder in children. I. Title.
>   RJ507.S77J64   1998
>   155.4' 18—dc21   97-31056
>   CIP

Ordering
Trade bookstores and wholesalers in the U.S. and Canada, please contact
>   Publishers Group West 1-800-788-3123   Fax (510) 658-1834

Hunter House books are available for textbook/course adoptions and bulk sales at discounts to qualifying community and health care organizations. For details please contact:
>   Marketing Department
>   Hunter House Inc., P.O. Box 2914, Alameda CA 94501-0914
>   Tel. (510) 865-5282   Fax (510) 865-4295
>   e-mail: marketing@hunterhouse.com

Individuals can order our books from most bookstores or by calling toll-free:
>   **1-800-266-5592**

Cover Design: Jil Weil Graphic Design   Book Design: *Qalagraphia*
Editorial Coordinators: Belinda Breyer, Dana Weissman, Jenny Moore
Copyeditor: Mali Apple   Proofreader: Lee Rappold
Production Coordinator: Wendy Low   Indexing: Kathy Talley-Jones
Marketing Director: Corrine M. Sahli   Marketing Associate: Susan Markey
Customer Support: Christina Arciniega, Edgar M. Estavilla, Jr.
Order Fulfillment: A & A Quality Shipping
Publisher: Kiran S. Rana

Printed and bound by Data Reproductions, Auburn Hills, MI
Manufactured in the United States of America

9 8 7 6 5 4 3   Second edition

Contents

DEDICATION

This book is dedicated to my son Trevor Losh-Johnson, and to my daughter Whitney Losh-Johnson, in fervent hopes that it never applies to them, and to my wife Wendy Losh. If it does apply to my children, however, I hope with equal fervency that the adults around them at that time possess the awareness and skills this book offers.

Acknowledgments

Grateful acknowledgment is first due Hunter House publisher Kiran Rana for his unwavering support of this book and the other books in the Hunter House trauma support series. Through his urging, the series has expanded to provide needed resource material for all aspects of school crisis management. Kiran is a dear friend, and he regularly provides the necessary challenge of honesty and commitment.

It is said that all wars are won first on the home front, and that is indeed the case with books. No book is probably important enough to warrant the time, anguish, expense, and psychological absence that it inflicts upon family life. Yet visionaries persist and families endure.

Thus heartfelt thanks are due to my wife, Wendy Losh, who never faltered in her support of this project. Wendy has always been a resonant sounding board for new ideas (after all, she is a musician), and she has time and again provided me with wise editorial advice. Our relationship has always been premised upon the idea that if something needed to be said or written, it had to be, and she has brought a fresh and compassionate perspective to our mutual interest in human behavior.

Two people lent energy to the first edition of this book. I owe a tremendous debt of gratitude to Dr. Jeffrey Mitchell of the Department of Emergency Health Services, University of Maryland. Jeff has provided me both direction and encouragement in this endeavor. More importantly perhaps, I have found his sense of mission highly infectious. Like this book, Jeff's work is devoted to easing human suffering. Over the years Jeff's innovations in the field of critical incident stress management have found acceptance among emergency responders and their supervisors.

Warm thanks are due to Spencer Eth, M.D., of the Brentwood V.A. Hospital, University of California, Los Angeles, and the Center for the Study of Psychological Trauma. I am honored by Dr. Eth's input, as his research and leadership at the Center have been groundbreaking in the field of pediatric psychotraumatology.

Many others contributed to this second edition.

The world does not wait for the slow scientific verification of principles and approaches. Incidents go ahead and happen, and practitioners are called upon to act. Three such people are Elizabeth Capewell, David Wee, and Nancy Sanford, profiled within. Each contribute to the accumulation of knowledge, but each have had to develop approaches to meet the needs of those suffering in the here and now. These people have shared their work and their enthusiasm with me, and I have learned much from our association. Francine Shapiro and Robbie Dunton of the EMDR Institute extended much assistance and encouragement, including Francine's much appreciated preface to this edition. In the process of learning about EMDR, I have incorporated it into my own practice. Through their network I received valuable contributions from Robert Tinker, Joan Lovett, Linda Cohn, Craig Penner, Chad Glang, and Ricky Greenwald.

I am honored by Charles Figley's contribution of the foreword for this edition. Charles has been at the forefront of psychotraumatology research and organization, playing a seminal role in the founding of both the Society for Traumatic Stress Studies and the *Journal of Traumatic Stress*. These organizations have been central to the phenomenal recent growth in the understanding of trauma and its treatment.

Kendall Johnson
Claremont, 1997

Foreword

My first experience with traumatized children began when I was twenty years old. During the year I spent in Vietnam I volunteered to work for the U.S. Marine Corps People-to-People Program in Danang. Our main job was to rebuild churches and schools and teach English and American games to Vietnamese students and teachers. I was so moved by the experience that I started a campaign to bring in hygiene and school supplies from my former high school in Springboro, Ohio.

That year of volunteer work with those orphaned children of war shaped the rest of my life. I wanted to understand and help children affected by war and other hardships. Soon I began taking courses at East Carolina College (now a university). My first summer job was working at a settlement house as the youth counselor. I was hooked completely. I declared social work as my major. In the meantime, marriage, a transfer to the University of Hawaii, and full-time employment intervened, but I graduated in 1970 with a degree in human development, specializing in traumatized children and families.

Following my master's and Ph.D. at Penn State University, I joined the faculty of the Department of Child Development and Family Studies (and a courtesy appointment to the Department of Psychological Sciences) and began to study the effects of war on individuals and families.

Now, over two and a half decades later, I am still interested in understanding trauma in the lives of children. It is a pleasure to recognize the contributions of Kendall Johnson, who has stimulated my interests and has substantially filled the gap in knowledge about the affect of traumatic experiences on children.

In 1989, the same year my *Helping Traumatized Families* was published, Kendall Johnson published *Trauma in the Lives of Children*. His book makes fundamental points that are basic reading for anyone interested in working with children. Dr. Johnson's book provides information that can be applied in practice to distressed children to relieve their pain, restore their joy, and identify the causes and effects of pediatric and adolescent emotional trauma from various stressors. This book gives parents, teachers, and counselors assessment tools to work with children on a preventive basis and provides child development education for the inexperienced so that they are able to discern how a traumatized child behaves in contrast to a nontraumatized child.

We know so much more about children now. We know that kids are programmed for sounds and grammar and begin to discern meaning even before childbirth. We know, thanks to an extraordinary flood of knowledge about the brain, that early child experiences are absolutely vital in helping to wire more neural circuits in the brain. All of this suggests what experienced parents have known all along: young children need lots of time and attention from those who love them. TV does not fill this need. Such things as cuddling and rocking a baby stimulate growth. In profoundly deprived children, such as orphans at institutions with inadequate resources, critical areas of the brain remain undeveloped.

The job of children is to play, according to the latest research. But what if play is disrupted by trauma? How do we know that the child is impacted and what should we do about it? Here is where Johnson's book is very instructive.

In chapter 2, Children's Reactions to Trauma, Johnson describes in detail children's acute, situational reactions to crisis situations, including those caused by traumatic memories. Emotional, physical, and behavioral signs of distress during or just after a crisis are detailed, including PTSD (posttraumatic stress disorder) and delayed traumatic stress reactions in children.

Of special note is Johnson's excellent description of EMDR treatment that focuses specifically on children. This approach has been hailed as one of the most significant contributions to psychotherapy in several decades. Johnson helps the reader grasp the critical concepts and clinical strategies adopted by EMDR–oriented therapists. Do not forget to read the material in the appendices at the end of the book, especially the results of an interesting study of the correlation between childhood trauma and maladaptive adolescent behavior. In an original study, Johnson asked students to report via questionnaires about their experiences with childhood trauma: how they coped with it, their age, the severity of the incident, the degree of support received, and their family stability at the time. This was compared to their answers about the responses of parents/adults using a parental/adult response-to-crisis checklist

These data were compared to current maladaptive adolescent behavior. The results show an empirically confirmed, direct relationship between childhood critical incidents and the frequency of maladaptive adolescent behaviors. Particularly harmful were negative parental/adult responses to the children's critical incidents. Also, it was confirmed that mothers' withdrawal and incompetence and the fathers' reactive/escapist responses to children's crises lead to maladaptive adolescent behavior. The study also suggests many ways that adults can respond that would lead to the children's effective coping with trauma and PTSD in particular.

Our research program at Florida State University includes testing various innovations in treating PTSD. EMDR was among the first approaches we investigated. Our findings so far suggest that treatments for one type of anxiety disorder such as PTSD show great promise in treating all the other disorders, such as simple phobia. If our findings continue to confirm this with children, readers should be alert that Johnson's approach may be applied to disorders including but not limited to PTSD.

All of the children I knew in Vietnam several decades ago are grown up, if they were fortunate enough to have survived the war. The traumatic memories they hold in their minds could be associated with a variety of maladaptive behaviors. Today, these adults would benefit from the help suggested by Johnson's work. Modern traumatology can not only help them heal the wounds of childhood loss, but also help their children free themselves of the bonds of trauma and live more productive happy lives.

Charles R. Figley, Ph.D.

Psychosocial Stress Research Program Director
and Professor, School of Social Work,
Florida State University

Preface

I began my career as a high school English teacher in Brooklyn, in an area now referred to as an "inner city." I remember especially one student who became an icon for me of the warring elements in this environment. I was teaching a class that was designed for the "slow learners" but also included the "problem students" who had acquired reputations as troublemakers. When I interviewed one of these students, he said that he didn't like to read—the only book he'd ever enjoyed was *The Prophet* by Gibran. So I started feeding him books and he began to open to me. Then one day, while driving home, I saw a young man on the street corner whose face was distorted with hate and rage—one of the most frightening sights I had ever witnessed. A I drove by, the boy saw me looking at him and his face melted into a smile—it was my student. In his environment he had to put on the mask to defend himself. He had to carry a knife to protect himself, while his beauty remained submerged. He had to do that to survive, and his reputation as a troublemaker in school showed that it was already taking its toll. The memory of this has haunted me for years, but this book has given me new hope for all those children caught in the bonds of trauma and pain.

I wish this book had been available then. *Trauma in the Lives of Children* provides a wonderful description of the field and practical instructions and resources for parents, teachers, and clinicians. There is no doubt that prevention of trauma is the best solution, but this is not always possible. This book provides guidelines to recognize the early stages of traumatization and direct ways to intervene before these problems have taken root. If the practice of EMDR has shown us anything over the last ten years, it is that the basis of most adult problems are earlier life experiences. Not only are these traumatizing experiences the cause of suffering in the victims, but they set the stage for revictimization and perpetrator behavior as well. Recent studies have indicated that at least 80% of those in prison have these types of experiences in their background.

As Wordsworth wrote so many years ago, "The Child is father of the Man." Each parent, teacher, and clinician can prevent years of suffering, and help stop the cycle of violence itself, by being sensitively aware of signs of distress, and using the excellent tools Ken Johnson has provided in this volume. The chapter on EMDR offers an excellent overview of how the application of this approach with children can liberate them from the influences of trauma. However, even more important, it provides all clinicians, regardless of their therapeutic specialty, with a wealth of resources and guidelines in order to involve parents and teachers in an integrated and comprehensive team approach.

Francine Shapiro, Ph.D.

Originator of EMDR, Senior Research Fellow
Mental Research Institute, Palo Alto, CA

Foreword to
First Edition

Children touch our lives, bring us joy, stir our souls. We cherish them as a delicate resource and a hope for a better tomorrow. Adults attempt to provide an environment that encourages their growth and gives them the courage necessary to improve the world. Adults do freely for children what they would resist vigorously if asked to do for other adults. They protect children, care for them, love them, and place hopes and dreams upon them.

Parents' and teachers' best attempts to provide a safe, uncomplicated environment for children is no fail-safe insurance policy against the traumas and distortions of human life. Unfortunately, some adults even participate knowingly and actively in self-serving destructive behaviors that leave the lives of children in chaos. Children, despite the very best efforts to protect them, are used in a wide assortment of dangerous, illegal, and destructive endeavors to satisfy the petty needs of adults. Children are cheated, sexually abused, neglected, ignored, injured, and even killed so that adults might be satisfied.

In addition, children face the same traumatic events that affect the lives of adults all around them. They become ill, experience accidents, and are exposed to fires and other disasters. Being a child offers no protection against loss, grief, or other emotional traumas. Neither does it protect them from illness, accidents, or death. Disturbing events in their own families, in the lives of their friends, or in the world may leave children feeling confused, uncertain, and frightened. Their self-esteem is frequently damaged as a result of traumatic experiences, and they may seek relief and reassurance in drugs. Under severe circumstances, children may try to escape the turmoil of their lives by running away or, even more tragically, in suicide. Children can be victims many times over before they reach adulthood.

Parents and teachers are frequently bewildered when faced with a traumatized child or group of distressed children. They turn anxiously toward health care professionals and psychological support services, only to find that specialists are frequently not adequately trained, skilled, or experienced to offer sound advice on how best to help damaged children. Research in libraries may be no more reassuring, because the existing literature on trauma in the lives of children is quite sparse; the literature that is available is usually not useful when applied to the real-life situations many children are facing.

Trauma in the Lives of Children needed to be written. It fills a serious gap in the literature on children. It provides teachers, school psychologists, health care professionals, mental health workers, and parents with practical information they might immediately apply to distressed children to relieve their pain. It explores the causes and effects of pediatric and adolescent emotional trauma. The information contained in this book will help adults, so they do not have to stand idle while children suffer. *Trauma in the Lives of Children* gives adults power to initiate changes in the care of children before the effects of traumatic events have the opportunity to become entrenched. The book provides information on the latest intervention strategies being employed in many areas of the country. These strategies have been designed to reduce the impact of traumatic events on children and to restore to children the happiest and most growth-enhancing circumstances possible in their schools and in their homes.

The author of this book, Kendall Johnson, has demonstrated consistent deep concern for children, both as a teacher and more recently as a mental health professional. He has spent considerable energy researching trauma and its effects on people. Dr. Johnson holds a Ph.D. in clinical psychology and serves as a consultant for California school districts and other organizations. He specializes in stress and crisis management as well as child sexual abuse and chemical dependency in children. He offers much to the field of child and adolescent development, and *Trauma in the Lives of Children* is another valuable contribution, devoted to the care of children after they have been exposed to the more painful aspects of life.

Jeffrey T. Mitchell, Ph.D.

Assistant Professor of Emergency Health Services
University of Maryland, Baltimore County Campus

Preface to First Edition

Society generally views childhood as a naturally happy time, free of responsibilities and worries. But the implication that children are somehow protected from the emotional effects of traumatic events is tragically false. All of us face the possibility of a disaster striking at any moment. A major earthquake, a plane crash, a fire, or a terrorist attack may be occurring as you read these words. Children are, in fact, as susceptible to trauma as adults, even though their suffering is commonly overlooked. Since the Second World War, mental health professionals have begun to recognize the dire consequences that can follow calamitous events. The first children studied were the survivors of the Nazi concentration camps. Many of these youngsters remained chronically frightened, depressed, and tormented. Today we find strikingly similar symptoms in Southeast Asian and Central American refugee children who have experienced war, confinement, and separation from their families.

American children have also encountered a series of catastrophes. In 1972, a flood washed away a West Virginia mining town. The displaced children reported a variety of persistent psychological and physical complaints. More recent studies of natural and human-induced disasters confirm severe distress in the child victims and serve to remind us that parents may be quite unaware of the extent of their own children's discomfort. My own work has centered on young witnesses of lethal violence. Each year in the United States more than 20,000 homicides are committed, often in the presence of the children of the deceased. The vast majority of these child witnesses develop the psychiatric syndrome of Posttraumatic Stress Disorder and are plagued by painful, intrusive memories, personality alterations, school difficulties, and behavioral disturbances. Although these children have usually escaped physical injury, in every case emotional wounds are the inevitable legacy of their exposure to violence.

Trauma in the Lives of Children confronts the neglect that traumatized youngsters have suffered for so long. In the pages that follow we are first introduced to the pathologic elements of crises that produce psychiatric symptoms. Identification of traumatic situations is a necessary first step in organizing a therapeutic intervention. We then learn of the spectrum of responses found in children and adolescents exposed to crisis. Several useful tables summarize the key signs and developmental features of Posttraumatic Stress Disorder. This term, PTSD, first appeared in the third edition of the American Psychiatric Association's Diagnostic and Statistical Manual (DSM-III) in 1980, and has become emblematic of the agony associated with Vietnam veterans, rape victims, and other disaster survivors. However, children are barely mentioned in the PTSD section of the current revision of DSM-III, an omission that underscores the value of this volume.

Ultimately, *Trauma in the Lives of Children* is about helping youngsters recover from overwhelming stress, and it contains a remarkable synthesis of useful techniques. Its view of children as embedded in a social context is instrumental in formulating a treatment plan. We see youth functioning in their families, schools, and communities, and see the subtle and dramatic effects that crises produce on these systems. This perspective naturally leads to a detailed exploration of strategies designed to assist traumatized children. The family, the school, and the therapist all have major and unique roles to play. Armed with the specific instructions found in later chapters, mental health professionals will be able to reverse the family's isolation and despair, to transform the classroom into an opportunity center for coping enhancement, and to empower themselves in their clinical encounters with traumatized children.

Trauma in the Lives of Children represents a sound foundation for the evolving field of pediatric psychotraumatology. By surveying the critical areas of concern, we also discover how much remains to be accomplished, especially with regard to primary prevention. Ideally, we would like to protect our environment from the ravages of disaster, or at least immunize our children from their devastating effects. So far we have not been successful in achieving either. But as this book so well documents, we can offer effective help to our young patients, their families, and their schools in the aftermath of trauma.

This work must be given priority attention both because of the prevalence of PTSD and because of its responsiveness to therapeutic intervention. Dr. Kendall Johnson, master teacher and therapist, is to be congratulated on an important contribution to the mental health literature. *Trauma in the Lives of Children* deserves to be read by every professional who cares for children in our troubled world.

Spencer Eth, M.D.

Associate Chief of Psychiatry
Veterans Administration Medical Center
West Los Angeles, California

Trauma in the Lives
of Children

Trauma:
Context and Concerns

> The kids come to school carrying unbelievable
> burdens! Here in L.A. they've had to cope with
> shootings here on campus, violence in their homes,
> and a riot, a firestorm, and an earthquake all in
> the past two years! It feels like we're going under!
>
> Excerpt from a debriefing of school crisis
> team members serving an urban, inner-city
> school in the Los Angeles area

Over the past few years the public has been inundated with reports of trauma in the lives of children. Combining concern for children with a morbid and sometimes tasteless fascination, the media rush to the scene of crisis after crisis, and viewers are treated to weekly dramas involving all sorts of catastrophes. And the world obliges. Los Angeles has not been alone in reeling from blow after blow by repeated disasters, both natural and social. Since the first writing of this book, violence has increasingly become an integral part of the school scene, even in elementary schools. Gang culture has become glorified, defining fashion trends and setting social standards. Single-incident crises and single-problem situations are becoming the exception to a brutalizing norm.

Social scientists, too, provide more accurate information every day regarding the prevalence of sexual crimes against children. Researchers compile frequency statistics and writers consolidate these studies into a wide assortment of books that range from theoretical dissertations to how-to-cope guides. Legislators respond to the public outrage with various types of legislation and funding for research projects, educational programs, and treatment facilities. All of this awareness and concern is, basically, good for children.

1

Professionals who work with children, however, greet the media coverage with mixed feelings. They recognize the value of public awareness and welcome the research and new programs now becoming available. They have committed their professional lives to the well-being of children, and they know that this new help is badly needed. Yet with the fervor comes new pressure. Much of the legislation creates new liabilities for child-care professionals—liabilities that can be severe. There is much to fear from a lawsuit for either overreacting or underreacting in child abuse situations, an area in which the law is still complex and vague. With today's media hungry for news about children's traumas, a professional's reputation can be shattered by one false accusation.

One hopeful sign developing over the past eight years following the publication of the first edition of this book is the gradual emergence of a nationwide movement toward the organization and training of crisis response teams. Trained to provide consultation, intervention, and postvention following school emergencies, these teams arm themselves with the skills and knowledge necessary to proactively mitigate the disintegrative effects of crisis upon individuals and schools.

In addition, many professionals who work with children are not trained to manage crisis situations involving those children. Teachers are rarely given any training in what to do during or following classroom crises. Most school districts provide little more than first aid drill and fire drill procedures. The training of therapists and social workers occasionally covers the *effects* of crisis but rarely includes training in crisis intervention. Program administrators normally receive no training in trauma work unless as a part of early training. Yet, each of these professionals either supervises someone who could be confronted by a child in real distress or may personally be called upon to deal with such a child. With little or no training in crisis management and with increased legal and social pressure to handle such incidents properly, professionals need solid information about trauma in the lives of children, with an emphasis upon practical aspects of crisis management.

Of particular concern is the increased need for interagency, interdisciplinary contact. In the school situation, teachers and administrators may be the first professionals aware of a child's trauma and the ones who maintain continuity of contact with the child over the course of the posttraumatic reaction. They are often in the best position to determine when to refer the child for specialized help. Yet, for most teachers and administrators, therapy is a black box, the workings of which they do not understand. They lack a knowledge of when referral is appropriate and why it should be made. Further, while they are in the position to provide useful "real-time" information regarding the child's recent behavioral changes, they frequently do not know (or feel they do not know) what information is relevant to therapists.

Therapists, social workers, and other mental health professionals often find themselves in a similar position. Although they are more familiar with school procedures and routines, they frequently do not know what to look for or what to recommend to schools when serving in a consulting capacity. With public exposure motivating schools to become more proactive in meeting children's posttraumatic needs, mental health professionals are increasingly called upon to provide consultation and assistance in crisis situations.

What happens to a child following a crisis? How might adults best respond to children in crisis to help them cut their losses? When is an incident psychologically critical? Counselors, teachers, and medical staff—anyone who works with children professionally—need to know the answers to these questions in order to intervene effectively. How do crises affect younger children differently than older children? What are the effects of background differences? Are there commonalities in response to crisis? What should one look for in identifying delayed reactions to crisis?

The answers to these and many related questions prove valuable for the professional when he or she is called upon to

— identify crisis situations

— recognize who is and who is not affected

— decide who is at risk in a given situation

— formulate options

— intervene appropriately

— monitor postcrisis recovery and

— determine when and how to follow up

The aim of this book is to address and answer these questions for teachers, administrators, counselors, psychologists, therapists, social workers, concerned parents, and others who work with, care for, or provide services to children. Because the audience is broad and the needs of different groups in the audience vary so widely, the chapters also vary in terms of content, style, and tone. Following is a brief synopsis of each chapter.

Chapter 1 investigates current research regarding crises. Providing general background information, "What We Know About Crisis" reviews and summarizes two types of studies. First, key reports that outline basic facts regarding trauma are presented. For purposes of review, children's traumatic events are classified into three groups: victimization, loss, and family pathology. The dynamics of each group are discussed in general, and then a representative example is presented in greater detail for illustration. This approach provides readers with the background information necessary for the management of such events. Chapter 1 is largely descriptive, outlining the role played by traumatic events in children's lives.

Adolescent crises are discussed separately in this chapter. The various types of adolescent maladaptive behaviors, such as substance abuse, running away, or self-destructive activities, are often reactions to prior traumas that create current crises as well. The resulting interactive effects of prior trauma and present individual and family crises due to adolescent acting out create unique problems. Because these situations so complicate the work of professionals, they need to be viewed separately from the general discussion of crises. Since the writing of the first edition in 1989, youth violence has increased to epidemic proportions; Chapter 1 discusses this.

Chapter 2, "Children's Reactions to Trauma," begins by describing children's acute, situational reactions to crisis situations. One child's excitement may be another's trauma, and this can create identification problems for professionals. Emotional, physical, and behavioral signs of distress during or just after a crisis are detailed in this chapter to increase the professional's ability to discern when a child is showing a traumatic reaction.

The concept of Posttraumatic Stress Disorder (PTSD) explains the delayed reactions children display toward crisis. Chapter 2 reviews current studies that outline the signs and symptoms of post-traumatic stress response in children. How this delayed response functions and the manner in which it manifests in the lives of trau-matized children are explored to aid in increasing professional awareness and crisis management skills. The fascinating developmental implications of childhood trauma are also discussed. New to the second editon are discussions of the DSM-IV conceptualization of posttraumatic stress reaction as it applies to children, recent research about changes in brain physiology following trauma, and child-specific reactions to trauma and their effects upon learning. The emerging diagnostic entity, Disorders of Extreme Stress Not Otherwise Specified or DESNOS, and Urban Violence Syndrome are explored.

Chapter 3, "What Schools Can Do," outlines the helpful, healthful steps school personnel can take in managing children's crises. Outside of the family, schools are by far the most influential institutions shaping children's lives. Because children normally spend a great amount of time in school, it may be considered a naturalistic setting compared to the clinician's office. Schools provide a potentially healing or hurtful environment for children who have been traumatized, depending upon the organizational climate and staff expertise. Because school personnel are leery of being accused of "doing therapy," which would be beyond their scope of practice, they sometimes ignore the very real and important role they can play in children's lives by creating a therapeutic context. Helping children to grow emotionally is clearly within the educator's scope of activity. Chapter 3 explores the many ways educators can interact with the traumatized child, allowing the natural healing process to take place. Toward this end, guidelines for individual conferencing are provided. Additionally, and unique to this book, classroom debriefings are discussed. Critical incidents frequently occur that affect an entire group. These events may either strengthen or weaken class cohesiveness, depending in large part upon how they are handled. Class debriefings are presented as a crisis management strategy, designed to maintain and strengthen class cohesiveness following an incident affecting the entire class.

Chapter 3 also discusses the school crisis response team developments of the past several years. The purpose, organization, strategies, and operation of CRTs in school environments will be described, circumscribing their role within the overall school crisis management picture.

This discussion of crisis management strategies in the school will be of particular benefit to mental health professionals. Increasingly, therapists, social workers, and other mental health professionals are being called into school postcrisis situations to provide consultation or direct intervention. Often these professionals are not familiar with school organization or practice and need practical guidelines to augment their theoretical knowledge. Chapter 3 presents directions, approaches, and strategies for providing effective assistance.

Chapter 4, "What Therapists Can Do," discusses how therapists can help traumatized children within a clinical setting. While a single chapter cannot provide a comprehensive discussion of treatment, this chapter presents a meaningful overview that will be useful to both therapists and nontherapists on several counts. While therapists have access to detailed literature about treatment modalities and outcomes, a general overview can address the central clinical task. Consideration of core therapeutic issues and direction is invaluable for coordinating the therapist's skills and resources with the traumatized child's needs.

Nontherapists, who are not familiar with the conventions and methodology of therapeutic intervention, are often unclear about where and when to refer. They are often not good consumers of therapy because they have no understanding of what the various approaches have to offer. Because they frequently do not know what the child can expect, they cannot help prepare the child for or assess the progress of treatment. Thus several standard therapeutic approaches are outlined, including the relatively new sandtray and narrative therapy approaches. Finally, nontherapists do not know which of their observations or impressions might be valuable, nor do they know what sorts of questions to ask. Many nontherapists make referrals to therapy and then just hope for the best. The information herein should assist nontherapists in knowing when and where to make wise referrals.

One of the strengths of this book is that it can provide nontherapists with a common ground, a translation of the direction, methods, and reasons behind posttrauma therapy. Accordingly, Chapter 4 describes the therapeutic task in treating posttrauma cases, beginning with on-scene crisis intervention. Following the discussion of acute, situational treatment, the longer-term treatment of posttrauma disorders is explored. This focuses upon the major therapeutic "kernel" of the reexperiencing, releasing, and reintegrating of traumatic experience. And because adolescents, always a class by themselves, raise treatment issues that require additional discussion, the chapter describes family mediation as an adjunct technique useful in posttrauma adolescent treatment.

In order to more fully describe therapeutic intervention with traumatized children, a new chapter, Chapter 5, has been added. In this chapter a specific therapeutic approach will be explored. Eye Movement Desensitization and Reprocessing (EMDR), relatively new to the clinical scene, has shown exciting potential as an effective treatment for trauma symptoms with children. Already gaining a large following among clinicians, and backed by ten years of clinical investigation and empirical verification of its efficacy, EMDR deserves investigation not only because of its usefulness in helping children, but also because of what it teaches us about trauma.

It is nearly impossible to deal with children in crisis without dealing with their families as well. At the very least this involves notifications, progress reports, or information queries by phone. More often, it entails discussion in which observations and resources are shared and problem solving occurs. In extreme cases, professionals may be "triangled" into conflictual or hopeless/helpless family situations in which they are either blamed for the difficulties or expected to solve them. Crisis affects families deeply and can create chaotic change. Whether the child's trauma occurs outside the family or within it, the family as a whole will be affected, and so, of course, will the task of the professional.

Thus Chapter 6, "Families in Crisis: The Ecology of Change," investigates the ways in which families react to crisis situations and their aftereffects. Beginning with the distinction between the process and content dimensions of family functioning, the chapter shows how those dynamics can affect the helping professional. Several critical dimensions are described and illustrated, with an emphasis upon the way they can present pitfalls for professionals. Pathological family functioning is outlined using the same critical dynamics as organizing principles. A three-stage model of family adaptation to crisis shows how crisis can serve to strengthen or disturb family relationships. Finally, an informal troubleshooting guide provides the assessment information regarding family health and stage-of-crisis response that professionals need to guide their interaction with the family.

Chapter 7, "Trauma Prevention Curricula," discusses the various elements of crisis prevention. The basic premise of this book is that, while crises themselves can never be eliminated, their effects can be softened significantly by effective intervention. Parents and teachers cannot keep airplanes from falling out of the sky or prevent grandparents from dying, but well-planned interventions can prepare children (and adults) for crises, thereby moderating their effects. This chapter explores some basic types of precrisis intervention that can go far in decreasing the harmful effects critical incidents can create.

First, children can be exposed to learning experiences designed to make them more stress resilient. Children need to be aware of their own feeling states and those of others so that they can communicate their feelings and needs; they need to have access to viable support systems, to know how to solve problems and make decisions, and to have a basically solid sense of self-esteem.

Second, children can be given trauma-specific instruction. Much of the difficulty with critical incidents comes from a sense of isolation and the compounding effect of secondary reactions. Children need to know the range of critical incidents; they need to learn what can be done about them and then face the fact that such incidents do, in fact, occur to people. When children do not know what reactions they are likely to have following a trauma, those effects may result in greater fear and disorientation. Finally, staff members are in the similar position of needing knowledge about their own stress reactions under such circumstances.

Thus Chapter 7 discusses the general elements of stress management, communication, support systems, and problem-solving and decision-making skills, and also outlines appropriate trauma-specific education. This diverse range of subjects, taken together under the broad rubric of prevention, provides the elements of a proactive program.

Chapter 8, "Managing Professional Stress," expands material begun in the first edition that has gained in importance. Professional stress, particularly among the new breed of professionals dealing with traumatized children, has skyrocketed. Not only has significant research been conducted in the area of vicarious traumatization, but that research points to a rapidly growing problem that must be addressed by each of us if we are to maintain our level of service and not burn out.

New to this edition is a study by David Wee and Diane Myers, both experts in the area of disaster psychology. Their paper on professionals' stress reaction to providing earthquake counseling, included as Appendix I, is seminal.

While much has been said relating specific childhood traumas to specific forms of adolescent acting-out, the general developmental connection has received very little empirical support. In addition, the actual outcome of different intervention behaviors has received little if any empirical verification. Accordingly, Appendix II reports original research addressing both the relationship between childhood traumas and subsequent adolescent development and the results of the style of intervention in terms of long-range effects. The results support the developmental connection between traumas and subsequent difficulties and clearly show five distinct interactional styles that have moderating or compounding effects on the behavioral outcome. This is exciting in that it provides empirical justification for setting directions in crisis management. This report is edited somewhat, as much of the literature and discussion appear elsewhere in the book.

Appendix III is a resource guide for professionals. The suggestions given and the agencies listed include sources of information, support, and referral.

The purpose of this book is to increase the understanding of children's trauma and provide directions for the management of the crises that create trauma. The book attempts to cross disciplinary lines and suggest helping strategies that focus and coordinate the work of both school and clinic. It is hoped that school personnel will explore the therapy chapter and that clinicians will familiarize themselves with the discussion on school intervention. Greater orchestration of posttrauma care is possible and sorely needed. It is further hoped that parents will investigate each chapter, so that they will know not only what to do, but what to expect of professionals in the event of trauma in the lives of their children.

This second edition of *Trauma in the Lives of Children* is considerably expanded over the first. And this is as it should be; in the intervening nine years, the field has grown enormously, both in terms of knowledge and involvement. I hope, in updating it as I have, that it maintains the practical usefulness for those who provide service to children in need.

CHAPTER 1

What We Know About Crisis

"My school is a war zone."

Chicago-area teacher in a workshop, 1995

OVERVIEW

Every professional dealing with children or their families needs to have an awareness of the types and frequencies of childhood traumas. Further, the manner in which adolescent crises are both a product of prior childhood traumas and also a compounding present crisis must be understood. This chapter presents basic background information concerning childhood and adolescent crises. Studies of the effects of victimization, loss, and dysfunctional families are reviewed, as are the various major maladaptive behaviors of adolescents.

Chapter Contents

Childhood Traumas

Adolescent Crises and Maladaptive Behaviors

Conclusion

This chapter provides a brief review of current research studies in the area of childhood trauma. A comprehensive review of all the research currently available or being done in this area is beyond the scope of this book, but a representative summary, suggestive and directive rather than exhaustive, is presented here. General background information is provided for those new to the field and, for

11

those more familiar with the territory, resources for further reading and research are suggested.

Childhood Traumas

The kinds of experiences and conditions that can seriously hurt children are legion. For purposes of review here they are classified into three groups: victimization, loss, and family pathology. In this chapter each group is discussed in turn. An investigation of the common characteristics among the various types of incidents within the group is presented, and then a representative example is discussed in greater detail.

VICTIMIZATION

The category of victimization includes assault, robbery, rape, incest, and serious accidents. Because incest, unlike the others, tends to be a long-term problem and a manifestation of serious family pathology, it could also be considered under the section on family pathology.

Bard and Sangrey (1979), in their theoretical discussion of victimization, identify three stages through which victims of crime tend to pass: impact, recoil, and reorganization. Their work is particularly relevant to this review because the reaction patterns they identify can be generalized to other types of victimization.

Impact

Victimization experiences tend to be of high intensity and short duration. Consequently, the first stage of reaction includes emotional shock symptoms such as numbness and feelings of vulnerability and helplessness. Lindemann (1944) identified the following somatic symptoms:

- tightness in the throat
- choking and shortness of breath
- an empty feeling in the abdomen
- lack of muscle power

Bard and Sangrey add the following to this list, treating the reaction to victimization as an acute grief reaction:

- sleep disturbances

- loss of appetite

Other symptoms may manifest during this period. Victims often feel shame and guilt concerning their state, blaming themselves for the ordeal. Lerner (1970) postulates a "just world" theory that may account for this reaction. In brief, the theory states that it is normal to believe that the world is rational and that consequences are in accordance with justice. Thus a person who is victimized might logically conclude that he or she must have somehow deserved it.

Bryant and Harvey (1996), in studying victims of automobile accidents, report that a large proportion—about one third—of those involved in incidents such as accidents report symptoms similar to those reported by clinical patients suffering long-term effects of trauma. They mention that while most of these symptoms turn out to be transient, the fear, shock, and recurrent anxiety symptoms are debilitating at the time.

Recoil

The recoil stage consists of the individual's attempts to deal emotionally with the victimizing event. Most individuals alternate between trying to go on with their lives as though the event never happened and returning periodically and almost obsessively to the event and its ramifications. The obsessional phases include compensatory fantasies and planning and, often, phobic reactions. This pattern of behavior seems to represent cognitive attempts at regaining equilibrium. In addition, probably as a further attempt to compensate for damage to the self or to provide enough cognitive coherence to allow them to cope, victims in the recoil phase frequently experience problems of blaming. Besides blaming themselves, they sometimes blame friends, family, or police (Bard & Sangrey, 1979). Horowitz and Reidbord (1992) point out that during this period victims may vacillate between intrusive thoughts and recollections of the event, and attempts to mute their distressing intensity by avoiding reminders, numbness, and distraction.

Reorganization

The third and final stage of response to victimization is character-ized by a return to psychological equilibrium. Obsessional fear and anger become modulated, though there are occasional flashbacks or extreme agitation. While recovery depends upon many factors (such as prior traumas, support, and extent of violation), the victim in the reorganization phase is able to focus upon life-enhancing activities rather than simply coping.

It might be said that victimization, or any trauma, represents an overwhelming assault on the person's sense of the world as an under-standable and safe place. Victimization ruptures the web of assump-tions that the individual developed and used to explain and predict what would happen and how to take sensible action in the world. Shapiro (1995) conceptualizes the process of reweaving this web of beliefs as "information processing" and conceives of the adjustment to trauma as a natural healing system. Symptoms of victimization, such as those discussed below, represent difficulties in processing the trauma and rebuilding an adaptive set of beliefs, assumptions, and perspectives necessary for the resumption of normal life.

This idea of a web of beliefs and cognitive constructs that is built over time and forms the basis for a sense of self has been given recent support (Horowitz, 1991). Janoff-Buhlman (1989) argues that victimization shatters necessary assumptions about a safe world. Our abilities to make predictions about events and to esti-mate the effects of our actions require such assumptions. When we are no longer able to do so, our ability to act in the world is limited. We become more fearful and less able to take the risks necessary to grow. This is of particular concern with children, whose lives are dependent upon growth and change.

The Effects of Sexual Abuse

Sexual abuse victims have reported depression, guilt, poor self- esteem, and feelings of inferiority in later life (Courtois, 1979; Herman, 1981). Interpersonal problems such as isolation, alienation, and dis-trust (Courtois, 1979), fear of men (Herman, 1981), transient and/or negative relationships (Herman, 1981), repeat victimization (Briere, 1984), promiscuity (Courtois, 1979), and sexual dysfunction (Kaplan, 1979) have also been associated with childhood sexual victimization.

Of the few studies that included nonclinical samples, two focused upon the long-term effects of childhood sexual abuse—those conducted by Tsai, Feldman-Summers, and Edgar (1979) and Briere and Runtz (1985). Tsai et al. compared psychotherapy clients with reported sexually abusive backgrounds to women in the general population with and without sexually abusive backgrounds. On the basis of MMPI scores, they concluded that sexual abuse need not produce long-term effects, and related positive outcomes to mediating aspects of the situation itself.

In their 1985 study, Briere and Runtz included a nonclinical abused group and used more appropriate instrumentation (symptom checklists) to measure postabuse trauma. Their results show significant long-term symptomatology associated with a history of sexual child abuse among nonclinical adult women.

They report that 15% of 278 university women had sexual contact with an older person prior to age 15. These women reported higher levels of dissociation, somatization, anxiety, and depression than did nonabused women. Briere and Runtz speculate that dissociation may initially function as a coping strategy and then later become an autonomous symptom. Anxiety and depression, they argue, appear to be conditioned or secondary learned responses to the sexual abuse, persisting into later life in a manner similar to unresolved rape trauma (Burgess & Holstrom, 1974). In addition, Briere and Runtz correlate abuse-related symptomatology with factors associated with the abusive incident such as perpetrator age, total number of perpetrators, use of force, parental incest, completed intercourse, and duration of abuse.

Reviewing clinical studies, Green (1985) concludes that despite methodological problems in the research, symptoms manifested by incest victims resemble those found in rape victims by Burgess and Holstrom (1974), including fear, sleep and eating disturbances, guilt, decreased or constricted levels of general functioning, sexual problems, and irritability.

Green (1985) presents three case studies of incest victims, ranging in age from 18 months to 28 years. Their symptoms included the following:

1. fear, startle reactions, and anxiety

2. repetition, reenactment, or flashback to the trauma

3. sleep disturbance and other depressive phenomena, including excessive guilt

4. ego constriction or regression

5. explosive and maladaptive expressions of anger (p.161)

Lenore Terr (1990) distinguishes between single-event and multiple-event traumas, citing more obscure memories among victims of prolonged trauma. Courtois (1992) cites memory loss and delayed recall among long-term childhood sexual assault victims. Cameron (1994) points out similarities between the reactions of sexual abuse survivors and Vietnam veterans with Posttraumatic Stress Disorder, another group suffering from prolonged exposure to trauma. Cameron also discusses amnesia symptoms lasting for extended periods of time following cessation of the abuse.

In attempting to differentiate long-term sexual abuse from other clinical subjects who were not abused, Zlotnick et al. (1996) discovered higher rates of somatization (physical manifestations of trauma), dissociation, generalized anxiety, difficulty expressing emotions, maladaptive behavior, self-destructiveness, and history of adult victimization. This study supported the notion of other researchers (e.g., Herman, 1992) that child sexual abuse symptoms are not identical to more short-term traumas in that they tend to be more physical, mood-oriented, and dissociative as well as characterological (that is, having to do with identity, the capacity for rewarding relationships, and the tendency to replicate harm to self). This is in contrast to trauma symptoms following intense, single-incident victimization, such as motor vehicle accidents, in which specific anxiety and fear, intrusive imagery (such as flashbacks, nightmares, and unwanted thoughts), and avoidance symptoms (Bryant & Harvey, 1996) predominate.

Loss

Literature related to loss generally focuses upon specific losses. These can be classified as apparent losses, losses as a part of change, and unnoticed losses (Frears & Schneider, 1981). Apparent losses include major losses that are obvious, resulting from such events as death of a relative or friend, permanent and involuntary separation, illness, or injury. Other losses are less dramatic and occur as a normal part of life changes. These can include divorce, moving, changing schools, or other significant changes in the environment, as well as leaving home, weaning, puberty, and aging. Finally, some losses are not normally identified as such but nevertheless trigger loss responses in many people. These are often difficult to deal with as they do not trigger normal social supports in the same manner as recognizable loss. Unnoticed losses can include marriage or remarriage, achievements, success, and growth. Although these changes are usually considered to be positive, they do represent the loss of an earlier lifestyle and coping pattern. Such a loss can create turmoil even though the overall life change is for the good.

The adjustment to loss requires an elaborate process whereby the subject gradually, in stages, accommodates to the changed reality. The process of bereavement has been outlined by Kübler-Ross (1969) as following the five major stages of denial, anger, bargaining, depression, and acceptance; these stages seem to apply to other losses as well. However, Frears and Schneider (1981) present a more elaborate six-stage model:

1. initial awareness (including shock, loss of equilibrium, and lowered resistance to infection)

2. strategies to overcome loss (including adaptive defense cycles of holding on and letting go)

3. awareness of loss (including exploration of extent of loss and its ramifications, such as loneliness, helplessness, and exhaustion)

4. completions (healing, acceptance, and resolution, freeing the energy invested in the loss)

5. empowering the self (in areas that were out of balance prior to the loss)

6. transcending the loss (growth following completions and rebalancing)

Children under 10 years of age have not yet developed the capacity to recognize, understand, and resolve loss. Not only are they likely to make incorrect assumptions regarding loss, but their dependent role and lack of ability to remove themselves from unbearable situations render them vulnerable to special problems. When loss affects the family, children may develop apathy and with-drawal behaviors because their basic needs are not being met during the parents' own grieving. Young children are not adept at limiting their helplessness (awareness) or resolving their loss (completions) (Frears & Schneider, 1981).

An appreciation of the development of the concept of death is central to understanding children's reactions to loss. Wass (1984) discusses this development from a Piagetian perspective; his correla-tion of predominant death concepts with stages of cognitive devel-opment is presented in Table 1.

Wass and Cason (1984) further discuss these phase-correlated death concepts in terms of the types of fears and anxieties associated with them. During the sensorimotor stage, death is not conceptualized and responses to death are simply responses to the immediate loss.

Preoperational-stage children, however, conceive of death as a temporary, reversible state, caused phenomenologically (that is, caused by whatever appears immediately preceding death), magi-cally, or psychologically (in terms of motives). Hence their fears have to do with motivations, magical controls, and things they have come to associate with a death, as well as fears regarding magical controls and motivations. How a body is treated after death is of great con-cern to children at this stage, as death is not perceived to be an irre-versible state. As a result, adults are often confused by the reactions to death of preoperational children.

During the concrete operations stage, children come to under-stand that death is irreversible. Causes of death are perceived to be external (such as violence, destruction, or accident). While anxiety related to the apparent capriciousness of death is lessened by this awareness, there is a focus upon postdeath decay. This preoccupa-tion may be a means of coping with the dread that awareness of dying raises.

In adolescence there is the final development of the concepts of the personal and universal nature of death. The anxiety attendant

Table 1: Development of Death Concepts

	Life Period	Predominant Death Concepts
1.	infancy	no concept of death
2.	late infancy, early childhood	death is reversible; a temporary restriction, departure, or sleep
3.	middle to late childhood, preadolescence	death is irreversible but capricious; external-internal physiological explanations
4.	preadolescence, adolescence, adulthood	death is irreversible, universal, personal, but distant; natural, physiological, and theological explanations

Source: Wass (1984)

upon this realization is somewhat contained, however, by the adolescent's ability to perceive death more as a personal threat in the very distant future.

While some sort of stage theory of grief processing, popularized by Elizabeth Kübler-Ross (1969), is accepted by most clinicians as basically correct, it sometimes confuses temporal stages with psychological tasks. "Stages," due to their "overlapping and fluid nature" (Shuchter & Zisook, 1993), might be better understood as issues to be resolved that follow an initial period of shock. Normal bereavement may last a long time and be accompanied by psychological and physical distress. Shuchter and Zisook point out that grief processing includes "affective and cognitive states, coping strategies, continuing relationship with the deceased, changes in functioning, changes in relationships, and alterations in identity" (p. 13).

Given the range of behavior associated with normal grief, it is sometimes hard to determine when grief has become pathological. Currently, mental health researchers and workers tend to find psychoanalytic or attachment theoretical models most useful in understanding normal and abnormal grief processing (Middleton et al., 1993). Psychoanalytic theory (Freud, 1917/1966) considered the elements of painful dejection, loss of interest in new objects of love, inhibition of activity, and loss of interest in the outside world to be normal, and the melancholia common to pathological grief based in ambivalence over the person lost or in self-blame. Resolution of grief involves freeing oneself from the one who was lost and forming new relationships.

Attachment theory (Bowlby, 1973) bases difficulty in overcoming loss in childhood patterns of separation anxiety from protective parents. Using this model, Parks (1965) identified three forms of pathological grief: chronic (aggravated symptoms lasting an indefinite period), inhibited (absence of normal symptoms), and delayed (painful feelings avoided). As Middleton et al. (1993) point out, sudden and massive loss can be traumatic, and distinguishing the signs of normal loss and reactions to trauma can be complex and confusing.

Horowitz and Reibord (1992) differentiate normal from pathological loss on the basis of degree of response. While normal grief can include outcry, numbing, ruminating, avoidance of reminders, and distress, pathological reactions are prolonged and intensified versions of the normal response.

The Case of Parental Death

These considerations regarding children's conceptions of death provide the background against which children's actual patterns of mourning take shape. On the basis of in-depth case analysis of 23 children of widely varying ages seen at a therapeutic school, Furman (1984) outlined basic elements of children's bereavement as a threefold task: (1) to understand and come to terms with the reality and circumstances of the death, (2) to mourn, and (3) to progress in the appropriate development of personality. This involves detachment (eventual resignation and withdrawal of emotional investment from what is no longer there) and identification (assimilation of attributes of the lost loved one).

Furman (1984) also discusses how detachment and identification affect the process of adjustment to a new stepparent. After a certain length of time, once the child has detached significantly from the lost parent, he or she may choose a parent substitute or redefine the relationship with the existing parent. If the parent remarries, however, this natural process is forced. Such a forced relationship is frequently experienced by the child as a violation of either an existing attachment to the lost parent or the child's internalized image of how a parent should be. In addition, unresolved mourning in children may lead them to avoid internalizing healthy attributes of the lost parent or to develop fears that they must avoid similar life decisions in order to avoid a similar fate.

Furman points out that the acute stage typically subsides after 6 to 18 months, but that it continues intermittently, triggered by anniversaries and developmental steps. Parent loss involves a loss of part of oneself and is experienced as diminution of self-worth and as isolation. Maladaptive coping with parent loss may take the form of intensifying detachment or increasing premature structuring.

Various authors have explored the relationship between specific significant losses during childhood and subsequent maladaptive behavior. In their review of the literature, Klagsbrun and Davis (1977) report that there is general agreement that a high correlation exists between substance abuse and parental loss. Bowlby (1961) indicates a high correlation between death of a parent and behavioral problems, particularly if the parent was lost prior to the child's reaching 5 years of age. Gregory (1965) correlates parental loss with delinquency and school attendance problems.

Such effects of parental loss upon subsequent development do not occur in a vacuum, however. Bowen (1978) states that "the intensity of the emotional reaction is governed by the functioning level of emotional integration of the family at the time, or by the functional importance to the family of the one who is lost" (p. 325).

Expanding upon this, Birchnell (1969) lists several factors that influence the degree of disruption the death causes:

1. the special relationship that existed between the lost parent and the child

2. the relationships that existed between the parent and the other family members

3. the controlling influence the parent exerted over other relationships within the family

4. the influences other family members exerted upon the relationship that existed between the child and the lost parent

5. the influence the child exerted upon the relationships that existed between the lost parent and the other family members (pp. 9–10)

The effects of parental death and its psychological processing are determined as well by the nature of the death itself. The extent to which the death involved trauma to the child will determine the manner in which it is grieved. This is discussed at greater length in the next chapter.

FAMILY PATHOLOGY

The family, although greatly changed in terms of structure and values through the past forty years, nevertheless remains a pervasive, formative force in children's development. Birchnell's discussion mentioned above illustrates this. Functioning as the primary learning milieu for individual behavior, the family provides the basic structure for children's values and expectations throughout their growth toward maturity (Satir, 1967). Consequently, families that show serious disturbance provide a faulty learning environment.

Coleman, Butcher, and Carson (1980) summarize the now-burgeoning family dynamics literature into four broad categories of family dysfunction that lead to a high incidence of problems in child development and later psychopathology:

1. *Inadequate families:* These families lack the physical or psychological resources for coping with normal life stressors.

2. *Antisocial families:* These families have values that differ greatly from those of their communities in that they may encourage dishonesty, deceit, or other undesirable behaviors.

3. *Discordant and disturbed families:* These families may be characterized by fraudulent interpersonal contracts and disturbances (including fighting, gross irrationality, and enmeshment of the family in parental conflicts).

4. *Disrupted families:* These families have inadequately adjusted to the loss of family members through death, divorce, or separation.

These four categories have been found to be associated with higher incidences of psychological disorders leading to various maladaptive behaviors and physical illness (Bloom, Asher, & White, 1978; Heatherington, Cox, & Cox, 1978; Langer & Michael, 1963; Lidz, Fleck, & Cornelison, 1965; Wolkind & Rutter, 1973; Davidson & Swartz, 1985; Emery et al., 1991).

Several specific patterns of parental influence appear regularly in the backgrounds of children showing emotional disturbances and faulty development. In their review, Coleman et al. (1980) indicate the following patterns as pathogenic: rejection, overprotection, unrealistic demands, overpermissiveness, faulty discipline, inadequate and irrational communication, and undesirable parental models.

As illustration, Richman (1981) reports a series of studies conducted by himself and Rosenbaum investigating characteristics typical of the family at the time of a suicidal crisis in one of its members:

- inability to accept necessary changes, including intolerance for separation, a symbiosis without empathy, and infantile fixations

- role disturbances

- affect disturbances, including one-sided handling of aggression and sexual difficulties with incestuous overtones

- interpersonal difficulties, including reliance upon scapegoating, double-binding, and sadomasochistic relationships

- close family system that is dominated by a fragile family member

- communication disturbances

- intolerance for crisis

Following an extensive review of literature relating to family life, delinquency, and crime, Wright and Wright (1995) conclude that marital discord combined with conflict and violence, parental rejection, poor monitoring and supervision, and lack of normative guidance and modeling, interact with social and community factors to produce maladaptive adolescent behavior and, in some instances, difficulties in adulthood.

The Case of Alcoholic Families

Whether alcoholism is or is not associated with genetic predisposition, studies of alcoholic families have shown that where one member is alcoholic, a dysfunctional pattern of interaction tends to emerge, affecting the children of the family to such an extent that subsequent maladaptive behaviors may be expected. Siegler, Osmond, and Newell (1968) describe the extreme manifestation of this pattern:

> Alcoholism, like drug addiction and schizophrenia, is best seen as a form of family interaction in which one person is assigned the role of the "alcoholic" while the others play complementary roles, such as the martyred wife, the neglected children, the disgraced parents, and so forth. As this deadly game is played by mutual consent, any attempt to remove the key actor, the alcoholic, is bound to create difficulties for the other family members, who will attempt to restore their former game. (p. 579)

Family systems theorists view the family as an operational system and observe that any change in the functioning of one family member is automatically followed by compensatory change in another family member (Bowen, 1978). They also observe that children in alcoholic families evolve compensatory roles in reaction to dysfunctional parenting in order to maintain family cohesiveness and equilibrium.

Black (1979) describes three such children's roles:

1. *The Responsible One:* the child who provides structure for him- or herself and others within the often inconsistent home environment

2. *The Adjuster:* the child who compliantly adapts to the inconsistencies

3. *The Placater:* the child who helps others, possibly in response to guilt over family dysfunction

Black claims that "Responsible" children carry the need to control into their adult lives and frequently end up alone or in unmeaningful relationships; "Adjuster" children tend to grow up manipulated by others, suffer from low self-esteem, and end up inviting into their lives someone who has significant problems (frequently an alcoholic); "Placaters" grow up minimizing their own needs and subjugating them to those of others.

Wegscheider (1981) provides a similar description of this role differentiation, adding a fourth role to the list:

4. *The Troubled One:* the child who acts out the family problems, frequently getting into explicitly maladaptive behaviors

Thus the parental inconsistency, faulty communication, and learned distrust common to alcoholic families force the children to adopt coping strategies that are often maladaptive.

The effects upon family dynamics of substance abuse patterns are pervasive and long-lasting. Treatment programs, in order to be effective, must address family issues as well as issues of the addicted parent's own dependency. Such services often combine interventions, including parent training and programs to develop parent-child interaction and bonding (Hawkins & Catalano, 1995).

SUMMARY

This review points out several similarities among experiences of victimization, loss, and pathogenic family structure in childhood. Each appears to create sufficient stress to cause behavioral symptomatology at the time of the experience, a finding that clearly has implications for involved professionals. When a crisis has occurred, sensitivity to the signs of trauma can help professionals determine whether or not particular children have been adversely affected by the event. In addition, this awareness can alert professionals to signs of trauma in children who have been in crisis prior to contact with the professional. These signs are discussed in detail in Chapter 3.

All three of the conditions discussed in this chapter tend to result in similar patterns of subsequent maladaptive behavior in adolescence or adulthood, although it is not clear whether different types of critical incidents predispose children to different specific maladaptive behaviors. This connection was given general support in the studies reviewed here, and Appendix II reports in detail the results of an independent study on this subject conducted by the author. The connection between critical incidents and maladaptive behaviors is of particular interest to those who work with troubled adolescents. As the next section points out, acting-out adolescents tend to report having experienced more trauma than do "normal" young people. This insight is especially useful to teachers, counselors, and medical staff dealing with youth. The practical implications of this finding for professionals are discussed in Chapter 4.

Finally, it appears that the degree of subsequent maladaptive response is moderated to some extent by various factors such as family or social support (Birchnell, 1969; Bowen, 1978; Pynoos et al., 1996). The effects of different styles of adult interaction with children in crisis were also investigated in the study reported in Appendix II, and specific recommendations for dealing with such children grew out of that investigation; these are outlined and discussed in Chapter 4. *Concerned* crisis management must be *aware* crisis management, and recommendations based upon empirical data are of particular value to professionals confronted with children in crisis.

Adolescent Crises and Maladaptive Behaviors

Why do the problems of young people seem so intense, so urgent? Those who work with adolescents in distress often remark that the crises seem to be more convoluted than those experienced by either younger children or adults. More often than not, young people's problems seem to become entangled with acting-out behavior, which complicates the work of any professional—therapeutic, medical, or educational—working with adolescents.

As these studies have indicated, children's traumas often result in maladaptive behavior later in adolescence. Thus, while adolescent crises are frequently situational (for example, loss), they are often compounded by the deleterious effects of acting out, which might include substance abuse or other self-destructive behavior. Professionals working with adolescents in crisis usually have to deal with elements of situational emergency, maladaptive behavioral patterns, and the residual effects of prior trauma in childhood.

Adolescence adds several dimensions to the general pattern of a child's response to crisis. First, the adolescent's conceptual abilities more closely resemble those of adults than they do those of younger children. Second, the emotional turmoil following adolescent developmental changes imparts a unique intensity to situational crises. Finally, adolescents usually have been through more prior traumas than younger children and bring with them certain special vulnerabilities.

While the previous section related a range of behavioral consequences in adolescence to certain specific critical incidents (CIs) in childhood, this section examines literature relating a range of antecedent critical incidents to specific maladaptive adolescent behaviors (MABs), including suicide, running away, serious school attendance problems, drug abuse, and alcohol abuse.

SUICIDE

Suicide is becoming an increasingly prevalent threat to children and adolescents. According to the National Center for Health Statistics (1996), while suicide ranks ninth among causes of death in the United States, it ranks third among the causes of death among persons ages 15 to 24. This rate is relatively stable. It must be kept in mind, however, that it may actually deserve a higher rank because many suicides are masked as accidents (Fredrick, 1985a). This amounts to some 5,000 suicides of young people annually, although this figure may be low. Shaffer and Fisher (1981), reporting on psychiatric clinic admissions in the United States and England, found that 7% to 10% of all referrals were for the investigation or treatment of threatened or attempted suicide. They further indicate that suicidal children make up an even greater proportion of total referrals to child emergency or crisis clinics. The Office of National Drug Control Policy (1996) reports that in a survey of nearly 200,000 adolescents, almost 7% of those ages 12 to 14 reported "thinking often/a lot about suicide," and nearly 8% of those ages 15 to 18 reported the same. A more startling figure is the estimate by the American Association of Suicidology (McIntosh, 1996) that while there are 8 to 20 attempts for every completion in the United States, among young people the ratio climbs to 100 to 200. The Office of National Drug

Control Policy (1996) reports that in a study of emergency department drug episodes, some 193,211 were specifically for suicide.

Michael Peck, director of the Los Angeles Suicide Prevention
Center, differentiates six categories of youth suicide (Peck, 1984).
These are useful in establishing both the age range and variety of
motivations of suicidal children.

The very young (ages 10–14). Two characteristics are often noted
in completed suicides among the very young. First, they tend to
have experienced loss of a parent; second, they have a disproportion-
ately high incidence of learning disabilities. Both factors tend to
diminish a child's self-esteem.

The loner. Frequently emerging from a family that defensively
denies the child's dysphoria, thus creating the child's distrust for his
or her own feelings, the loner is characterized by loneliness, isolation, lack of friends, and poor interpersonal communication. This
type of suicidal youth represents a relatively higher potential for
completed rather than failed suicide attempts.

Those who act out depression. Adolescents in this category use
action as a coping mechanism in dealing with depressive feelings.
They find actions that are rewarding in the short run, often illegal,
dangerous, disruptive, harmful, or hostile behaviors such as drug or
alcohol abuse, running away, petty crime, assaultive behavior, and
serious violence. On the basis of clinical observations with 150 such
patients in a psychiatric unit, Lustig and Zeitlin (1985) find two primary psychodynamic themes triggering the initial episode:

1. enormous fear of failure, creating a marked anxiety

2. reduced capacity to tolerate separation from people upon
   whom the youth is dependent

Failure means loss of identity and overwhelming anxiety, triggering
antisocial behavior (Lustig & Zeitlin, 1985).

The crisis suicide. Representing less than 15% of all youth suicides,
the crisis suicide presents no unusual background characteristics. The
crisis, typically diagnosed as a reactive depression, follows sudden
traumatic incidents and is characterized by dramatic behavioral
change, hostility, and signs of confusion and disorganization.

Those whose suicidal behavior is a form of communication. This is a category characterized more by suicide attempts than by completed suicides. The behavior appears to be a "cry for help," usually does not follow prior attempts or accompany an "at-risk" profile, and sometimes results in an accidental death when a low-lethality plan goes wrong.

Discussions of background factors that are common among suicidal adolescents frequently reveal a broad range of factors, often cumulative in nature. Anderson (1981) points out that adolescents who have experienced significant object losses during childhood and who have grown up in unstable or hostile environments show greater suicidal risk. Teicher (1979) cites loss themes such as parental death, divorce and separation, stepparent problems, parental alcoholism, and frequent school changes as correlating significantly with suicide attempts.

Anderson's three-stage model of suicide provides some indication of why these background events are so significant. In the first stage, critical incidents and chronic problems together form a history that affects development, a history of vulnerability or risk. Adolescence creates a second stage of escalation of these problems. Behavioral changes that occur under the new stress of adolescence frequently serve to undermine social support and increase the experience of stress. The final stage involves a trigger situation, culminating in the suicide attempt. Thus a long-standing history of critical incidents provides the context within which a suicidal crisis develops.

While trauma may dispose young people to suicidal ideation and suicide attempts, completed suicides cause great upset in the lives of those who knew the victim. Each of the 5,000 completions per year represents 100 to 200 attempts, and each attempt is estimated to affect at least 6 other people (McIntosh, 1996). This means that three to six million people are so affected each year. It must also be noted that McIntosh's estimate may be quite low, being based upon the general population rather than upon children. Children tend to be in school classes and extended families more than do adults. Thus each attempt creates many crises.

Runaways

The National Center for Health conducted a study of the frequency of adolescent runaways in 1975 and reported that 10% of all youth between the ages of 12 and 17 run away one or more times (Justice & Duncan, 1976). This amounts to some one million children under the age of 18, according to Walker (1975), who finds very little consensus in a literature survey regarding reasons to run away, except general agreement that disturbed family relations are involved. The figures presented by the National Center for Health are somewhat at odds with a later study discussed by Sedlak et al. (1990), although it is difficult to tell whether Sedlak's lower figures represent a decline over time, or whether they simply reflect differing data-gathering methods.

Nilson (1981) compared runaway children to a control group in the areas of problem-solving abilities, coping skills, and background experiences. The control group consisted of nonrunaway referrals to counseling services, although the procedures used in selecting the sample were not clarified and so generalization is limited. Runaways did not differ significantly from controls with regard to coping or problem-solving skills, but ten times as many had family divorces, remarriages, and placements outside the home.

In a continuation of that study, Nilson explored the psychological profiles of 46 children: 28 runaways and 18 referrals from the same agency sources who approximated the runaways in terms of "need for supervision" but who had not run away. While family structure was similarly unstable and dysfunctional in both groups, runaways tended to have been abused or neglected more. Further, the runaway group tended to act out depressive features, showing higher rates of suicide ideation, gestures, and attempts.

Russell (1981), in his comparison of psychological profiles of runaways with delinquent referrals other than runaways from the same agencies, found more similarities than differences. Runaways differed from controls only in that there were a higher number from chaotic homes, and a greater percentage of runaways placed in the highest and lowest IQ ranges. Otherwise the groups were similar, showing the following exaggerated adolescent traits: self-centeredness, immature ego structures, interpersonal difficulties, and defective self-image.

Half of the sample showed depression, while a third showed poor impulse control, regressive tendencies, emotional immaturity, and identity conflicts. Some 10% showed definite self-destructive signs.

On the basis of his research and a review of the literature, Russell (1981) makes the following generalizations about runaways:

1. Running away is easier and a more socially acceptable form of protest in adolescence today

2. There appear to be more neglectful, abusive, and conflictual homes today

3. There are a greater number of incomplete or inadequately structured families unable to provide the emotional supports necessary to help accomplish the tasks of adolescence

4. Most runaways manifest immature or incomplete development

5. Running away can be seen as self-harming, or as a measure taken for protection against parental relationships, or as the adolescent's own expression of rage (p. 72)

In terms of background and stressors, Russell's study bears further comment. Using his sample of 100 runaways drawn from a population of 2,000 juveniles who were court-referred for clinical evaluation, Russell reports the following background critical incidents:

- divorce/separation, 49%

- serious parental illness, 26%

- severe parental alcoholism, 26%

- death of a parent, 16%

Plass and Hotaling (1995) considered the histories of parents of runaways to explore a possible fourth category of factors leading to runaway behavior. Citing current literature, they acknowledge personal difficulties in the child's life, high levels of parental conflict, and physical, emotional, or sexual abuse of the child as being well-documented precipitators. In their studies, Plass and Hotaling explore the interesting notion that children who run away may be reliving and reenacting the experiences of their parents' adolescence.

Plass and Hotaling determined that 24% of runaways they interviewed reported that their parents had run away from home when
they were adolescents themselves. This points to some sort of intergenerational transmission of runaway behavior as being a factor in a
significant number of cases. The exact nature of the transmission is
unclear, however. It is doubtful that modeling would directly account
for running away, because the parents' behavior occurred prior to the
birth of their children. However, the parents may indirectly model
conflict avoidance in ways that make running appear to be the best
alternative under such circumstances as abuse or conflict. Plass and
Hotaling report three likely means of transmission:

1. Child victims are more likely to become adult perpetrators,
   thus creating the reason for their own children running

2. Child victims become "damaged" in ways that later affect
   their ability to parent, again setting the stage for intolerable
   conditions from which their children must then flee

3. Children model their behavior on their parents' past or
   present running away, in ways discussed above

The significance of this study is that it moves the discussion
beyond the correlation among stressful events, conflict, and abuse in
runaways' lives, and focuses upon the need for greater understanding
of the specific interactional dynamics in the families of runaways.

SERIOUS SCHOOL ATTENDANCE PROBLEMS

Serious attendance problems continue to plague schools, despite the
existence in many states of alternatives, such as the continuation
school system in California, where each school district must provide
a special setting for students at risk of dropping out.

According to Fossey (1996), while the prevalent opinion holds
that dropout rates are declining, the reverse may in fact be true. The
National Center of Educational Statistics (1994) reports that 11% of
youth ages 16 to 24 are high school dropouts (that is, not graduated
and not enrolled). Citing widespread reporting of declines in graduation rates and increased participation in GED programs, Fossey questions the data collection methods used in the federal survey. The

government considers GED recipients as high school graduates, despite the fact that they often do not complete programs until their early twenties. This suggests that the percentage of youth graduating on time in traditional programs may be declining.

Fossey also points to flawed and nonstandard reporting practices at the district as well as state levels. He feels that many districts, particularly those in urban areas, are faced with large numbers of at-risk adolescents with combinations of discipline problems, learning disabilities, and unmet emotional needs. These districts may be practicing an unconscious educational triage—concentrating on the needs of those students who they feel will be more successful and letting marginal students slip away. Thus suspensions, expulsions, and grade retentions provide a means by which a fairly large number of students drain away without being accounted for because of flawed tracking systems. Because of such inaccurate reporting, limited educational resources may not be used appropriately, districts' performance comparisons are likely to be distorted, and communities in crisis may go unidentified. Thus Fossey points out a self-reported estimate of a 15% dropout rate in a major East Coast city while an article in a leading educational journal estimates the same district's rate at 56%, one of many such discrepancies. The bottom line seems to be that we really do not know what the current dropout rate is.

In an early, comprehensive study of middle-class dropouts, Lichter, Rapien, Seibert, and Sklansky (1962) differentiated between what they called "psychological" and "reality" problems underlying serious nonattendance. Reality problems included lower IQ scores, economic need, and physical illness. Psychological problems, which accounted for the majority of dropout behavior, chiefly crystallized around issues of dependency and hostility, with parental characteristics projected upon teachers by students (p. 40).

This projective dynamic may explain the reasons students frequently give for nonattendance, as summarized by Thorneburg (1975):

- lack of interest

- failing grades

- relationship problems with teachers and peers

- negative attitudes toward school
- wanting to find a job
- marriage and/or pregnancy
- military enlistment
- expulsion

The proposed relationship between underlying psychological needs and school nonattendance (as well as other maladaptive behaviors) is given support by the frequency of traumatic background factors among nonattenders. Harris (1980) provides the most thoroughly controlled documentation of this relationship, as previously discussed in this chapter. She showed significantly higher incidence of the following background events among nonattenders and at-risk-for-dropout subjects than among controls:

- physical abuse
- incest
- sexual assault
- death of a family member
- divorce of parents
- death of a friend
- frequency of school transfers

In addition, Harris found that dropout-prone students exhibited a higher total number of traumatic events, appeared to be more emotionally disturbed and in need of mental health services, and experienced higher levels of family stress within the past year than did controls. Finally, Harris found that these students exhibited more of the following maladaptive behaviors:

- pregnancy
- running away
- delinquency
- substance use/abuse

- suicide attempts

- self-mutilation

One of the major causal factors predicting dropping out seems obvious: school failure beginning in the late elementary grades. School failure experiences increase risk of drug abuse, delinquency, violence, and pregnancy, as well as dropping out (Brewer et al., 1995).

DRUG AND ALCOHOL ABUSE

Drug and alcohol abuse continue to plague young people, both as a result of and as a cause of trauma. As a traumatogenic factor in adolescents' lives, the results of drug and alcohol abuse during adolescence are manifold. Accidents, overdose, physical and mental deterioration and disability, relational difficulties, and diminished work and school performance have all been traditionally associated with drug and alcohol abuse among those ages 14 to 24 (Millman et al., 1981). Currently, however, the wave of youth violence now overwhelming the young people of this and other developed countries is fueled by substance misuse, as outlined in the next section.

Drug and alcohol abuse differs from other maladaptive coping behaviors (such as running away, gambling, and risk taking) because, in addition to psychological dependence, it involves physiological dependence. Rehabilitation thus requires altering physiological as well as psychological cycles. Another differentiating characteristic is the wide acceptance of substance abuse among peers, making such abuse nearly a given in the social milieu.

It is difficult to estimate abuse frequencies among adolescents, as the use of alcohol and drugs is such a pervasive part of the contemporary youth culture (and indeed of the general culture), and strict delineation of use from abuse is largely dependent upon the purpose of the person rendering the judgment. Millman et al., as early as 1981, conceptualized substance abuse as having moved through an epidemic situation (precipitously increased usage) to the then-endemic situation in which use was an integral part of the rites of passage in this and many societies. Currently, however, we may have moved back into an epidemic mode due to fresh escalation.

While in 1977, Schukit et al. estimated that 80 to 90% of young people had imbibed alcohol on at least one occasion, and Abelson et al. (1977) determined that 15% of 14-year-olds had used marijuana at least once, current figures show increased usage among younger children and increased usage of harder drugs.

The Office of National Drug Control Policy (1996) reports a study conducted during the 1994–95 school year involving 198,241 students in sixth through twelfth grades from 32 states across the country. They found data, consistent with other recent studies, supporting the following conclusions:

- Cigarette and marijuana use is at an eight-year high, with one third of high school seniors reporting smoking marijuana within the past year and one fifth reporting smoking marijuana at least monthly. In junior high school, marijuana use has risen 111% from 1989. Cigarette use has increased at the high school level, up from 37% in 1989 to nearly half. Nearly one third of all students from sixth to twelfth grades report smoking, 20% regularly.

- More than one third of all high school seniors say they engage in heavy drinking, reporting having five or more drinks in a row on at least one occasion in the two weeks prior to the survey.

- The average age of first use of alcohol or marijuana dropped to 13 years of age.

- Hard drugs, predominately cocaine and hallucinogens, show a similar increase: in 1995, 36% more students in ninth to twelfth grades used cocaine over those in 1989, and 75% more used hallucinogens.

Even more troubling is a U.S. Department of Health and Human Services report cited in the Office of Drug Control Policy (1996) that, in 1995, 2.4 million youth ages 12 to 17 admitted using an illicit drug at least once during the month prior to the survey. This is 11% of those surveyed. However accurate the survey is in reflecting actual usage, the most disturbing part of the report is that it represents double the usage reported in 1992 using the same methodology.

Another sobering consideration is that the above figures represent only those young people in school. Adolescents who are either incarcerated or on the street are not included and are likely to be more heavily involved. This may constitute 15 to 20% of youth the age of high school seniors.

In many ways, alcohol and drug use makes sense to young people. In the process of moving from a position of relative dependence to one of relative independence, adolescents normally lack the sense of identity and personal competence to "be adult." In the short run, substance use provides peer acceptance, a sense of control, and a medicinal effect, enhancing self-esteem and relieving anxiety and tension. Typical use begins with occasional experimentation in association with friends, usually beginning with alcohol and progressing to marijuana. Some adolescents move on to try depressants, stimulants, and psychedelics, culminating in opiates or cocaine. While most adolescents stop and stabilize at some point along this progression, some develop a poly-drug abuse pattern that varies according to the availability of the drugs, the situation, and the needs of the user (Millman et al., 1981). The American Probation and Parole Association (1992) outlines a convenient and practical four-stage model of substance involvement:

1. Experimental and social use, in which occasional usage provides a temporary high and satisfies various needs common to growing up. This stage usually produces little noticeable change in behavior.

2. Purposeful misuse, several times a week, including use that begins during the day. A state of euphoria is the goal, and coping with stress is a desired spinoff. Behavioral indicators may be a change of friends, mood swings, more rebellious behavior, and the beginning of school problems.

3. Almost daily usage, frequently alone. Substance is used not to attain a high, but rather to return to "normal" and escape pain, depression, and general discomfort. Indicators include poor school or work attendance and performance, deviant peer group, drug culture appearance, poor family and social relationships, personality changes, and a consuming focus upon using.

4. Dependency and addiction, characterized by continuous and out-of-control use. Indicators include dropping out of school, inability to maintain work or relationships, deteriorating cognitive and physical condition, emotional and mood swings, and an exclusive focus upon procuring and using drugs.

A substantial determinant of early-use patterns is peer group influence. In a review of the literature on the relationship between peer pressure and drug and alcohol abuse, the Office of National Drug Control Policy (1996) concludes that adolescents derive progressively more support and information from peers, although the extent varies considerably.

Negligent or extreme parental styles often push adolescents into precocious identification with the peer group. This is borne out in the literature concerning background variables antecedent to problematic substance use. Robins, Davis, and Wish (1977) document increased incidence of parental divorce and separation in the backgrounds of substance-abusing adolescents. Similarly, Barnes (1979) found higher rates of family pathology among solvent abusers. Family alcoholism has also been found to be predictive of substance abuse.

Family pathology is one background factor predictive of substance abuse. Both victimization and loss during childhood are also predictive. Klagsbrun and Davis (1977), cited earlier, report a high correlation between parental loss and subsequent drug and alcohol abuse during adolescence. Similarly, Harris (1980), in her study of dropout-prone adolescents, showed substance abuse to be common among her sample and found high frequencies of both physical abuse and sexual assault in their backgrounds. More recently, a multipath model of delinquency is being increasingly adopted to examine the interactive factors leading to substance abuse among other maladaptive adolescent behaviors. See the discussion in the next section on youth violence.

Even if usage never reaches stage 4 (as outlined above), the consequences of substance abuse constitute a profound crisis facing youth who choose to abuse. Important developmental tasks are not completed, the development of autonomy is thwarted, physical health is at risk through accident or illness, and higher operational learning is affected. Relationships with family, friends, the community, and the legal system are compromised, all of which constitute a set of over-whelming burdens to young people trying to grow up. Thus, while substance abuse may be the result of prior trauma, it creates new crises as it follows its progressive course.

YOUTH VIOLENCE

During the past several years, a new area of adolescent maladaptive behavior has become vogue. Youth violence is epidemic, perhaps reflecting a growing desperation in the larger society, and is having a devastating effect upon the young people of countries worldwide. Newspapers reflect the adult world's concern over youth violence in headlines announcing drive-by shootings, campus killings, murders by teens and preteens, and gang-related crime. Members of posses compete for predatory sex, murder has become a rite of passage, and children are maimed or killed for their fashionable clothing.

In the United States, gun violence is particularly frightening. One of every four teenage deaths is caused by firearms, and one in three inner-city male students has been shot at, stabbed, or other-wise injured with a weapon at or in transit to or from school in the past few years (Office of Juvenile Justice and Delinquency Prevention, 1995). The number of arrests for violent crimes reflects the increase in youth violence, jumping 36% between 1989 and 1993, more than four times the increase for adults. Similarly, juvenile arrests for homicide soared 45% during that same period (FBI, 1994). These increases illustrate another trend: crimes committed by youth are increasingly against persons, not property. The same FBI report cites crimes against persons having increased 47%, while those against property only rose 8%.

Much of the increase in violent crime is attributable to the rise in gang affiliation, behavior, and style among young people. According to the Department of Justice (Howell, 1994), gang affiliation per se is fairly large; there are an estimated 4,441 identified gangs with 249,324 members nationwide. Furthermore, law enforcement leaders have reported the migration of Los Angeles Crips and Bloods to as many as forty-five western and midwestern cities, although Howell cites ongoing studies as indicating that this trend is caused by a combination of family migration and local genesis rather than gang relocation. Howell goes on to cite studies indicating that gang affiliation per se is involved in a relatively low proportion of criminal acts.

Of greater concern is a general identification on the part of young people with gang-style behavior and values. Brewer et al. (1995) cite several risk factors associated with increased violence, many of which are family and community based. Some of these factors appear obvious: family discord and violence, economic deprivation, low neighborhood attachment and community organization, transience and mobility, and the availability of drugs and firearms. However, two stand out: community laws and norms favorable to drug use, firearms, and crime; and media portrayals of violence. It is not news that this is a society that is fascinated by violence, and clearly our entertainments of choice favor flash, glitter, and quick resolutions. But even more so, the entire youth clothing and entertainment industries make fortunes pushing violence-oriented music, gang-theme fashions, and the glorification of external symbols of power, however they are acquired.

The Office of Juvenile Justice and Delinquency Prevention (1995) conducted a wide-ranging study of delinquent behavior. The survey, which polled 198,241 students in sixth through twelfth grades in 32 states from California to New York, had startling results.

The results from high school students include the following:

- More than 6% carry a gun to school

- More than 13% take part in a gang

- Nearly 8% think often or a lot about suicide

- More than a third have threatened to harm another student or a teacher

- More than 27% are getting into trouble with police

- More than 35% are afraid another student will hurt them

- Nearly 14% have been hurt by another student at school

Even more dramatic are the results of the junior high school students:

- More than 3% carry a gun to school

- More than 14% take part in a gang

- More than 6% think often or a lot about suicide

- Almost 30% have threatened to harm another student or teacher

- More than 21% are getting into trouble with police

- More than 38% are afraid another student will hurt them

- Nearly 22% have been hurt by another student at school

These students are 12 to 14 years old! Clearly, schools in America in the 1990s are not safe places to be. Educational goals and strategies, once the central staff problems of the day, are being eclipsed by issues of behavior management and personal safety.

The causes of violence on an individual level are currently understood on a developmental basis. The risk factors organized by Hawkins and Catalano (1995) into the areas of community, family, school, and individual have a different effect depending upon the stage of the individual's growth and development.

From birth to age 4, family bonding and parental skills are critical. Parents' failure to establish clear expectations for behavior, negligent supervision, and severe or inconsistent punishment are predictors of later delinquent and violent behavior (Mendel, 1995), as are physical abuse and neglect (Thornberry et al., 1995).

During the ages of 4 to 6, community norms favorable to crime and substance abuse, availability of drugs and weapons, frequent transitions, and exposure to media violence have an adverse effect predicting later violence, as does early academic failure (Institute of Medicine, 1994).

Among children ages 7 to 12, transitions, the availability of firearms and other weapons, association with delinquent and violent peers, and academic failure predict violence and delinquent behavior. Drug use, association with delinquent peers, gang membership, as well as domestic violence and child maltreatment place 13- to 18-year-old adolescents at risk (Huizinga et al., 1994).

One of the great difficulties in dealing with violent youth is that adolescents tend to view such adult helpers as school personnel, law enforcement, and mental health professionals as extensions of the parental control system. The "multiple path" etiology of violence and delinquency presumes the synergistic effect of the various sources of risk to youth that together make violence more likely. This conceptualization is outlined in Chapter 7.

Conclusion

The research discussed here provides basic background information regarding childhood and adolescent crisis, and the connection between the two. The major forms of adolescent acting-out behaviors have been outlined in a manner designed to give professionals an overview of the central variables and dynamics of each. More important, these studies point to a relationship between childhood trauma and adolescent crisis that underscores the need for effective management of childhood crisis and illuminates essential dimensions of adolescent crisis.

Studies reviewed relating a range of antecedent experiences in childhood to subsequent specific maladaptive adolescent behaviors indicate a commonality of antecedents. Studies of adolescent alcohol and drug abuse, runaways, and serious school attendance problems show each to be positively correlated with incidents from the three thematic areas of critical incidents: family pathology, victimization, and loss. Only suicide was not correlated with all three; studies reviewed on suicide correlate that behavior with family pathology and loss, but not with victimization. It should be noted, however, that Briere, Runtz, and Lightfoot (1978) have associated adult suicide with prior childhood sexual abuse.

This review of the literature relating to childhood critical incidents appears to support the contention that—in general—such incidents are related to maladaptive behaviors in adolescence. The one study that addressed this question directly established a connection (Harris, 1980). In addition, although each was limited in scope to specific childhood incidents or to specific behavioral consequences, the studies taken together add direct evidence to a general relationship and useful discussion of the dynamics of each aspect studied.

Appendix I reports original research supporting this general relationship and suggests approaches and management strategies for adults that are empirically associated with more healthy outcomes for traumatized children. The implications of this association will be discussed further in Chapter 3.

Prior to that discussion, however, a major task remains. In order for professionals to determine appropriate steps to meet the challenge of childhood crises, it is essential that they know not only *that* an association exists between crisis and subsequent behavioral difficulties, but also *why* it exists and *how* it functions. We turn in the next chapter to this task and focus upon posttraumatic reactions in childhood.

CHAPTER 2

Children's Reactions to Trauma

"This whole year has been just too crazy for me
I guess. If things keep going on the way they are
I am just going to bust out and seriously hurt some-
body. I just want everybody to know one thing: I
am _____ from 62nd St. East Coast Crips and
I will always be a Crip no matter how old I get."

> 16-year-old who lost six cousins in unrelated
> deaths, three of which were gang-related,
> over a one-year period

OVERVIEW

When crisis occurs, school personnel need relevant, developmentally accurate information regarding children's reactions to trauma. This chapter provides detailed descriptions of children's reactions to crises, including typical after-effects and developmental implications.

Chapter Contents

Most professionals who work with children—educators, therapists, social workers, or others—will encounter children whose lives have been changed by trauma. Effectiveness in dealing with such children during or after a crisis requires knowledge. To be aware of possible signs of trauma, professionals should first be able to recognize situations that are potentially traumatic. One doesn't need a Ph.D. to realize that most children will be traumatized by a parent's death, but there are other far less dramatic situations that are also potentially traumatic. For example:

> One woman in therapy for agoraphobia (fear of public places) had her most violent reactions when contemplating eating out in a restaurant. While the background factors were numerous and complex, one childhood event stood out in her mind. At about 11 years of age, following a move to the city and enrollment in a new, urban school, she was asked to give an oral report on her second day of school. Already having an upset stomach, she involuntarily vomited in front of the class. Not only had she never forgotten the incident, but whenever she went out in public she felt nauseated and frequently had to return home.

An experience that is only moderately difficult for one person may be unbearable and traumatic for another. Thus professionals cannot always gauge whether situations will be traumatic or not without observing the reactions of those involved.

Professionals in fields related to child care and child development need to become aware of the signs and symptoms of trauma. These symptoms may appear at times seemingly unrelated to crisis. While some children may have acute situational reactions to critical incidents that may manifest at the time of the incident or in the hours or days just following, a different set of symptoms may occur in the weeks, months, or years after the incident, and these delayed reactions may take many forms.

In this chapter the signs and symptoms of both acute situational stress and delayed stress reactions to critical incidents are outlined. The concept of Posttraumatic Stress Disorder is discussed as an explanatory construct, and the developmental implications of trauma are explored.

Acute Situational Reactions to Crisis

While much has been written about delayed stress reactions follow-ing crises, little empirical research has been done documenting chil-dren's stress reactions during or immediately following critical incidents. Such information would be quite useful to those who work with children who are traumatized, although such studies are difficult to conduct. Data now available are largely anecdotal and retrospective.

Some studies have described behavior in the weeks following traumatic events. Creamer et al. (1992) and Bryant and Harvey (1996) have discussed stress reactions in the immediate aftermath of disasters and other emergencies. The studies state comparable rates of impairment, although they differ in instrumentation. Further, they are not correlated to the more recent DSM-IV classification of Acute Stress Disorder. The studies differ most on the alleged connec-tion between premorbid variables such as preexisting mental illness or prior incidents, and subsequent posttrauma reactions, and it is generally held by researchers and clinicians that the severity of the trauma is a more significant factor than the premorbid condition in determining the severity of reaction. Neither of these studies consid-ers children's reactions.

Very little hard research has been (or can be) conducted on chil-dren's situational reactions to traumatic events. Much of what is recorded consists of inferences based upon secondhand reports of children's behavior during crises. Usually, rescue workers, police, and medical workers provide the most reliable information, and this sec-tion will draw heavily from such sources, as well as from the work of Eth and Pynoos, discussed later in the chapter. Their discussion of symptomatology is based upon observation of and interviews with children shortly after the children had witnessed a parent's death (Eth & Pynoos, 1985c).

Children's immediate responses to critical incidents can range from hysteria to shock. Often there is no apparent reaction—a visi-ble response may set in only later. This is usually the result of denial: The child cannot make sense of the relevant sensory information and simply shuts it out. Sometimes the child lacks the conceptual maturity to comprehend what has happened. It is probably also often the case that adults observing children's reactions during such incidents are themselves caught up in the events, and therefore misread the children's subtle signs as lack of response.

In general, a child who is experiencing a traumatic reaction will show extremes of behavior, either underresponding or overresponding to the crisis situation. The signs and symptoms of acute stress in children can be grouped under the following classifications: cognitive, emotional, physical, and behavioral.

To obtain firsthand information regarding the specific reactions children go through following trauma, this author questioned 28 adolescents about their traumatic experiences. These adolescents were all at risk of dropping out of school, the majority were from middle-class families, and most were Anglo. Their experiences included rape, accidents, parental suicide attempts, divorce, death of parents or close friends, family problems, and abuse. Despite the fact that sexual abuse tends to be underreported, some 36% of the females reported having been molested or raped.

The reactions listed below were each reported at least once by the group and are representative of children's responses to a wide variety of critical incidents:

Signs and Symptoms of Situational Trauma

Cognitive	*Physical*
confusion	pounding heart
difficulties solving problems	nausea
time distortions	cramps
problems in setting priorities	sweating
	other signs of shock
	headaches
	muffled hearing

Emotional	*Behavioral*
irritability	slowness
fear	aimless wandering
anxiety	dejection
frustration	memory problems
anger	hysteria
	out-of-control behavior
	hyperactivity

This same group was asked which symptoms appeared weeks, months, and even years after the incident. They related the following signs of delayed response to the event:

Signs and Symptoms of Delayed Response to Trauma

Cognitive	*Physical*
confusion	fatigue
fear of going crazy	increased illness
preoccupation with the incident	
orientation toward the past	
denial of importance of the event	

Emotional	*Behavioral*
fear of reoccurrence	sleep problems
phobias	social withdrawal
oversensitivity	need to talk compulsively about the event
depression	
grief	relationship or family problems
guilt	
resentment	flashbacks
worry about physical health	avoidance of incident location
self-destructive behaviors	substance abuse

The delayed reactions listed here differ from immediate responses to trauma in some ways that might be expected. Yet the severity of the symptoms—sometimes years after the event—coupled with the fact that this group of young people had significant school attendance problems, higher-than-average rates of substance abuse, and other self-destructive behaviors, raises several interesting questions about posttraumatic stress reactions in childhood.

The most useful explanatory construct available for making sense of the relationship between traumas and later reactions is that of Posttraumatic Stress Disorder (PTSD) and its recent addition, Acute Stress Disorder (ASD) (American Psychiatric Association,

1994). In the sections that follow this construct will be explored, with particular emphasis upon the manner in which posttraumatic stress interacts with normal development and the evolution of symptomatology among children and adolescents.

Posttraumatic Stress Disorder

HISTORY

Over the years, practitioners have gradually formulated, applied, tested, and refined the concept of posttraumatic reactions. A quick review of the development of the concept may be useful, given that different aspects of the concept were the main focus in different eras. Freud's emphasis upon the stimulus barrier, for instance, is still of interest, even though current application of the concept does not employ Freudian terminology.

The concept of Posttraumatic Stress Disorder has a long and distinguished history, despite its fairly recent appearance as a diagnostic category in the American Psychiatric Association's (APA)(1980) *Diagnostic and Statistical Manual,* third edition (DSM-III). The disorder was described, at least symptomatically, in the writings of Shakespeare, Samuel Pepys, and Charles Dickens.

The concept of posttraumatic neurosis was introduced in the late nineteenth century and soon became a focus of controversy within English compensation laws following the expansion of railroads from freight to extensive passenger hauling (Trimble, 1981). In cases involving railroad passenger accidents, postaccident symptomatology was argued to be of psychological rather than physical origin, and this clearly had implications for settlements in court (Trimble, 1985). Subsequently, controversy over posttraumatic symptomatology spread to the battlefield, focusing upon whether "posttraumatic neurosis" was a legitimate clinical entity or simply a form of malingering.

Freud discussed traumatic experiences and their sequelae in several writings, hypothesizing a protective shield, or stimulus barrier, that provides a threshold for the perception of stimulus (Freud, 1920, 1926). Once this stimulus barrier is breached, the pleasure principle no longer functions and the victim regresses to a more primitive form of functioning in order to master the stimulus. Helplessness is experienced, and obsessive repetition of the traumatic theme occurs. Defensive reactions may be utilized in order to avoid the painful repetitive stimulus (Freud, 1939). Elements of Freud's construct are found in contemporary theories of posttrauma reaction.

CONTEMPORARY THEORIES

The two major contemporary theories that explain the process of posttrauma reaction are based in cognitive psychology and learning theory, respectively. These theories are useful because they account for three common phenomena associated with posttrauma reactions: denial and numbing, reexperiencing, and depressive and phobic symptoms.

In the report of their work with Veterans Administration staff who treated Vietnam veterans, Horowitz and Solomon (1975) discuss two major dynamics that accounted for the delayed nature of the vets' stress responses. The first dynamic is what Freud had previously described as a "completion" tendency. In order to accommodate to a radically different situation that has changed as a result of a traumatic experience, memories, associated information, and implications are assimilated through a gradual process of integration. Primarily a cognitive process, this includes the intrusion of recurrent nightmares, daytime images and painful emotional reexperiences, unpleasant moods and emotional storms, and compulsive behavioral repetitions. This process may include secondary signs such as aggressive or self-destructive behavior, fear of loss of control over hostile or violent impulses characterized by apparent good functioning, and impaired social relationships. With veterans, such behavior often did not arise until years after return to a civilian life.

The second major dynamic is a "denial/numbing" tendency, serving as a defense against the intrusion of intolerable ideas and emotions. This tendency consists of denial, numbing, alienation, compartmentalization, and isolation of the traumatic experience from everyday life. Horowitz and Solomon believe that the denial/numbing tendency interrupts the intrusion/repetition process, accounting for the delayed nature of Vietnam veterans' stress responses.

The intrusion/repetition process serves the healing function of integration and adaptation. The denial/numbing function appears to protect the individual from having to assimilate too much too soon. Horowitz and Solomon indicate that difficulties in integrating the Vietnam experience with the veterans' pre- and post-Vietnam lives leads to such psychological problems as low self-worth, shame, depersonalization, frustration and reactive rages, and various psychosocial disabilities.

Horowitz and Solomon's discussion builds upon Freud's, using essentially psychodynamic concepts. A learning model of post-trauma reaction is provided by Seligman and Garber (1980) in their discussion of learned helplessness. This is useful, as it presents a rationale for such symptoms as depression and phobias. Seligman and Garber describe traumatic situations as those in which adverse consequences follow a situation in which the victim perceives little or no control and little predictability. An externalized attribution of control is learned from the experience, forming a learned helplessness. On the basis of this, motivational deficits follow, and the victim ceases to initiate adaptive responses. Withdrawal, isolation, and depression are logical outcomes, as are anxieties and phobias resulting from the perception of the world as both threatening and unpredictable. Central to both Horowitz and Solomon's and Seligman and Garber's discussions is the nucleus of the posttrauma reaction: reexperience of the event, numbing of experience, and various forms of maladaptive behavioral change.

Horowitz (1991) expands his discussion of alternating intrusion and numbing phases by elaborating why this takes place. Trauma presents an assault upon fundamental beliefs, which are necessary for the individual to act constructively in the world. The overwhelming stimulus and emotions generated by the incident present a threat to the existing conceptual framework by which the world is understood. To protect this framework, the mind automatically inhibits its own perception of the event, thus reducing the information being processed. This "perceptual inhibition" is a defense mechanism designed to maintain a stable sense of self and world.

Horowitz postulates a set of inner models of expectancies (schemata) by which ongoing experience is organized and decisions orchestrated. The various types of experienc-processing he notes include the following:

- New stimuli are matched with expectancies based upon current needs

- New information is matched with schematic representations of the world

- Current body sensations are related to body images

- Images are matched with relevant labels such as words

- New demands are matched with available coping strategies

When experiences do not fit existing models, the models must be revised and the experiences reinterpreted until a "fit" is found. Horowitz calls the predisposition to actively store and continually rework memories of incompletely "processed" experiences a "completion tendency." Completion can be accomplished by

> a combination of conscious and unconscious processes, by revisions, learning, and the creation of new solutions . . . , decisions . . . that revise inner schemata and plans for action. The goal is continuity of the traumatic experience with other life memories, and the reintegration of personal aims. (1987, p. 99)

Internal defense mechanisms such as inhibition and facilitation serve to manage the degree to which such experiences are processed, and people—and their posttrauma symptoms—differ as to their characteristic controls. Such controls can include seeking information, switching among attitudes, sliding meanings and valuations, arranging information into decision trees, revising schemata, and practicing new modes of thinking and acting (Horowitz, 1987, p. 100). Controls can be used in an adaptive manner (e.g., problem solving, emotional balancing, identification) or in a defensive manner (e.g., denial by rationalization, intellectualization, avoidance), or they may fail altogether (e.g., helplessness, meaninglessness, emotional flooding).

Much recent work on understanding how trauma occurs has focused upon neurobiological dimensions of brain changes following overwhelming incidents and upon memory research. In reviewing recent work on the psychobiology of Posttraumatic Stress Disorder (defined below), Van der Kolk (1996) points out two types of abnormalities following trauma. The first consists of heightened responsiveness to trauma-specific stimulus. Reminders of the event can result in increased levels of those chemicals that trigger autonomic nervous system arousal. The second type of abnormality consists of overarousal to intense stimuli that are not trauma-related. Victims of trauma tend to have a pronounced startle reaction as well as other arousal symptoms to loud noises or other abrupt but trauma-neutral experiences. This overactivation of the autonomic nervous system, Van der Kolk feels, results from a lack of integration of highly emotionally charged memories with the cognitive structuring of experience.

Van der Kolk points out that specific psychophysiological effects include release of those neurohormones that accompany stress reactions, including the following:

- increased levels of catecholamines (epinephrine and norepinepherine), resulting in increased sympathetic nervous system activity

- decreased corticosteriods and serotonin; the lowered levels of cortisol and serotonin result in inability to moderate the catecholamine-triggered fight or flight response

- increased levels of endogenous opioids, resulting in pain analgesia, emotional blunting, and memory impairment

Van der Kolk cites a recently growing body of research that is beginning to outline the psychophysiology of trauma among children. The developmental effects of these neurohormonal responses appear to include disruption of the functional areas of numerous cortical and subcortical areas, including loss of synchronization and integration. Left hemisphere activities seem to be more affected, impacting language and recall abilities in particular. While the evidence is limited so far, it seems to provide support for observations leading to the new complex Posttraumatic Stress Disorder discussed below, which has particular relevance for children traumatized early and for prolonged periods. The potential for connections with a wide range of thus far poorly understood learning and adjustment problems among young people seems to be great.

Finally, as indicated above, researchers have narrowed the search for the brain centers responsible for these posttraumatic biological changes (Van der Kolk, 1996) to two structures in the limbic system (the part of the subcortical brain responsible for self-preservation and survival). The amygdala evaluates the emotional meaning of incoming stimuli and integrates the representation of external events with emotional experiences associated with their memory. The hippocampus categorizes, relates, and stores incoming stimuli in memory, a vital part of the process of creating declarative memory.

Van der Kolk cites reports linking posttrauma chemical activity as described above with shrinking of the hippocampus (due to increased levels of cortisol—a hormone toxic to the hippocampus) and increased activity in the right hemisphere, site of parts of the limbic system connected with the amygdala. This would correlate with findings that activity in these areas corresponds with posttrauma symptomology. As research develops in the psychobiology of stress disorders, new avenues of prevention and treatment will emerge.

These findings make sense of diverse phenomena, yet they appear to complicate understanding of the reaction with a wide variety of signs and symptoms. In order to provide a more cohesive description of the reaction, practitioners have sought to unify contemporary understanding into a single diagnostic formula in the latest edition of the APA's *Diagnostic and Statistical Manual*, revised in 1987 (DSM-III-R) and again in 1994 (DSM-IV). The reaction has been named Posttraumatic Stress Disorder, and the revised criteria for PTSD are now formalized as follows:

Diagnostic Criteria for 309.81: Posttraumatic Stress Disorder

A. The person has been exposed to a traumatic event in which both of the following were present:

1. The person experienced, witnessed, or was confronted with an event or events that involved actual or threatened death or serious injury, or a threat to the physical integrity of self or others.

2. The person's response involved intense fear, helplessness, or horror. (In children, this may be expressed instead by disorganized or agitated behavior.)

B. The traumatic event is persistently reexperienced in one or more of the following ways:

1. Recurrent and intrusive distressing recollections of the event, including images, thoughts, or perceptions. (In young children, repetitive play may occur in which themes or aspects of the trauma are expressed.)

2. Recurrent distressing dreams of the event. (In children, there may be frightening dreams without recognizable content.)

3. Acting or feeling as if the traumatic event were recurring, which may involve a sense of reliving the experience, illusions, hallucinations, and dissociative flashback episodes, including those that occur on awakening or when intoxicated. (In young children, trauma-specific reenactment may occur.)

4. Intense psychological distress at exposure to internal or external cues that symbolize or resemble an aspect of the traumatic event.

5. Physiological reactivity at exposure to internal or external cues that symbolize or resemble an aspect of the traumatic event.

C. Persistent avoidance of stimuli associated with the trauma and numbing of general responsiveness (not present before the trauma), as indicated by three or more of the following:

1. efforts to avoid thoughts, feelings, or conversations associated with the trauma

2. efforts to avoid activities, places, or people that arouse recollections of the trauma

3. inability to recall an important aspect of the trauma

4. markedly diminished interest or participation in significant activities

5. feeling of detachment or estrangement from others

6. restricted range of affect (e.g., unable to have loving feelings)

7. sense of a foreshortened future (e.g., does not expect to have a career, marriage, children, or a normal life span)

D. Persistent symptoms of increased arousal (not present before the trauma), as indicated by two or more of the following:

1. difficulty falling or staying asleep

2. irritability or outbursts of anger

3. difficulty concentrating

4. hypervigilance

5. exaggerated startle response

E. Duration of the disturbance (symptoms in B, C, and D) is more than one month.

F. The disturbance causes clinically significant distress or impairment of social, occupational, or other important areas of functioning.

Specify acute if duration of symptoms is less than three months.

Specify chronic if duration of symptoms is three months or more.

Specify delayed onset if onset of symptoms is at least six months after the stressor.

(American Psychiatric Association, 1994, pp. 424–429)

The DSM-IV also added a new category, *308.3 Acute Stress Disorder*. Acute Stress Disorder closely follows Posttraumatic Stress Disorder, differing mainly in terms of time of onset and duration (within four weeks of the incident, lasting a minimum of two days to a maximum of four weeks) and in terms of some of the symptoms. While ASD symptoms are similar to those of PTSD, the DSM-IV emphasizes some types of dissociation more in ASD than in PTSD. The new edition does not provide much information regarding the application of the new category of ASD to children. It should be remembered that the DSM-III (1980), prior to its revision, did not address the diagnosis of children with its new category at that time, PTSD. Presumably, clarification will be forthcoming. It should be noted that, because dissociation has recently been found to be predictive of the later development of Posttraumatic Stress Disorder (Van der Kolk, 1996), the diagnosis of Acute Stress Disorder focuses upon dissociation as the key pathological element during reactions in the immediate aftermath of a critical incident.

CONTINUING CONTROVERSY

The discussion over how to best characterize children's reactions to traumatic events continues despite, or perhaps because of, the burgeoning research findings of the past ten years. One issue concerns the advisability of maintaining one umbrella diagnostic category such as PTSD, particularly when specific symptom clusters within the category appear associated with trauma of long duration. In an excellent current paper, Zlotnick et al. (1996) discuss the controversy over whether the symptoms of childhood sexual abuse are (Rowan & Foy, 1993) or are not (Herman, 1992) best described as PTSD. Herman suggests that stress responses to trauma be viewed as a "spectrum of conditions" rather than as a single disorder (1992). She argues for an "expanded" concept of posttraumatic stress reaction for victims of repeated, prolonged trauma (Disorder of Extreme Stress Not Otherwise Specified). DESNOS refers to three symptom clusters—physical, dissociative, and mood—as well as relationship disruption, changes in identity, and repetition of harm. Zlotnick's study supports a complex PTSD/DESNOS symptom picture following childhood sexual abuse, including somatization, dissociation, anxiety, alexithymia (the inability to verbalize feelings), social dysfunction, maladaptive schemas, self-destruction, and adult victimization. It may be that further studies will support a clear symptom cluster for long-term repeated abuse, sexual or otherwise. Similarly, it is hoped that researchers will be able to specify in the future how the long-term posttraumatic reaction surfaces in childhood. In any case, it is clear that profound symptoms follow from childhood victimization into adulthood. Van der Kolk (1996) summarizes the DESNOS indicators as follows:

1. The older the person at the time of the traumatization, and the shorter the duration of the trauma, the more the symptoms follow the intrusion/numbing/arousal cluster associated with the current conception of PTSD

2. The younger the person, and the longer the duration, the more the symptoms approach the complexity of the DESNOS formulation, involving disorders of self-regulation, stimulus discrimination, and characterological development

Specific DESNOS indicators are the following:

A. Alterations in regulating affective arousal

    1. chronic affect dysregulation

    2. difficulty modulating anger

    3. self-destructive and suicidal behavior

    4. difficulty modulating sexual involvement

    5. impulsive and risk-taking behavior

B. Alterations in attention and consciousness

    1. amnesia

    2. dissociation

C. Somatization

D. Chronic characterological changes

    1. alterations in self-perception: chronic guilt and shame; feelings of self-blame, ineffectiveness, and of being permanently damaged

    2. alterations in perception of perpetrator: adopting distorted beliefs and idealizing the perpetrator

    3. alterations in relations with others; an inability to trust or maintain relationships with others, a tendency to be victimized, and a tendency to victimize others

E. Alterations in systems of meaning

    1. despair and hopelessness

    2. loss of previously sustaining beliefs

A careful reading of the DESNOS indicators shows a transition from intrusive imagery/overreactivity/numbing to more characterological traits.

PTSD in Children

The manner in which children are affected by PTSD is of great interest among educators and therapists because it directly affects the learning, behavior, and progress of children. While all but the most naïve accept that children are negatively affected by critical incidents in a lasting manner, *how* they are affected is less clear. Of equal importance to educators and others who work with children, however, is the need to know when to refer the child for extra services.

Until recently, little work had been done on articulating the specific manner in which PTSD is manifested in children. In general, there was a presumption that 1980 DSM-III criteria applied, but few verification studies had been done. Empirical studies regarding PTSD in children are beginning to surface through studies of specific situational stressors. Following the kidnapping of a busload of children in Chowchilla, California, Terr (1979) published the first of a series of studies describing the children's posttraumatic reactions. As early as 1976, Newman reported children's reactions to the disastrous Buffalo Creek flood. Pynoos and Eth (1984) describe children's reactions to witnessing parental homicide, and Earle (1979) studied the psychological effects upon children of mutilating surgery. Through these studies a clinical picture of PTSD in children is emerging.

In a brief review of contemporary thinking regarding childhood trauma, Benedek (1985) summarizes children's posttraumatic symptomatology as it applies to DSM-III PTSD criteria. Benedek cites in particular daydreams, fantasies, and nightmares (recurrent recollections), and behavioral changes linked to sudden visual and auditory stimuli that may remind children of the traumatic event. In addition, she notes emotional numbing in children, which she feels is in fact a defensive reaction:

> Particularly prominent in children are sleep disturbances, with inability to fall asleep, night terrors and nightmares. Traumatized children are described as regressing in the following ways: climbing

in bed with their parents, sleeping in strange places, sucking their thumbs, and becoming enuretic. (Benedek, 1985, p. 8)

Benedek concludes that childhood symptomatology does indeed fit DSM-III criteria. As will be discussed below, the revised edition of the DSM-III and the DSM-IV (American Psychiatric Association, 1987 and 1994) begin to address some of these issues.

Much remains to be done to clarify differences between childhood and adult Posttraumatic Stress Disorder. Diagnostic criteria and associated features must be refined further to provide a more precise clinical picture. As research and clinical knowledge sharpen, many children who have been diagnosed and treated as depressive, anxiety disordered, and adjustment disordered will be recognized to be suffering from PTSD. This change of diagnostic focus will bring about changes in treatment, as will be elaborated further in this chapter. Before treatment is addressed, however, the effect of developmental level must be considered, as well as the implications of PTSD in traumatized groups.

PTSD AND DEVELOPMENTAL LEVEL

Eth and Pynoos (1985c), working with a subject pool of traumatized children who had witnessed a parent's homicide and who were referred by various agencies for evaluation, describe developmental-level-specific posttraumatic symptomatology.

Based upon clinical interviews and treatment of 40 children who witnessed the homicide of a parent, Eth and Pynoos present a general phenomenology of posttraumatic reactions in childhood. They delineate specific developmental characteristics of preschool, school-age, and adolescent groups and, on the basis of their literature review and observations, list common reactions to trauma occurring in children irrespective of their age. These general features include deleterious effects in the following areas:

1. Cognition
    recurrent and intrusive recollections
    decline in school performance
    learning problems
    misperception of duration and sequencing

2. Affect
   psychic numbing
   feelings of detachment
   constricted affect
   fear of repeated trauma
   anxiety
   feelings of guilt
   pessimistic expectations of the future
   intolerance of fear response

3. Interpersonal Relations

4. Behavior
   inhibited
   hypervigilant, avoidant, or phobic
   startle reactions
   reenactments; unknowing performance of similar acts
   repetitive, unsatisfying play involving traumatic themes
   counterphobic
   nightmares

5. Vegetative Function

6. Symptom Formation, including personality change

Posttraumatic features specific to preschool-age children include the following:

withdrawal; subdued and mute behavior
denial
participation in reenactments and unsatisfying plans involving
   traumatic themes
anxious attachment behaviors, including greater separation or
   stranger anxiety, clinging to previously cherished objects,
   whining, crying, clinging, and tantrums
regression to previous levels of functioning
relatively brief grieving period
denial of permanence of change

Posttraumatic features specific to school-age children include the following:

lowered intellectual functioning; decline in school performance

inner plans of action (attempts at denial, compensation, rever-
    sal, or retribution through fantasy)

obsessive talking about incident

isolation of affect

constant anxious arousal

behavioral alterations

problems relating to peers

more elaborate reenactments

psychosomatic complaints

Posttraumatic features specific to adolescents include the following:

premature closure of identity formation

acting-out behavior (including truancy, substance abuse, and
    sexual activity)

self-criticism

fear of repetition of event in future (fate)

In general, Eth and Pynoos (1985c) point to the child's progress
over developmental lines being accentuated, retarded, or fixated as
current life circumstances are eroded by traumatic anxiety. Learning
can be affected by constant reworking of traumatic memories,
relationships can be altered by changes in emotional life, and major
life decisions can be influenced by focus upon the past (p. 50).

PTSD AND TRAUMATIZED GROUPS

In a fascinating paper, Terr (1985) discusses three subjects, each of
which provides interesting information regarding children's reaction
to trauma: the findings from the Chowchilla Group, which illustrate
the differences between adults' and children's PTSD symptomatology; phenomena-specific group trauma; and five new findings concerning the experiences of children within traumatized groups. These
discussions are summarized below.

The Chowchilla Group

In the late 1970s, Terr studied 25 youngsters who had been kid-
napped as a group in Chowchilla, California. On the basis of field

studies at the time and subsequent observations of children traumatized in separate, small-group incidents, Terr draws the following
conclusions regarding *PTSD symptoms unique to children:*

1. For the most part, children over 3 or 4 years of age do not
   become amnesiac about their traumatic experiences. Unlike
   adults, who frequently deny external traumatic reality or
   repress memories, children tend to remember the
   experiences vividly. Children under 3 or 4 do tend to forget
   their experiences, due in part to repressions normal to the
   first few years of life and in part to nonverbal encoding of
   memories. Some children under 3 or 4 will remember
   traumatic events, however.

2. For the most part, children do not experience the psychic
   numbing common to adults, with the exception of response
   to chronic stressors (such as parental abuse) as opposed to
   acute stressors (such as auto accidents).

3. For the most part, children do not experience intrusive and
   disruptive visual flashbacks. Probably this is because
   children tend to daydream intentionally and have not
   engaged in significant denial of reality in the manner of
   adults.

4. Children's school performance usually does not decline in
   cases of acute trauma for as long a duration as adults' work
   performance is impaired.

5. Play and reenactment increase in frequency.

6. Time distortions are more frequent, including a
   foreshortened view of the future. (Terr, 1985, p. 51)

Group-Specific Posttrauma Phenomena

On the basis of clinical observations of Chowchilla children as a
group and of four small groups of children who had, as groups, experienced traumatic events, Terr describes *posttraumatic group phenomena.* These phenomena do not automatically arise, nor is it possible
to separate individual versus group determinates of a particular individual's manifesting a group symptom without extensive background

investigation with that individual. These group phenomena are as follows:

1. symptom contagion affecting the group members and then their siblings, families, and associates (symptom contagion appears to be a large-group phenomenon, as it was relatively insignificant among the small groups studied)

   a. posttraumatic play (trauma-theme specific)

   b. reenactment

   c. omens (irrational beliefs regarding the future based upon the event)

   d. foreshortened future (belief that a long-range future is not possible)

   e. fears and misperceptions

2. lack of group cohesiveness or breakdown of cohesiveness

3. failure of child victims to communicate verbally regarding the critical incident

Five New Findings

Terr's study of particular individuals within these different groups revealed several findings of interest regarding posttraumatic reactions among children:

1. *Ghosts:* Terr reports that children who have experienced sudden and shocking death sometimes see "ghosts," apparitions Terr attributes to posttraumatic misperception and hallucination.

2. *Time distortion:* While children prior to 12 years of age have not yet matured their time operations, observations of greater than expected time distortions are common among posttraumatic children. Overwhelming anxiety can distort time sense during critical incidents, leaving confusion and feelings of inadequacy later, particularly if the child must appear on the witness stand. Specific distortions include time compression and expansion. In addition, time

distortions can make sequencing in memory difficult. A related phenomenon is future foreshortening, or the perception that future possibilities do not exist or have been precluded.

3. *Symbolization:* Parts of the traumatic experience may become associated by the child in forms more easily processed. What symbol is chosen and what part of the experience is chosen to be symbolized depend upon personal variables such as background experiences and issues, developmental level, and current situation.

4. *Condensation:* Separate ideas, symbols, or objects can be symbolized together. These condensations can be confusing, and astute observation is required to sort them out.

5. *Preverbal memories:* Experiences of children under the age of 2 are sometimes encoded nonverbally, consequently the children are unable to speak of a traumatic event. However, they can play out, reenact, or even show in concrete modes or fear responses what has happened to them. These memories appear to be preverbal and preconceptual.

Posttraumatic Stress Disorder is becoming accepted as a childhood clinical entity, as illustrated by studies over the past decade. Arroyo and Eth (1985) diagnosed 10 of 30 referred children who had experienced war as suffering from PTSD. Fredrick (1985b), reviewing various literature sources, listed several psychiatric disturbances found among children. PTSD ranked seventh of ten in cases of disasters, first in cases of child molestation, and fourth in cases of physical abuse, although the sources of these figures are not clear.

In 1987 the diagnostic criteria for Posttraumatic Stress Disorder in DSM-III-R were adjusted to reflect the research that had been surfacing since 1980. These criteria include the following two unique to children:

B. (1) recurrent and intrusive distressing recollections of the event (in young children, repetitive play in which themes or aspects of the trauma are expressed)

C. (4) marked diminished interest in significant activities (in young children, loss of recently acquired developmental skills such as toilet training or language skills)

(American Psychiatric Association, 1987, p. 250)

In addition, further distinctive characteristics are discussed in a section on age-related features in the DSM-III-R (American Psychiatric Association, 1987, p. 249).

The DSM-IV has added the following new criteria, which further reflect later findings. These criteria focus upon the importance of disorganized or agitated behavior satisfying the criteria for reaction of fear, helplessness, and horror at the time of the trauma, and traumatic reenactment indicating reexperience of the trauma. These behaviors reflect the inability of children to vocalize their distress. Interestingly, the DSM-IV does not include the loss of recently acquired developmental skills such as language and toileting as being diagnostically important, as did the DSM-III.

Two recent additions to the range of children's reactions to trauma bear mention. The first is the failure of the startle reflex to return to normal following trauma (Ornitz & Pynoos, 1989), resulting in delayed development of a number of skills acquired during the latency period. Included are control over activity level, capacity for reflection, academic learning, and focused attention. The second is the impact upon mechanisms regulating sleep control and aggression (Pynoos, 1990), both of which lead to irritability and difficulties in concentration, attention, and relationships. These additions are reflected in the DSM-IV in both the Acute and Posttraumatic Stress Disorder diagnoses.

In a wonderfully informative review of his own recent work and that of his colleagues and other leading researchers on children's trauma, Pynoos et al. (1996) summarize what we have learned lately about children's reactions and the developmental effects following traumatic exposure. Whereas until recently the majority of research dealt with PTSD symptomology, current work is extending that focus to include other symptom clusters, more specific symptom manifestation, and developmental impact of trauma.

Outlining current research trends in children's posttrauma reactions, Pynoos et al. point to developing a wider spectrum of diagnosis and exploring the interaction among the various symptom clusters of depression, separation anxiety, and complicated grief, as well as posttraumatic onset of attention deficit hyperactivity disorder, phobias, conduct disorders, and substance abuse. Citing his ongoing study of children and adolescents in Armenia following the earthquake of 1988, Pynoos notes the interactive relationship among PTSD, depressive symptoms, and anxiety disorders. He observed that

- distress caused by PTSD symptoms exacerbated anxious attachment, especially clinging and the need for proximity to loved ones.

- anxious attachment aggravated PTSD symptoms, particularly arousal symptoms.

Similarly, he has found PTSD to be a risk factor for depression, and depression to inhibit resolution of PTSD. These, together with the secondary adversities (changes in life conditions brought about by the traumatic event) create what he terms a "pernicious interactive matrix."

The result of this new evidence argues for a developmental perspective. According to Pynoos et al. (1996), differing symptoms and personality traits reflect a layering effect over time of several factors, including:

1. specific features of traumatic exposures at varying points in development

2. secondary adversities

3. disturbances in developmental expectations and in the acquisition and integration of developmental competencies

4. the disruption of developmental transitions

5. disturbances in biological maturation

6. the expression of traumatic expectations and intervention fantasies (p. 351)

TYPICAL POSTTRAUMATIC BEHAVIORS

On the basis of the differing reports discussed so far, we see that children's reactions to crisis are varied, complex, and profound. However, patterns emerge that are cohesive, if not entirely predictable. Individual response patterns are limited by the child's state of development and personal history. The following summary description of typical posttraumatic behaviors may be useful to professionals observing children in their care. Note that each progressive age may involve previous levels of functioning or malfunctioning in response to crisis.

The descriptions are keyed to general developmental stages. They will prove useful for professionals in observing students in the classroom setting for two reasons. First, observation of these behaviors can alert staff that a trauma may have occurred in a particular child's life, recently or in the past. Appropriate steps can be taken to corroborate this by questions or indirect inquiry. Second, if the trauma has definitely occurred and remedial steps have been taken, the knowledge that these behaviors are, in fact, typical of posttraumatic children can give staff the needed perspective to deal effectively with the child in the school setting. Knowing that certain abnormal behaviors are normal under abnormal conditions is helpful and provides feedback for therapists and parents.

It should also be noted that regression in functioning level is a common response to anxiety. Thus posttraumatic behaviors typical of an earlier level of functioning may appear in an older child or adult.

Preschool/Kindergarten Children

Posttraumatic behaviors that occur among preschool and kindergarten children are likely to include the following:

Withdrawal. Children frequently react to trauma with a generalized response of distrust. Perhaps because their cognitive discriminatory processes are newly emergent, they cannot feel safe from further harm. Also, children may try to assimilate their new and very negative learning about the world. They may become unusually quiet or subdued and seemingly detached from others, and may even become mute with adults or peers.

Denial. Children may deal with overwhelming experiences and unbearable changes with denial. Denial may take many forms, including denial of facts and memories of events, avoidance of certain themes or issues, and ignoring of certain people or conditions. This may be compounded by perceptual distortions and memory gaps or embellishments that may occur with anyone, but particularly with younger children. This makes it difficult for adults to discern when the child is denying, not remembering, or confusing facts.

Thematic play. As children try to make sense of traumatic experiences and the resulting life changes, the attempt must be cognitive, emotional, and relational. The best way for children to accomplish this is through play. Play is the medium they use normally to incorporate new ideas, realities, and feelings into their existing world, and it is not surprising that they use this medium in attempting to process the bigger issues they face. This includes frequent participation in reenactments or ritualistic play following a theme of either trauma itself or life upsets that are secondary to the trauma (such as family problems or physical changes). This can include playing horses, dolls, soldiers, or other such games either by themselves or with others. Children's art projects may also reflect traumatic themes and issues. Less obvious forms of play include ritualistic interactions with parents or friends, a fascination with certain themes in books or television, and solitary activity of a symbolic nature.

Anxious attachment. Clinging, whining, not letting go of parents or favorite objects, and tantrums are frequently signs of anxious attachment. Since attachment behavior occurs during this developmental stage with many nontraumatized children, changes in frequency and intensity are the best indications that such behavior may be influenced by trauma.

Specific fears. Common specific fears include fear of new situations, strangers, males, confinement, violence, or certain objects. This may be noticeable in the classroom when a student becomes inappropriately emotional in an otherwise moderate situation, refuses to read a particular story, or won't talk about a certain subject. Sudden avoidance of the playground or reluctance to go home may surface. Problems with sleep may be fear reactions. Fear of going to sleep, nightmares, and frequent waking at night often develop because the cognitive dreamwork involves trauma-specific content or content having to do with loss brought about by changed circumstances.

Regression. Under severe stress, children attempt to master the situation by reverting to behavior patterns that were successful in earlier developmental stages. This represents a search for a comfort zone.

Younger School-Age Children

One or more of the above behaviors among preschool children are likely to resurface with school-age children in the face of posttraumatic adjustment stress. Posttraumatic behaviors likely to occur among school-age children include the following:

Performance decline. School and intellectual performance as well as performance in sports, music lessons, and hobbies could all be affected. In the classroom a quiet child may drop from mostly A's to mostly D's in a short period of time with no explanation for the change. An athlete may begin missing practice or having a string of "off-days." The performance decline may be due to acting out, or it may be due to the child's preoccupation.

Compensatory behavior. Behavior designed to compensate for the critical incident or its resulting loss, injury, or unwanted changes may be evident. Such behaviors may be attempts to deny or reverse the traumatic event, or to gain retribution through fantasy, play, or interaction. Compensatory themes in play include killing the perpetrator, acting as if nothing had changed, and undoing the damage.

Obsessive talking. Once the child feels free to talk about the incident, he or she may talk about it continually. Like a dam breaking, details about facts, interpretations, or reactions may spill out, unrestrained. The child may recount the incident again and again, and may repeat the theme in written work or in art. He or she may make resolutions, uncover feelings, and establish intimacy with others, but all this may be quickly undone when the processing is through. This necessary process of assimilating the event will be temporary.

Discrepancy in mood. The child may exhibit feelings or moods inappropriate to the immediate situation or to the events he or she is describing. Sometimes this represents an attempt to avoid full realization, and at other times it is the result of the child's preoccupation with past events. It may simply be a way of blocking communication regarding the event, possibly because the child is not ready to reopen wounds or because he or she does not yet trust the adult.

Behavior changes or problems. Children may exhibit changes in normal patterns of behavior. These changes do not always take the form of "problem" behaviors, but may nevertheless indicate underlying turmoil. These children get into trouble or show sudden changes in interest or regressive behavior. Often such changes result from children's attempts to relieve anxiety, gain needed attention, or sort through new, troubling information about the world and themselves.

More elaborate reenactments. School-age children's play tends to be more complex, abstract, and sophisticated than that of preschoolers; various personal themes and meanings permeate their activity. In their play, reenactments of traumatic events may become progressively more sophisticated, although often no more satisfactory than during early childhood. Developmental and incident-specific themes become scripts governing interaction and prompting tasks, decisions, and choices. As the child grows older, reenactments become less a function of indirect play and more a property of real-life transactions in the world.

Psychosomatic complaints. If the excess stress caused by faltering attempts at posttrauma adjustment does not manifest itself in problematic behaviors, physical problems may occur. Some children show the effects of their difficult experience with physical complaints. Stomachaches, headaches, digestive upsets, and other physical disorders are often very real symptoms of psychological distress. Sometimes they are thinly disguised bids for extra time and attention. Such complaints are often indirect communications about other things.

Older School-Age Children/Adolescents

Behaviors specific to preschool or school-age children can resurface due to the tendency toward regression as a coping mechanism. Posttraumatic behaviors likely to occur among older school-age children and adolescents include the following:

Acting-out behaviors. Perhaps because of a combination of peer influence and a need not to defer to parental support, adolescents often act out their distress in ways that are ultimately misguided and self-destructive. Typical patterns include isolation, drug and alcohol abuse, sexual activity, violence, delinquency, running away, and suicidal expressions or attempts. While not every adolescent who engages in these behaviors has experienced trauma in the past, the majority have. The trauma may have been recent or long ago; even events distant in time may resurface with the increased developmental pressures of adolescence.

Low self-esteem and self-criticism. Adolescents are quick to blame themselves and to condemn their own reactions to crisis situations. They often have fanciful expectations regarding their control over situations; thus anything going wrong is a blow to their sense of power and independence.

"Too old, too fast." Adolescents who are "too old, too fast" are often very reluctant to come to terms with their past experiences and resist interactions. Traumatized adolescents sometimes develop lifestyles several years in advance of their age. This is particularly true for poor children, who must compete in the street with adults, and child prodigies, who constantly deal with adults. Such adolescents seem to expect a generally joyless existence; their life choices often confirm their expectations. They may take on unnecessary full-time jobs before high school graduation, or other heavy responsibilities such as a planned pregnancy or a decision to keep a baby when circumstances and attitudes clearly dictate otherwise.

Displaced anger. Teachers or other school personnel may be the safest people the adolescent confronts during the day, and may become the unwilling, undeserving recipients of anger that has no other place to go. This undeserved aggression certainly increases staff stress and makes schoolwork unpleasant. Anger of this sort tends to be depersonalized and may seem ritualistic in nature.

Preoccupation with self. Adolescents tend to see the world through self-colored glasses. They interpret an event on the basis of its impact on them first. Trauma and the resulting inner processing that must be done to sort through the meaning of the incident can intensify the adolescent's normal self-centeredness.

DEVELOPMENTAL IMPLICATIONS

A psychological trauma can interrupt the normal progress of development, causing more difficult resolution of current life issues and impeding growth. How this transpires is interesting in the sense that it provides a framework for understanding why a trauma can have its particular effect upon a child's later life.

Human development consists of a gradual unfolding of personality wherein new learning and skills transform the individual from one state to another. Erickson (1968) describes this process as one of increasing differentiation, following a universal epigenic sequence. Individual development is shaped by cultural and familial influences interacting with genetically based aspects of personality. As social expectations change according to age and as hereditary traits manifest themselves, the individual is confronted with different demands. Each phase has certain inherent tasks that must be resolved to form the basis for further change. Erickson (1968) describes these steps as "crises."

> Each successive step then is a potential crisis because of a radical change in perspective. Crisis is used here in a developmental sense to connote not a threat of catastrophe but a turning point, a crucial period of increased vulnerability and heightened potential, and therefore the ontogenic source of generational strength and maladjustment. (p. 96)

Erickson describes developmental crises as ontogenic sources of maladjustment *as well as growth*. Each successive stage of development, resulting from the external demands of environment interfacing with internal readiness for new levels of functioning, causes a specific vulnerability. A stage is a time when a given capacity or set of skills requisite to further development occurs—a turning point or crucial moment when the individual, as a result of both the acquisition of skills and capacities and the necessary cultural and biological pressure, must change. Unlike crisis in the sense of catastrophe, where the individual's resolution entails reestablishing a previous level of functioning, crisis here denotes an event or stage the resolution of which involves reaching previously unattained levels of functioning.

Development, then, is a process of transformation through stages characterized by specific demands, opportunities, and vulnerabilities. As Erickson suggests, adverse conditions may affect development in stage-specific ways. This disruption affects not only the stage during which the event occurred but also resolution of tasks in subsequent stages.

Two concepts are worth mentioning at this point, prior to exploring the effects of critical incidents upon developmental patterns: developmental anxiety and premature structuring.

In a discussion of the assessment of trait versus state anxiety, Saarni and Azara (1981) advance the concept of developmental anxiety. An extended state anxiety, developmental anxiety represents a reaction to the transition involved in the giving up of old forms of coping that worked at one level of development and the acquisition of new ones appropriate to a new level of development. The acquisition of new forms of coping can be a prolonged process of differentiation and experimentation and generates considerable anxiety.

Saarni and Azara interpret Erickson's "crisis" as a growth stage in which developmental anxiety "emerges and spurs the organism on afresh and with a new adaptiveness to synchronize forms of coping with the inherent conflicts of being alive" (p. 579). Thus developmental anxiety increases or decreases across the life span of the individual as that individual attempts resolution of each new set of demands raised by changes of biological and societal expectations.

Elkind (1981), in a book about the "hurried child" directed at a general audience and based upon an unclear methodology, discusses a concept that has some heuristic value. Premature structuring is a process by which character or personality formation of the child is accelerated due to the demands of the environment. This acts to constrict future personality development. Elkind cites child prodigies and children of slums as examples of children who must grow up too quickly, deal with grown-up demands and stressors too early, and develop certain aspects of their personalities at the expense of others. These children tend to become overspecialized and overdifferentiated in a manner that provides immediate survival value but closes off further learning and balanced growth. Particularly with prodigies, this premature structuring has serious consequences when the child reaches adolescence.

PTSD, VIETNAM, AND IMPLICATIONS FOR TRAUMATIZED CHILDREN

The notion of subsequent developmental implications following trauma was applied by Wilson (1978) in a major study of Vietnam veterans. The first part studied 56 veterans from the Cleveland area and examined their personal attributes and their perceptions of society. As might be expected, Wilson found significant changes in ego-identity, ideology, and attitudes as a consequence of their involvement in the war. Adequately controlled by a sample of veterans who did not serve in Vietnam, this study utilized Erickson's developmental issues as a basis for determining developmental consequences of Vietnam combat.

Wilson found a wide range of symptomatology consistent with PTSD. He also determined that, as a group, combat veterans could be characterized as struggling with the developmental task of identity versus role confusion. Particularly difficult were adjustment to the existent social system of values and maintenance of a sense of self-sameness and continuity. Wilson characterized failure to develop a strong sense of coherency in a person as indicating a strong likelihood of suffering profound existential despair. The typical soldier in Vietnam was about 20 years old and had not had the opportunity to experience the sort of psychosocial moratorium Erickson considers essential for the exploration of ego boundaries and values as preparation for adult commitments. Combat critical incidents—indeed the social and moral tenor of the war itself—"constituted a series of social, moral, and psychosocial conflicts which were not easily assimilated into pre-existing cognitive structures or easily handled by emotional coping patterns" (Wilson, 1978, II, p. 1). Further, economic difficulties and social ambivalence toward the war deprived the veterans upon their return of the sort of support needed for healing; thus they struggled against identity diffusion.

Compared to controls, Vietnam veterans' specific symptoms included the following:

- difficulty in establishing a coherent and integrated sense of identity and successful intimate relationships

- difficulty coping with interpersonal problems

- more interpersonal conflict with significant others

- greater drug use

- lower career and educational aspirations

- greater political and social alienation

- psychic numbing

Wilson's results provide support for Erickson's (1968) contention that trauma during a particular psychosocial stage undermines the internal control mechanisms essential to development of the specific ego strength being formed during that period, or may exacerbate previously poorly developed ego strengths (such as mistrust, shame, and feelings of inferiority). Thus areas of potential weakness in ego development become at risk.

While the first volume of Wilson's study explored the manner in which combat experience negatively affected the successful resolution of the identity versus role confusion stage, the second focused upon the effects of the Vietnam combat experience upon subsequent developmental stages.

At the time Wilson wrote, the typical veteran was about 30 years old and faced with social demands for resolving the crisis of intimacy versus isolation. Wilson studied the love relationships and intimate personal friendships of the veterans, and found greater difficulty in relationships among Vietnam veterans than among controls. He also found in Vietnam veterans increased incidence of the following maladaptive means of dealing with interpersonal difficulties:

1. frequent and heavy use of drugs and alcohol

2. fits of anger

3. rage and hostility

4. emotional ambivalence toward loved ones

5. irresponsibility toward jobs and other commitments demanding propriety, reliability, and trustworthiness (p. 10)

Of particular note is Wilson's support of Erickson's notion of *distantiation,* or withdrawal from the sort of intimacy required to bring affection, sexual pleasure, love, and affiliation. Purposeful distantiation, a learned adaptive behavior in Vietnam, proved maladaptive at home, isolating the veteran from social support and impeding resolution of issues of identity.

Wilson's study supports Erickson's observations that each life stage is characterized by a particular psychosocial crisis and that each crisis bears the risk of specific types of ego-regressive attributes; sufficient stress and trauma during a specific stage will increase the risk of failing to master the critical issues and of developing the related ego-regressive attributes. Table 2 illustrates Erickson's regressive attributes of the various stages of child development as outlined by Wilson (1978, p. 28).

What was learned from Vietnam veterans can be transferred to the classroom, providing direction to professionals dealing with children who have been traumatized. Critical incidents require interventions geared toward the prevention of maladaptive behaviors in later development.

Trauma and the Development of Maladaptive Adolescent Behaviors

Further research is needed to establish the correlation, if any, of the risk of specific types of maladaptive behaviors occurring as a result of childhood critical incidents (CCIs) taking place during specific developmental stages. PTSD, however, does provide an explanatory construct that is of value in understanding the high correlation of

Table 2: Developmental Ego-Regressive Attributes

Life Stage	Crisis	Ego-Regressive Attribute
infancy	trust versus mistrust	hopelessness, dependency, anxiety, withdrawal
play age	autonomy versus shame/doubt	overcontrol, impulsiveness, order, structure, predictability, helplessness
younger school age	initiative versus guilt	guilt, loss of rootedness, need for protectors, loss of purpose
older school age	industry versus inferiority	sense of futility, work paralysis, incompetence
adolescence	identity versus identity diffusion	self-consciousness, lack of commitment, prolonged moratorium

Source: Wilson (1978)

CCIs and maladaptive adolescent behaviors (MABs) in general. Traumas occurring during a specific developmental stage do create special vulnerabilities by impeding successful resolution of growth issues during that stage, leaving the individual less able to resolve future issues successfully. Adolescence is a crucial stage, and the successful resolution of the issue of identity is particularly stressful and anxiety-provoking when underlying issues (of mistrust, guilt, or feelings of inferiority) remain unresolved. The anxiety generated by outmoded coping mechanisms and new, seemingly insurmountable demands creates a propensity to adopt maladaptive coping strategies rather than no coping strategies at all.

Trauma, Development, and Learning

Opening the discussion to long-range consequences of trauma and secondary adversity, Pynoos et al. (1996) discuss the effects of traumatic stress upon children's long-term development. They point out recent psychological studies that indicate interference in narrative coherence (ability to organize material into beginning, middle, and end), emotional regulation (including differentiating affective states, expressing those states, and understanding the origin and consequences of negative states), developmental transitions, and transitions in peer relationships. These four areas are each affected differently according to developmental level, and the subsequent development of each is itself affected. These abstract psychological factors seem at first far removed from the classroom. Yet school personnel wrestle every day with the consequences of trauma.

Learning in school may be compromised by neurobiological effects of trauma, much of which seems related to alterations in the normal development of modulatory mechanisms—the mature organism's means of blocking reflex reactions when they would be inappropriate. Activity level, capacity for reflection, academic learning, and focused attention can all be impacted by loss of inhibitory control over the startle reflex (Ornitz & Pynoos, 1989). Irritability and difficulties in concentration and attention can result from chronic sleep disturbance caused by reaction to trauma (Pynoos, 1990). Aggressiveness and social withdrawal can follow the reduced ability to modulate aggression, typical in posttrauma children (Pynoos et al., 1991). Diminished self-concept can result from posttraumatic focus upon external stimuli and neural overresponsiveness to trauma-related cues (Krystal et al., 1989). Each of these neurobiological reactions to trauma can affect general information processing (Reider & Cicchetti, 1989).

Urban Violence Syndrome

As discussed earlier, the 1990s have endured increased urban deterioration and violence. Nowhere has this been worse than the inner city, and no one experiences it more closely than the staff of an inner-city school. In discussing the effects of working with inner-city children, Parson (1994) coined the term Urban Violence Traumatic Stress Response Syndrome (U-VTS) to refer to the unique developmental reaction children sustain to enduring, frequent acts of violence within the urban setting.

High rates of various pathogenic factors create a vulnerability to trauma with the inner-city child, and traumas abound. Such factors include abusive, neglectful, and inadequate parenting, which is often brutalizing and nonprotective. This may be compounded by a lack of functional secondary family systems and support networks, and a lack of a culture of strong values. Chronic cynicism and distrust of and by the adult authority figures, including racism, inequality, and prevalence of instrumental violence, remove potential sources of safety and resources. Prevalence of drugs, pervasiveness of dependency, and a culture that condones violence all create a climate against which individual acts of violence punctuate a bleak, hostile background.

Existing diagnostic categories fail to address the social/environmental dimensions and issues of urban violence. Symptoms of U-VTS above and beyond PTSD symptoms are noted by Parson to include a damaged self-syndrome, in which retaliatory violence seems the only way to repair damaged self-esteem. Further, he notes that "traumaphobia" apparently transforms into a "traumaphilia," or attraction to violence in order to manage the internal effects of violence. Internal fragmentation and dissociation predominate, replacing meaning, purpose, and feelings for safety with cynicism, apathy, shattered values, and distrust. Death-related anxiety is common, and rage, rather than grieving, becomes the normal response to loss.

Growing up in the inner city can result in a loss of self and future. These are extreme reactions to extreme and chronic life conditions characterized by grinding social conditions. Hopefully, future diagnostic standards may come to better describe children's reactions in these contexts.

Conclusion

The concept of PTSD provides a direction to use when approaching critical incidents as well as maladaptive behaviors. By recognizing the possible developmental outcomes of CCIs, clinicians, teachers, and other professionals can better plan comprehensive intervention approaches with traumatized children. Similarly, by recognizing the likelihood of prior CCIs in the lives of adolescents whose behavior is maladaptive and problematic, clinicians and student service professionals can plan interventions that can better address underlying causative and developmental factors.

Thus trauma produces psychological disequilibrium that is anxiety provoking. Attempts at coping with this anxiety affect the child's ability to tolerate the normal anxiety created by developmental transitions. The resulting combination can block successful developmental task mastery, and maladaptive attempts to cope with this anxiety can produce further complications. Such attempts can include typical adolescent acting-out behaviors such as premature structuring, extreme sensitivity to emotional issues, and self-defeating life choices.

With this understanding of the manner in which crises affect children's development, the way is cleared for an exploration of what professionals can do to minimize posttraumatic reactions and subsequent developmental difficulties.

CHAPTER 3

What Schools Can Do

In order to see clearly the alternatives we face,
we must first distinguish education from schooling, which means separating the humanistic
intent of the teacher from the impact of the
invariant structure of the school.

Ivan Illich, *The Alternative to Schooling*

OVERVIEW

Despite the alarming increase in crises at school, school personnel are rarely
trained in crisis management. They need guidelines to follow when confronted
with crisis situations. Therapists and other mental health consultants would
often like to help, but feel unable to provide the programmatic approach teach-
ers and administrators frequently want. This chapter provides such an
approach.

Chapter Contents

School plays a unique role in the lives of children, through teachers, administrators, and other personnel. A child spends approximately six out of thirteen to fifteen waking hours in school. That is one-third to nearly one-half of the child's weekly life. Further, the school experience is a socializing and normalizing influence on children's lives. Events that happen to students individually affect their performance in class and affect the class as a whole. Events affecting the entire class have far-ranging effects in terms of classroom cohesiveness, school performance, learning, interpersonal relationships, behavior out of school, and the tendency toward behavioral problems later on.

This chapter explores what school personnel can do when students are exposed to traumatic events. Within one recent year, students watching television in their classrooms experienced the tragedy of the explosion of the space shuttle *Challenger*, students in the Midwest were held hostage by adults who placed a bomb in a classroom, and in Los Angeles a student put a gun to his head in an adult education classroom and pulled the trigger (fortunately, the gun did not discharge). More recently, in Illinois a young woman entered a second-grade classroom and began shooting, killing one child and wounding five others. These media-covered events are just examples of the thousands of critical incidents that affect the nation's classrooms annually. The manner in which school personnel respond to such events affects the traumatic impact they have on the children involved, both inside and outside the classroom.

Critical incidents are events that overwhelm an individual's capacity to cope. They are psychologically traumatic, causing emotional turmoil, cognitive problems, and behavioral changes. The effects of a critical incident can be lasting, depending upon the quality of the individual's experiences during or shortly after the incident. The degree and rate of recovery is determined in part by the extent to which the individual is surrounded by supportive, caring people who help him or her deal with the aftereffects of the experience.

The classroom is fertile ground for critical incidents. The group kidnapping at Chowchilla, the 49th Street School shooting in Los Angeles, and the shootings in Illinois are testimony to the possibility of large-scale, dramatic traumas. Yet far more frequent in the life of a class are such events as the victimization or death of a class member

84 Trauma in the Lives of Children

or the witnessing of shocking incidents by the group. Because class-rooms are not insulated from the world, classroom events often occur in response to world events.

Following are responses to some questions frequently asked by school personnel about critical incidents:

How often do they happen in a classroom? Quite likely any given class will experience one and possibly several critical incidents in a year.

How do they affect a class? An event that happens to one child affects other classmates vicariously. A class is an intimate group, and just as experiences of individual family members affect the rest of the family, one student's experiences will affect the rest of the class. Shared difficulties can bring classes together or pull them apart, affecting class climate, behavior, and performance.

What is "delayed stress response"? The immediate, situational response to a critical incident is called *acute stress response*. It is characterized by temporary problems in thinking, emotional over-reactions (or underreactions), and behavioral changes. These responses are detailed in Chapter 2. Sometimes the effects of the trauma do not surface for weeks, months, or years. This is called *delayed stress response*. Delayed stress response is generally thought to occur when the strategies used to cope with the critical incident pro-hibit the person from emotionally processing the event. Later, as the individual attempts to adapt to the changed circumstances, memo-ries and feelings about the incident emerge, causing distress and fur-ther attempts at coping. Details about such responses to critical incidents may be found in Chapter 2.

Why must I become involved? School personnel must become involved in students' crises for two reasons. First, studies have shown that the way in which an adult responds to individual chil-dren and groups of children following a crisis can significantly affect the outcome of the experience. Through effective, caring interven-tion, negative delayed stress responses to trauma can be minimized. Second, the process of effectively intervening with individuals or groups is a tremendous group builder, creating a sense of cohesive-ness in a class.

School staff, particularly teachers, can provide several valuable services to their students that ultimately serve educational goals. First, by becoming aware of the nature of incidents and posttraumatic behaviors, staff are in a position to observe student reactions and respond correctly. Second, staff can conference individually or work with an entire class for early intervention in a crisis situation. Third, they are in a position to provide effective coordination and follow-through with students, other staff, and parents. Finally, school personnel can interface in a knowledgeable manner with the school's mental health consultants or outside therapists to utilize these resources, when available, to best effect. The following sections outline what an effective school team can do to assist and benefit from mental health specialists.

What to Expect:
Posttraumatic Behavior at School

The classroom setting is essentially naturalistic. This means that students are there in the normal course of events, not because they have been identified as "having a problem." Teachers and other school personnel observe children there day after day for hours at a time, so changes in the children's behavior are fairly obvious and changes over time are noticeable. When children's normal behavioral processes and development are altered by traumatic events, the school is one of the first places these changes are seen outside the home. Whether the original incident occurred in the classroom or elsewhere, classroom behavior is affected. Even if the child is under medical or psychological treatment for the trauma, school personnel will be in a situation to observe and deal with posttraumatic behavior. For purposes of identifying children who have been traumatized and for keeping perspective with children who staff already know have been traumatized, knowledge of posttrauma behavior is essential.

In dealing with children following a traumatic incident, it is useful to know what to expect. Recovery behavior is different from everyday, regular behavior, in part because a great deal of inner work goes on in the process of assimilating the traumatic experience.

Teachers need some sense of what is and is not "normal" during this unusual time.

In coping with the extreme stress of a critical incident, those going through it often suppress certain thoughts and feelings. This process allows the individual to do what must be done to maintain psychological and physical equilibrium. Traumatic experiences too threatening and disturbing to be assimilated at once gradually surface later to be fully integrated. This is a natural process of self-healing.

Trauma involves change. More than a simple emotional process, trauma forces the child to accommodate new, discrepant, and frequently threatening information about the world. The sudden realization of vulnerability, the loss of support or loved ones, or large-scale rejection requires difficult adjustments. As the child attempts to accommodate this new information cognitively, thoughts and feelings associated with the incident begin to surface. The child reexperiences fear, anger, helplessness, and guilt. As the new changes in the child's life begin to be experienced, anxiety, fear, and depression may follow. The emotional reactions to this process can themselves make up a frightening, stressful, out-of-control experience.

Several general concepts regarding posttraumatic behavior in the classroom should be noted. These concepts provide an overall perspective regarding behavioral changes after trauma. Adults who work with traumatized children will benefit from this perspective because coping with posttraumatic behavior can be difficult, prolonged, and thankless. A realistic overview of the situation can do much to temper expectations and sustain willingness to persevere.

Normalcy. Emotional upset and faltering attempts to work out coping systems following a crisis are not indications of mental illness. Rather, they are very normal reactions to abnormal circumstances. To classify a person going through such reactions as "crazy" and assume that only psychologists are qualified to talk to him or her deprives that individual of much-needed support and healthy interaction. Staff members frequently feel that their training and scope of practice preclude them from being able to provide helpful contact with posttrauma children. This notion is mistaken; indeed, the opposite is the case. While psychotherapy is quite likely important, the *normalized* context of everyday life is essential to healing.

Whether or not to refer a child to psychotherapy is another question that should be brought up with other staff members. See the section in this chapter titled "When to Refer."

Instability. Critical incidents alone, even the most severe, do not cause mental illness. Preexisting mental instability, however, may be reactivated by extreme stress. See the section "When to Refer" for further discussion regarding signs of more serious instability. Mental illness is an interesting concept within this culture, and great mystery surrounds its origin and treatment. Posttraumatic behavior may indeed be quite different from "normal" behavior, as the next section describes in detail. If posttraumatic changes are seen as attempts at adjustment, however, they will be less threatening. Staff must develop sufficient communication with the child to be able to talk about the behaviors within the context of school life.

Epicycles. Normal recovery can be a long process and probably will include times when it appears as though the child is getting worse, not better. Again, this is normal and is quite likely a part of the natural healing process. As the child becomes stronger, he or she is able to deal with more intense memories, thoughts, and feelings. Reactions to these intrusive memories and feelings can strain newly developed coping skills. Particularly difficult times can include anniversaries of the incident, similar situations, or events that preceded or coincided with the trauma event. These times can reawaken old hurts and cause difficulties. Often these appear to the child involved as reversals in progress. They may, however, represent real progress as the child deals with information thus far avoided.

Ages and stages. Often years of relative calm go by without difficulty, and it appears that the crisis is really over. Then, suddenly, new problems arise. Normal developmental transitions create new realities, and these changes make a child's previously successful coping strategies obsolete. As short-term coping skills become outworn, new ones must develop. Until they do, painful memories become more intrusive and more difficult to manage. Often during these transitional times maladaptive behaviors develop as misguided attempts at coping. Adolescents, in particular, are likely to foster maladaptive attempts at adjustment.

Just as each person's experience of a particular incident is unique, responses to critical incidents are unique. Some patterns of behavioral change can be seen among individuals who have been traumatized, and the patterns of response to crisis particular to children show some common ties. The patterns manifested by an individual child, however, are limited by the child's own traits, personal background, and stage of development.

Classroom behaviors that can be expected following trauma were discussed at length in the previous chapter. Existence of these behaviors may indicate prior traumas, although they are not in themselves conclusive; more information is needed to corroborate these observations. The responsibility of educators is, however, to be aware of signals and to begin to try to account for children's posttrauma-type behavior. Gentle, general inquiry often leads to confirmation, as though the child was waiting for someone to ask. Other behaviors, put together, may form a pattern. The best context for such inquiry, as well as for providing support for the child, is the individual conference, discussed below.

Guidelines for Individual Conferencing

Sometimes the disclosures of critical incident experiences are direct and done in such a context that the class is not affected. When this is the case, teacher intervention can take place in individual conference without involving other students. Sometimes the individual disclosure is not direct, but the staff member observes suspicious behavior, writing, or artworks. At this point nothing is known, but hypotheses can be formed. These hypotheses must be confirmed by corroborative information gathered through discussions with other staff, phone calls to the child's home, or direct conferences with the child.

Individual conferencing can occur in several situations. A student may have mentioned a critical incident in class discussion or in a writing assignment, prompting the teacher to inquire further. A student may ask to speak privately and then may take the teacher into his or her confidence. A student's performance or behavior may alert the teacher to a possible incident. Or perhaps the teacher has heard a disquieting rumor and wishes to provide the right context in case the student chooses to talk.

Approach styles differ among professionals. Some individuals can be very direct, while others are uncomfortable with this approach. Some may share their feelings openly, while others do not. Some styles of interaction are more helpful than others, however (see Appendix I). Styles that project judgmental attitudes, blaming, or general incompetence in dealing with the person or the content of disclosure tend to worsen the situation. Styles projecting warmth, caring, and a nonjudgmental attitude tend to be helpful. Beyond these basic differences, however, much latitude exists for personal style differences. In general, an authentic, honest approach is more conducive to trust than one that attempts to emulate the preconceived "right way."

The following strategies have proved helpful in dealing with distressed students in individual conferences:

1. Find a comfortable, private place for the conference. If the conference is individual, it must be private in order to engender trust. Audiences are inhibiting. A traumatized child or adolescent is usually embarrassed about his or her predicament. The social repercussions of gossip and hearsay are intimidating and will discourage disclosure. For this reason, providing a socially safe context is important. A word of caution is necessary, however. Educators must avoid placing themselves in compromising positions, particularly in the case of male teachers counseling female students. Stay visible to others.

2. Maintain calm. In all probability, the student is experiencing uncertainty and self-doubt. Presenting a calm demeanor tells the student that what he or she is about to say will be accepted. On the other hand, the child must feel that the teacher is really present, attending, and nonjudgmental. This involves showing reactions. Professionals who are not normally as expressive as others should remember that in such situations they can express more without undermining the child's need to have an adult who can be trusted to handle information they consider revealing. In the study reported in Appendix I, adolescents reported that the worst thing their parents could do when facing the child's crisis was to fall apart and not be able to manage themselves or parent their children. While the proper balance between expression and calm is often hard to determine, a balanced demeanor is helpful.

3. Be honest with yourself. We all have days in which we are less effective than we can be. Further, we all have difficulty relating to certain issues or types of people. Recognizing such situations is essential. To attempt a conference with a troubled child in these circumstances would be a disservice to the child. Professionals need to keep in touch with their own feelings and their own reactions—to students, issues, and situations. If a teacher feels unable to handle the conference situation, he or she should ask someone else to take over, and should arrange a satisfactory transition, so that the child does not feel "passed off" or rejected.

4. Read between the lines. Often behavior belies speech. While a child is saying one thing, his or her body position, gestures, or facial expressions may be saying something else. Such incongruity may be significant. The professional should watch the student's behavior during a conference, and should be aware of subtle messages from which inferences for further exploration may be drawn. Finally, the professional should keep in mind how overt, nonverbal messages may be reflecting his or her own discomfort, judgments, or impatience.

5. Validate feelings. Feelings are often barely, if at all, under control in times of crisis. They can be confused, contradictory, "inappropriate," or noticeably lacking. Feelings may be very strong under the surface, while the exterior may seem impassive and social. Feelings are neither right nor wrong. Whatever feelings the student is expressing during the conference, the professional should validate them as being present. Often many feelings clamor for expression; if the professional can help the student clarify them, it is very likely that they will change.

6. Listen well. Listening is more than hearing. Listening implies attention, focus, and empathy. Children especially need to be listened to in a manner *they* recognize to be listening. Good listening involves several skills: gentle probes for clarification and elaboration, good eye contact, and the use of increasingly focused questions when appropriate (this is especially important when the professional suspects that harm has been done to the child). Professionals should trust their hunches and check them out.

7. Show belief. It is tempting to seek answers to questions about culpability. After all, if wrong has been done to the child, the conference provides an opportunity for the teacher to identify the wrongdoer and prevent further harm. It is also tempting to assume that the story is embellished, one-sided, or distorted, and that may indeed be the case. It is not the professional's role at this time to determine the accuracy of the child's report. To pursue the quest for truth or accuracy at this point is to violate the child's need to be heard. The professional's job is to listen and to facilitate expression. Not a judge, jury, or investigator, the professional serves as simply a helper or contact. He or she should show confidence, trust, and faith that the student is telling the truth as the student sees it. If the professional does believe that the child is being abused, however, he or she has a moral and probably a legal responsibility to report those suspicions to the proper authorities.

8. Dispel fault. Children sometimes feel that a death, accident, or divorce is their fault, especially if they had thought angry or destructive thoughts prior to the event. In the need to stabilize their situation, they may assume responsibility for events that are out of their control. Because they lack conceptual ability or experience, children may believe it when someone else tells them that they are at fault for a crisis. If the student has been victimized, the professional should make it clear that the incident was not the student's fault. The professional should be proactive about this, because victims tend to distrust and blame themselves.

9. Explore fears. Individuals often are able to tell what happened to them, but unable to express assumptions they have made, questions they have, or fears they hold about the incident. Helping a child to express these assumptions, questions, and fears may empower the child to deal with them. However, a cautionary note is in order. Because perceptions under extreme stress are often inaccurate, even delusional, discussion of these perceptions may be an opportunity for the professional to provide the child with needed reality checks. However, it is important to contradict the child's perception as little as possible. The reality is that the child needs *support*. What he or she reports may be what is *true* or it may be what he or she *fears* is true. The fears must be explored, facts that are clearly wrong and causing anguish must be clarified, and care must be taken to respect the child's need to express whatever needs expression at the time.

10. Provide information. Providing the right information can be very helpful. If the professional knows something about the incident, normal reactions to that type of incident, or actions that could be taken, he or she should consider sharing them. He or she should be sure not to preach, however, and be sure that his or her own need to "do something" is not taking precedence over the child's needs. The most important consideration is whether or not the child is really ready for the information. The following questions can help the professional clarify whether children involved in a critical incident are ready for information:

> Do they need to vent feelings or to retell the incident more?
> Have they reached the point where the information meets a felt need?
> Do they have other investments in the situation that override the importance of the information?
> Do they want to hear the information?

11. Walk through the process. Many processes are predictable in any particular situation. Loss of a significant person will predictably involve the grief process. Disclosure of crime victimization will predictably involve police and legal procedures. When the time is right, the teacher's sharing what he or she knows about certain procedures can assist the student in predicting and planning for his or her near future. In addition, the professional's expectations for the present need to be stated.

12. Explore resources. As soon as possible, the professional should explore with the student the resources available and what the student's support system provides. The professional should assist the student in deciding who is in his or her support group, and when and how to reach out for that support.

13. Find friends. The professional may need to help the student to contact friends or family members, decide who at the school is available, and locate agencies or individuals in the community who could be of assistance. Professional and student should start with defining the needs and then move toward the solutions.

Teachers often shy away from dealing with troubled children, believing that they are not trained psychotherapists and are not being paid for this responsibility. The crucial distinction, however, is the difference between *doing therapy* and managing a crisis in a manner that does not further traumatize the child through mishandling or neglect. Through individual conferencing in which the situation is shared, feelings are validated, and resources are explored, the negative impact of the trauma upon the overall educational experience is minimized. This is simply concerned crisis management in the service of learning.

Classroom Debriefings

Sometimes an entire class as a group is affected by a critical incident. A good example might be sharing the experience of watching the space shuttle explode on television. The death of a student, a natural disaster occurring during school hours, witnessing a violent crime as a group—these and many other situations present a need for group intervention. When the critical incident affects the entire group, it must be addressed with this group in mind.

Not only are crisis management courses not offered in teacher training, but basic principles of managing groups are similarly ignored. Students in teacher education take courses in educational philosophy, curriculum considerations, and discipline. However, this does not equip them to deal with groups of children who go through something out of the ordinary. A growing need exists for the development of principles and procedures that teachers and other educators can follow during times of crisis.

Procedures used by fire and rescue teams provide a useful and productive model for a group intervention. Jeffrey Mitchell of the Department of Emergency Health Services, University of Maryland, uses a group crisis intervention model with traumatized emergency teams. Critical Incident Stress Debriefing (CISD) holds promise as a structured intervention approach with groups of children, and the classroom debriefing format described here follows Mitchell's model. This model provides a definite procedure and system of rules for conducting such an activity, which is important when one is dealing with emotionally sensitive content. Students must feel secure before they can benefit.

Classroom debriefings are structured group discussions. Not intended or recommended to be psychotherapy, classroom debriefings allow the class as a group to sort out the events leading to the incident and to express reactions to the incident. Their purpose is to develop understanding and increased feelings of personal control. Debriefings are an attempt to salvage group cohesiveness from the disintegrating effects of a crisis.

Debriefings vary from group to group and from situation to situation, but they tend to follow five main phases:

1. **Introductory phase.** The leader presents basic facts regarding the incident and lays down basic rules for participation. Rules for participation provide security for students. Talking about disturbing events is difficult; having a clear format spells out what the student can expect in terms of sequence of events in the group, confidentiality, what others will be talking about, and whether or not his or her feelings will be heard and respected. Much is at risk if the expression of feelings is allowed to have social backlash. The introductory phase is where the leader sets the tone for the entire session.

2. **Fact phase.** Students explore and reach concurrence on the sequence of events and the role each played in the incident. Each student must be given several opportunities to describe each phase of the incident from his or her own perspective. By the time this is done thoroughly, the events will have been clarified for all, and everyone involved will have gained some realization that he or she was not alone in the experience. They will see that others were similarly affected, and a shared perspective of the incident will begin to emerge.

3. **Feeling phase.** Feelings about the incident are explored in a supportive context. Each student is given the opportunity to share. Feelings are neither right nor wrong; they just are. Students have the right to express what they need to express and the responsibility to

listen uncritically and supportively to what others are feeling. Again, it is important to stress that every student be given an opportunity—or several—to share his or her feelings, but that no student should *have* to share. Always announce the right to pass; to be coerced to share things that are uncomfortable is another victimization. It is important to explore what feelings were present during the incident and what feelings are present *now* concerning the incident.

4. Teaching phase. Facts about posttraumatic response are shared with particular emphasis upon validation of individual experiences. The leader provides information to the students regarding normal reactions to the incident and anticipated reactions later. Any misconceptions regarding the incident or its effects can be cleared up. Finally, discussions and explorations of available resources can point out where to get help.

5. Closure phase. A debriefing can be a significant event in the life of the group and can affirm group cohesiveness and the value of the group to the individuals within it. This can be summarized and final comments made by each student. It is often important to devise some actual plan of action the class can take to regain a feeling of at least partial control over fate. Invite further discussion at a later date on an individual or group basis.

The group's sense of security needs to be reestablished by a return to a normal routine at the conclusion of the debriefing. The incident will have provided enough change for a while. Traumas are extreme disruptions, and the changes following traumas are further disruptions. Even class debriefings, designed to help students adjust, are themselves unsettling. A sense of continuity will be provided by a return to the normal events of the day. After the debriefing has run its course, the leader can do much for the students by letting them know clearly that the time has come to resume a normal routine.

The five phases of a class debriefing provide a structure that supports the individual and guides group process. Within this structure students can work toward a better understanding of the incident and its ramifications. The five stages are timed so as to maximize trust and sharing.

Following are some general suggestions for leading a group discussion after a crisis:

Leadership style. The style of the leader can vary, but qualities of warmth, acceptance, and a nonthreatening nature combined with the ability to control the group process quietly are particularly helpful.

Opportunity for sharing. Following a critical incident, students need a chance to talk about it. They do not, however, need to be coerced. The leader should make sure each student is asked questions at each step of the process, but should also set a rule that anyone can always say "pass" and not answer. Some clarification of this must be made in the introductory phase, during rule setting. This clarification is essential in lowering the anxiety level. A student can learn much, process much, and be helped a great deal simply by observing others and their reactions.

Ground rules. Ground rules can vary from group to group, but some standard and helpful ones are given here:

- confidentiality ("What's said in here stays in here.")

- no put-downs

- no interrupting

- speak only for yourself

Other rules can vary from group to group depending upon student needs, instructor preference, and the situation. Students may wish to specify particular rules with which they feel comfortable. The leader must be sure to check professional liability regarding the duty to report child abuse, dangerousness, and so on. These liabilities vary from state to state and can be a source of jeopardy for the unaware. The leader must make it clear to the group at the outset what the limits of his or her confidentiality are.

Format. One good way to handle the fact and feeling phases is for the leader to first go around the room asking individuals what they *saw* when they first became aware of the incident. Later, he or she should ask what individuals *heard,* and, finally, ask what they *felt.* This pattern establishes the principle of sharing while it moves from cognitive to affective material. The use of the term *felt* within the movement through the senses exploits the ambiguity of sensations versus feelings. This is a natural move and conducive to sharing and expression. Also, relating the material by "round robin" allows the reality of the experience to emerge and gives each individual increased opportunity and practice in participating before the content becomes uncontrollably emotional. In the event students jump at volunteering information, the leader can use his or her own judgment as to whether or not to allow open discussion. If open discussion is the decision, then care must be taken to ensure that each member has several opportunities to contribute. Further, the leader can choose to regulate the timing of the group in order to keep the discussion comfortable.

Needs. Students may need to talk about similar incidents, both current and past. This is all part of the sorting-out process and may occupy the majority of the time allotted. Often the present experience may be less serious than past incidents and a student may be talking about different events interchangeably or simultaneously without realizing it. The leader's clarification may be necessary to avoid confusion. Often one student will dominate the discussion, and the leader will be forced to balance between the more acute needs of one or two individuals and the less acute needs of the majority (some of whom may also have acute needs, but may be quiet). The length of the session will be determined by the amount of obvious energy in the group. As long as the session is focused and constructive, it should go on. If the session becomes unnecessarily uncomfortable for some member or digresses into unproductive chatter, it should be ended. Again, the tenor of the group will be fairly obvious and will provide the key to timing.

Reactions. Students' emotional reactions can vary widely. They can range from unaffected or amused to quite shaken. An "unaffected" reaction, however, may actually be numbness, and general amusement is often a defense against anxiety. Such students may need to be protected from others seeking to displace anger. In general, while reactions are bound to be strong, behavioral extremes are of concern. These are spelled out in this chapter in the section "When to Refer."

When it's over. The leader should keep the discussion gently focused until it has run its course, and then get the classroom back to its normal routine. It is likely that students will still refer to the event and return to discussing it in the future. The object of debriefing after critical incidents is to open up discussion regarding the event. The teacher's job after debriefing is to be open to further discussion with students, whether it takes the form of class discussion, small-group or individual interchange, written expression, or artwork.

Assess. If students need further support (that is, if individuals are uncontrollable or seem to be in shock), the teacher should immediately refer them to the office or to whatever backup is available. This is discussed further in the section "When to Refer."

Teachers, auxiliary staff, and administrators need not be trained in psychotherapy in order to fill a therapeutic role effectively. The debriefing process modeled here is a management tool. The group being managed consists of students whose well-being coincides with the well-being of the group, and whose future academic learning depends in part upon their coming to understand an event that has befallen them. The purpose of classroom debriefings is not psychotherapy; rather, it is crisis management in the service of education. The key actions involved include establishment of ground rules, exploration of facts, sharing of feelings, and learning about future possibilities.

What Not to Do

Much has been said so far about what to do with individuals and groups who have experienced traumatic situations. It would be irresponsible to indicate, however, that *any* interaction is preferable to no interaction at all. In the study reported in Appendix I, adolescents who had experienced trauma during childhood were questioned about how their parents had responded to them during and shortly after their critical incidents. The resulting styles of response were then matched with the children's subsequent adjustment. What emerged was a fairly clear picture of what does and does not work with children who have been subjected to traumatic experiences.

After a critical incident, the traumatized person is highly suggestible and emotionally vulnerable. Careless messages, heavy judgments, and bad advice can leave a lasting impression. Feelings of guilt, inadequacy, and social stigma can follow from well-meaning but hurtful "help" after a crisis. Such bad medicine can amount to retraumatization; the person is taught to hurt.

The study also indicates that there are two general types of interchange that are helpful to children in crisis. The discussions about individual conferencing and class debriefings have incorporated the helping behaviors common to those styles. The study further indicated that there are three styles of adult response that are *hurtful* to children following a crisis. These can be labeled as the withholding, incompetent, and reactive/escapist styles. Withholding parents tend to focus upon their own needs and deny the seriousness of the child's experience, shrugging off the child's feelings. Incompetent parents make false assurances, discourage discussion about the incident, and are themselves unable to cope or to continue fulfilling their normal role functions as parents. Reactive/escapist parents initially make false assumptions regarding the child's role in the incident and blame the child; later, these parents close communication regarding the incident. These three parenting styles during crisis were correlated with many problems for the children later, during the already difficult period of adolescence.

The study reported in Appendix I provides some indication of what *not* to do with a child or a group following a crisis. The following types of interaction should be *avoided* when talking to a student or class following a critical incident.

1. Falling apart. It is essential that teachers and other professionals demonstrate empathy and understanding. It's all right for them to shed some tears in sympathy or express what they feel, but it is vital that they remain in emotional control. They must not fall apart or react with excessive emotion, because that sends a message that they can't be trusted with the information a student may give them. The student has enough to cope with; he or she does not need to be forced to take care of adults emotionally as well.

2. False promises. Professionals must not tell the individual or group things they are not really sure of or that are not true. If unsure of something, professionals should be careful to say so: "I'm not sure, but I will find out for you." They should not say, "Everything is going to be all right," unless they have some way of knowing that for sure.

3. Making judgments. Facial expressions, body language, inferences, and questions can each communicate judgments. Even "Why did you take so long to come to me?" signals an implied judgment that may be more than a traumatized student can handle. The professional should focus upon the person, not on what's "right." The child's needs must take precedence at this point.

4. Inquisition. The professional should not play detective, searching for information to identify the perpetrator. Pushing for information at this point comes across as using the child for other purposes. Such inquisition will only drive the student away or make things worse. Instead, the professional should assist the student in revealing what he or she feels necessary, and then work with that.

5. Role defection. During crisis situations it is important for teachers to maintain control and not relinquish the leadership role. Students may complain about and resist classroom structure and discipline—the leadership of the teacher is sometimes seen as both a problem and a solution—yet students rely upon that structure for their sense of well-being. Discipline and leadership provide a secure base for the developing sense of self, a base against which to define one's individuality and personal values. The role filled by the teacher is important for any student; for the child in crisis, it is essential. Crisis threatens the existing structure of the world and the teacher, so it is important that the teacher in such a situation maintain a strong leadership and class structure, to provide a system of security.

6. Withdrawal. Professionals should not withdraw from children in crisis emotionally—enough stigma is attached to trauma as it is. If the trauma occurred at school, parents, relatives, and nonschool friends are likely to withdraw from traumatized children because they do not know what to do and feel incompetent. If the trauma occurred at home, school staff and students are likely to withdraw for the same reasons and also from the fear that they will make it worse. While the child in crisis does not need to be in the limelight, he or she does need to have supportive, normalizing, and affirming contact with others.

Students who have just been through traumatic situations do not need to be retraumatized by clumsy, heavy-handed intervention or by isolation and withdrawal. The maintenance of an ongoing classroom structure with caring, supportive, and listening school staff provides a healing context whether or not additional psychotherapy is needed or available. Important to the long-range management of student crisis is the follow-through that aware staff can provide. The following two sections discuss when referral is critical and ways in which school staff can provide helpful follow-through.

When to Refer

School personnel find themselves in a difficult predicament. While not trained as mental health specialists, they find themselves on the front lines when it comes to behavioral disturbances. When traumas occur at home—and sometimes they occur *because* of the home—school personnel are the first in the community to become aware of the children's behavioral changes. The section "What to Expect" outlined what school personnel can expect following a crisis. The behaviors outlined are "normal" following trauma. This section discusses behavior that is clearly extreme. The information will be useful to teachers and other professionals in determining when children should be referred for consultation with mental health specialists.

The question of when to refer is not a simple one, and no list of conditions can do more than provide general indicators. One difficulty is the question of degree of need. Anyone who has experienced trauma could probably benefit from professional consultation, if only to assess whether or not further intervention is needed. Specialists can provide support, perspective, assistance in family matters, and information about other resources. This would be a referral for purposes of *optimal* health and is optional. Many children who have experienced trauma can probably get along without treatment by a specialist. Some very serious signs, however, can indicate that mental health referral is important for the short- and long-term interests of a child. The teacher or administrator should always bring up concerns with guidance personnel and parents when questions arise, but this section addresses occasions when referral is critical.

The following guidelines are presented in an attempt to sharpen school staff perception of situations in which consideration of referral is essential. The main difference between normal and serious reactions to critical incidents is one of degree rather than kind. Serious reactions are simply normal reactions taken to an extreme; thus this section will differentiate between the normal reaction and its more serious counterpart. These signs will be grouped according to cognitive, emotional, and behavioral signs.

1. Cognitive signs. A reaction may be said to be serious when

— slight disorientation has become the inability to tell one's name, the date, or relate what has happened over the past 24 hours

— too much concern over little things has become exclusive preoccupation with one idea

— denial of the severity of the problem has become wholesale denial that a problem exists

— visual or auditory flashbacks have become out-of-control hallucinations

— self-doubt has become a feeling of unreality, disconnectedness, and fear of "losing my mind"

— difficulty in planning practical things has become the inability to carry out basic life functions

— light confusion has become bizarre, irrational beliefs, and these form the basis for action

2. Emotional signs. A reaction may be said to be serious when

— crying has become uncontrolled hysteria

— anger or self-blame has become fear or threats of harm to self or others

— blunted emotional response or numbing has become complete withdrawal, with no emotional response

— appropriate expression of despair or depression has become self-destructive

3. Behavioral signs. A reaction may be said to be serious when

— restlessness or excitement has become unfocused agitation

— excessive talking or nervous laughter has become uncontrolled

— frequent retelling of the incident has become continual or ritualistic

— pacing, hand-wringing, or fist-clenching has become ritualistic or uncontrolled

— disheveled appearance has, over time, become an inability to care for oneself

— irritability has become destructive

Referral is sometimes made for reasons of optimal adjustment. Sometimes, in cases such as those described above, in which a child's behavior indicates serious disturbance, the care of specialists is required to prevent even greater decline. While teachers are usually the ones who raise the questions, referrals themselves are usually made by district psychologists or administrators. Often the teacher is then left with no indication of what might happen to the child. Chapter 4, "What Therapists Can Do," is designed to shed light upon the black box of therapeutic process, and school personnel are urged to read that chapter to obtain greater understanding of what happens in therapy. In addition, the next section addresses the issues involved in school follow-through.

Follow-Through

The process of classroom management of crisis does not end after a formal conference or debriefing or even with referral of some students for mental health services. Staff follow-through is important in four particular areas: in the classroom itself, with other staff members, with auxiliary personnel such as outside therapists, and with the child's family.

In the classroom, the fact that the trauma occurred is inescapable. After conferences and debriefing, the cognitive, emotional, and social processing of the event continues. If the event occurred outside of class to one student, it is quite likely that little explicit mention of the incident will be made. Instead, the child may deal with it indirectly through art, writing, thematic play, or choice of reading material. The child may talk to the teacher or to a circle of friends about it. The teacher, school psychologist, or other staff member can encourage or even facilitate this attempt at dealing with the changes the trauma has brought about.

If the event occurred to the group as a whole, it is likely to occur as an object of discussion as well as in the indirect ways mentioned above. This is an opportunity for group building of the class, and the honesty and straightforward nature of the debriefing can extend to other classroom contexts. The processes of assimilation and accommodation should be encouraged, and the teacher can raise the issue through various class activities. Eventually, if given sufficient attention over time, the traumatic event will become old news without being repressed by group taboo. Some groups may resist rehashing the event. Since there is a tendency to avoid confronting painful material, initial reluctance may occur.

Activities in the Classroom

Classroom activities can be used—directly or indirectly—to assist the class in accommodating to the crisis. The decision to address the crisis through crisis-related activities should take several factors into consideration. Postcrisis classroom activities are useful when

— the group or class would benefit from a structured process

— students are feeling isolated and need assistance in sharing about the incident

— discussion would benefit from impetus, direction, context, and leadership

— activities are chosen and implemented with consideration toward student sensitivities and needs

Such activities can be didactic, interactive, or employ various media such as writing, art, and simulation. Didactic presentation is useful where the flow of information should be controlled, the students need a more structured and less interactive presentation, and the process requires greater control. Didactic presentation is less personal and involving, and so tends to be less threatening.

Interaction and discussion, whether in a structured class debriefing format or a less structured, more spontaneous free-flow rap session, is more personalized, involving, flexible, and potentially more powerful. At the same time, this format is less manageable, provides less control of material and interpretation, and can miss material needing to be covered.

The use of writing, art, and simulation experiences can be very involving and thus quite powerful. Writing is more organized, individual, and less threatening than art. Of the three, simulation exercises can be the least controlled and most volatile.

It should be noted that students who are exhibiting signs of Acute Stress Reaction (extreme reaction to an incident) or signs indicating the need for immediate referral should not participate in either discussions or follow-up activities that address crisis issues until they are properly screened by mental health professionals competent to evaluate postcrisis functioning. Similarly, certain conditions indicate that groups or classes should not use such activities. Group warning signs include the following:

- the group or class has a history of being nonsupportive, hurtful, or divisive

- the group's needs relative to the crisis are polarized (that is, some students are deeply affected while others are untouched; for some the incident represents loss while for some it creates opportunities)

- some class members are highly traumatized or have suffered serious loss

In general, most activities—art, writing, or enactment and simulation—can be modified to change their impact. The impact of activities can be softened when prompts

— involve individual rather than group activity

— require cognitive rather than affective responses

— encourage general rather than specific responses

— invite universal rather than personal or individual responses

— involve principles or lessons learned rather than relating experiences

— involve problem solving rather than dwelling upon the impact of the crisis

— require global impressions rather than sensory images

— involve writing rather than art activities

— involve art rather than enactment or simulation activities

Follow-through with staff members varies in form depending upon the interpersonal makeup of the staff, its normal mode of communication, the roles staff members have played in the crisis, and the types of specialists available.

If the crisis occurred outside of the school and was limited to one student, follow-through may be needed only with the teacher, the administrator, and any other support personnel who have been involved. This may consist of informed periodic status reports, but it may also include consultation for brainstorming and problem solving to ensure that educational services to the child are well maintained through the aftermath of the crisis.

If the crisis occurred in the class, more personnel are likely to be involved, particularly district staff. The event will be more organizationally visible and perhaps more visible to the community. There may be more pressure upon the organization to portray a proactive stance in dealing with the crisis. Administrators may exhibit more involvement with activity planning and may ask the teacher for more frequent and formal status reports and articulated action plans. Other staff members will be more interested, and periodic updates will be expected. The stress on the teaching staff and students will be more intense. In addition to situational management, teachers in particular will need extra support during and following the incident to help them manage the varied stressors with which they must deal.

Finally, if the event occurred to several classes at once, the visibility will be even greater. Besides the need for greater resources and thoughts regarding methods of meeting the diversity of personal needs, new levels of organizational needs will emerge. Resources will

have to be allocated effectively. Information will have to be organized and communicated consistently. School activities will need to
be coordinated appropriately. There is likely to be increased community awareness, and this may entail media coverage. Media coverage
will affect staff members, increasing staff stress and contributing to a
general sense of emergency. Uninvolved students will pick up on the
excitement and need to be given as much information as is appropriate. To avoid the effects of rumormongering, a consistent, regular
updating of information is essential. In addition, all students will
need time to talk about not only the crisis and its residual effects but
also the current situation and subsequent developments.

Follow-up can also be conducted with any mental health professionals who are involved. While updating is a major part of such an
effort, it has more to do with enhancing treatment. Therapists
become involved in two major capacities. First, they may be consulting with school personnel or even working with students or whole
classes. In this capacity, their primary source of valid information
consists of the observations of the classroom teacher. The information they will seek will include the general class mood, specific incidents that are indicative of underlying issues, the extent to which
children are communicative about these issues, problems that have
arisen, and particular individuals who seem to be having a rougher-
than-average time. Contact between the consultant and school personnel regarding progress and the effects of specific activities can
increase the effectiveness of the consultant.

The other major capacity in which therapists become involved is
in treating individual students outside the school. Once school personnel make referrals to therapists, they often assume that the problem is gone. This severance of services limits the effectiveness on
both sides. Educators need information regarding the progress and
needs of their students who are receiving mental health services in
order to manage wisely for educational gain. Therapists can similarly
gain from teacher feedback regarding a child's classroom behavior.
The school exists in "real time" for children. It is a natural setting,
while the clinical office is not. Therapists deal mainly with inferences drawn from second-hand information and self-report. Teachers
can provide the therapist extensive observation of the child's individual and social behavior in his or her normal world. However, to

most teachers, therapy is a "black box." The lack of experience shared by teachers and therapists limits their communication. With the perspectives provided in this book, teachers and therapists may begin to utilize their knowledge of each other's function in order to ask the right questions and give the right answers.

Parents represent the final area for follow-through. As mentioned earlier, families often present significant resistance to communication about their children's traumatic experiences. No one raises a child to be hurt. Most parents are appalled at the idea of their children being hurt, even in some cases where they themselves are inflicting the pain. The natural first reaction to bad news is denial, and parental resistance to dealing openly with children's hurt is a form of denial. Second, a child's hurt may cause unpleasant memories of the parent's own past hurts, and this may spark a desire to avoid thinking about it. Another source of resistance lies in the fact that trauma often uncovers weaknesses in the fabric of the family relationship. If that is the case, a child's needs may go unmet because to deal with them might cost the whole family. Another source of resistance is feelings of shame because the event has occurred. Finally, many forms of resistance are grounded in the family's general resistance to being intruded upon by yet another bureaucratic institution.

Whatever the source of resistance, it makes the task of the school more difficult. However, the degree of resistance is usually a good indication of how much the child needs the school to make the contact and to open up communication. The specific form of parent contact need not differ from other school-home communication, except that it needs to be personal contact and not form letters. Further, if the trauma involved a group, continued information about what activities are being done in class to deal with the incident helps keep parents involved. Likewise, calls or questionnaires with personal notes requesting information about behavioral changes noticed at school not only provide helpful information, but also keep the door open for future contact.

USING OUTSIDE RESOURCES

Many rich resources can be tapped by school personnel to assist them in dealing with school crises. Private mental health professionals often seek contact with schools as a means of boosting their private practices, and health maintenance organizations and employee assistance groups often seek to build a public presence by contributing expertise. Public mental health and social service agencies often want to make their services more accessible. These resources, whatever their motivations, can often provide much to beleaguered school professionals in support of students.

Some cautions are in order before utilizing community resources. First, make certain that the services offered are appropriate to the need. Be clear with regard to what is actually offered and how it will be delivered. Clarify the limits of the services and the extent to which providers will be supervised by school personnel. Clarify legal liabilities, particularly concerning the scope of practice delineations set by the state, county, and local jurisdictions. Make sure the services can legally be offered by the school.

Second, when accepting trauma assistance from the community, determine whether the provider is oriented toward trauma treatment or trauma containment. Many clinicians wish to conduct research and need a crisis for material. The school is not a treatment facility, nor are students in crisis appropriate subjects for experiment. Services should be rendered for the good of the school and in service of stabilization of the school environment.

Third, clinicians often have unrealistic views of the conditions under which school personnel work. They do not think in terms of whole classes or large groups of students. They frequently are insensitive to the political factors or the social fishbowl position of the school in the community. In their zeal to advocate for children, they may do long-term political damage to the school.

Fourth, clinicians frequently do not accept the necessity of prioritizing the smooth operation of the school in situation management. In the lives of many children, the school stands as the single stable element, and routine is essential to that stability. Whether a crisis occurred inside or outside the school, school stability reinforces the child's emerging sense of self. To compromise that stability, no matter how worthy the cause, is to compromise the child. Disruptions must be justifiable.

Finally, clinicians often do not understand or appreciate the nature and extent of staff stress. Teachers and support staff work under difficult conditions of multifactored stress, and for many the balance between resources and demands is tenuous indeed. Crises exacerbate those stressful conditions, and the last thing school people need is to have to deal with additional stressors introduced by well-meaning but misguided outside resource people.

Outside resources cannot be expected to understand or assist the school crisis environment without formal preparation, and they can be best utilized when introduced to the school prior to an emergency. Proactive crisis management involves active recruitment, training, and role definition. A preexisting working relationship and adequate supervision will turn outside resources into assets rather than liabilities.

SCHOOL CRISIS RESPONSE TEAMS

Since the initial appearance of the first edition of this book in 1989, school districts all over the country have initiated and developed crisis response teams to deal with emergencies on campus. The typical development of a team follows an almost predictable pattern.

Several individuals, often school psychologists, who work with students in difficult situations, become familiar with the literature about crisis response. Then an emergency occurs, and the school or district experiences distress regarding their efforts in dealing with it. The several individuals, reinforced by others who were involved in the incident and now feel the need to prepare for possible future incidents, form an ad hoc task force with the express purpose of organizing and preparing a formal team. An initial organization is formed, interested people recruited, preliminary administrative blessing granted, and initial training scheduled. The team meets, receives training, and begins to provide services during small incidents. Then a large incident occurs. The team often feels defeated by the nature and scope of the incident and secures more specific training. During this advanced training, an actual debriefing of the troubling incident often takes place.

It was after providing a number of these later, more advanced trainings to intact teams that this author formalized the training curriculum into book form; see *School Crisis Management* (Alameda, CA: Hunter House, 1993). During subsequent training of crisis response teams in New York City schools, and following the riot, firestorms and floods, and earthquake during the period of 1992–94, further materials have been formalized and are available.

The cardinal virtue of such crisis teams lies in their unique ability to assist the school in being able to respond to student and staff needs while reinforcing the smooth operation of the school. The supportive climate of the school is increased, and the school is recognized as a caring place that protects its children.

PROFILE: ELIZABETH CAPEWELL

Schools in the United Kingdom have traditionally been slow to place school crisis intervention on their agendas—that is, until a local man entered the primary school in Dunblane, Scotland, shooting and killing sixteen children and their teacher and injuring twelve other children and three teachers. Elizabeth Capewell assisted school personnel and community agencies in dealing with the aftermath of the shootings.

With a background in school teaching and social work, Capewell is ideally suited to meeting the need for community and school crisis management. Her Centre for Crisis Management and Education in Newbury, just outside of London, challenges complacency and fear and presses schools and other helping agencies to prepare for crisis. She has an impressive record of both intervention and consultation, having presented trainings and lectures in Australia, New Zealand, Israel, and the United States. She has also been part of a UNICEF training project in Croatia and is now engaged in long-term consultancies in northern Ireland and Dunblane.

Capewell knows whereof she speaks. Her first involvement with large-scale crisis work followed the Hungerford massacre in 1987, when a deranged resident methodically burned his parents' home and set out on a six-hour rampage that resulted in sixteen dead, fifteen wounded by gunfire, and a community under seige for six hours. Her work began the day of the shooting and continues.

She provided consultation to a school in the area that had recently accepted Croatian refugee children and was experiencing conflict between those children and the local children who had been involved with the shootings two years before. Despite the similarity of the experiences, each group's posttraumatic reactions were triggered by the other group's behavior. The cultural and linguistic differences made reconciliation difficult.

Working with the staff in her own agency, the local schools, and young people in the community, Capewell noticed how the needs of the young were generally not understood and that there was much dissent about what schools could do. Similar observations were made in subsequent work following the Pan Am 103 disaster at Lockerbie (1988) and the Hillsborough football stadium disaster (1989). Since then she has coordinated school and community responses to major and minor school-and-community-based traumas, such as the London Docklands IRA bombing (1996) and the impact of the death of her own daughter, Anne Capewell. The Centre for Crisis Management follows the principle that preparation for and management of an incident are critical to the effectiveness of reactive help. What the classroom teacher does or does not do or say is seen as important to recovery, as is individual counseling. Capewell believes that, ideally, school interventions should be teacher led, specialist (e.g., school psychologist) supported, and—where the school structures are overwhelmed—external-consultant coordinated. Teachers must be prepared and trained so that they know how to apply their usual skills to trauma situations, so that their responses to students and parents are informed, and so that they have the emotional capacity to deal with distressing situations.

Capewell's center makes great use of methods learned from colleagues in Israel, educational methods that do not stigmatize children. Of particular use is the empowerment model of debriefing developed by Dr. Ofra Ayalon of the University of Haifa, and employed for more than two decades. The model relies heavily on metaphor as the mediator between the child and the distressing event, giving children the opportunity and skills to work through their own stories at their own pace. Simple assessement and monitoring methods are taught to teachers to help them be aware of the full range of the ripple effect and its long-term consequences.

PROFILE: DAVID WEE

David Wee does disaster. Working in the aftermaths of the Loma Prieta earthquake, Hurricane Andrew, the Los Angeles civil disturbances and firestorms, the Northridge earthquake and winter storms, the Oklahoma City bombing, and the Great Heishin earthquake, Wee has emerged as one of the most experienced disaster mental health service delivery specialists in the United States. As the mental health program supervisor and disaster coordinator for the city of Berkeley, California, he spends much of his time preparing for disaster service delivery.

Working directly with students in school, Wee has found that children of all ages can benefit from the opportunity to tell the stories of their disaster experiences and receive acknowledgment that others have heard their fear, sadness, uncertainty, and relief. Children can learn that they are not alone and that others felt like they did. Crisis intervention with children in the classroom provides a powerful buffer for children who have been given distressing misinformation. They are offered a safe place to ventilate feelings, express their concerns, get accurate information, and give support to as well as receive support from teachers and other children. All of this assists their coping with their postdisaster world.

To accomplish this, Wee uses a form of art therapy, "draw and talk," with younger children (discussed in Chapter 4), Critical Incident Stress Debriefing with adolescents and staff, and parent education. While they differ in method, these approaches seek the same end: to allow those affected by disaster to move ahead with the tasks of recovery and rebuilding.

In assisting school personnel who had to contend with children following disaster, Wee found that administrators and teachers were also affected by the incident. Many wanted to talk about what had happened to them when the disaster occurred. Before work with the children could begin, they needed time to tell their own stories, to have themselves heard, and to receive reassurance, support, and direction in coping with the situation.. Teachers wanted to do the best for their students and needed information, techniques, and support.

Wee feels that those who would help children after a disaster must be sensitive to the needs of the adults who work with those children. Disasters disrupt everything in some way, impacting routines, relationships, and anything that provides feelings of safety and security. Interventions can help the school recover, or they can be seen as yet another obstacle. Working with school personnel must be a partnership among administrators, teachers, parents, and those who would help. School intervention isn't easy work. Wee allows that it "takes clear vision, and volumes of energy, compassion, and patience."

PROFILE: NANCY SANFORD

Disaster is the mother of large-scale invention. When the Northridge earthquake hit in the early morning hours of January 17, 1994, the sprawling Los Angeles Unified School District found itself facing a calamity of monstrous proportions. Some schools were closed outright, many had some damage necessitating changes in their way of conducting the business of education, and the district was forced to take emergency measures impacting thousands of children and employees. Most importantly, the learning environment needed to be stabilized.

It was determined that debriefings would be helpful, yet the numbers were staggering. The Federal Emergency Management Agency sponsored Project Rebound to provide crisis and recovery counseling for earthquake victims. Rebound logged services for 28,500 adults and 125,000 children. A sizable proportion of those counseling sessions with children were provided by L.A.U.S.D. Mental Health Services, a department headed by Nancy Sanford, M.S., R.N.

District mental health services began with an initial training by Sanford of 450 facilitators who taught a modification of Jeffrey Mitchell's debriefing format (discussed earlier), which provided a limited debriefing with a structured educational component. This group of facilitators went on to conduct a series of large-scale debriefings with district employees, parents, and selected groups of students. In all, some 3,000 employees were debriefed. It is impossible to determine how many students were then debriefed, because those 3,000 employees would each have conducted informal and unofficial smaller scale debriefings with the students they encountered as part of their normal duties. Sanford alone conducted more than 50 classroom-size or smaller debriefing sessions with students. Assessment of effectiveness is difficult; however, since the earthquake, no students receiving debriefings have been reported as referred to district mental health clinics with complaints of earthquake-related trauma symptoms.

While the debriefing format had been significantly modified, it could hardly have been otherwise. The numbers of children, parents, and staff who were in need were immense and would have quickly outstripped the numbers of trained interveners available. Disaster planning is rarely realistic because the aftermath of disaster is usually surrealistic. Planning for the Los Angeles civil disorder, firestorms, and earthquake would have seemed a ludicrous exercise in paranoia. Yet having the basic concepts of prevention and the basic models of intervention in place allowed Sanford and those with whom she worked to make a creative and productive response.

Conclusion

Crisis can occur in or out of school, but in either case the school is involved. The child's behavior is affected and the class climate and productivity will undergo change.

Teachers and administrators can assist the child and the class by providing a context within which the child is safe. This entails doing some things and avoiding others, as was discussed. The gravity of the crisis should not create a fear of contact with involved students and professional therapists. Much can be done by people without specialized training, and, in fact, much should be done by school personnel. While certain types of interaction need to be avoided, specific positive steps can be taken in the proactive management of the crisis situation. These steps have been outlined in the sections on individual conferencing, class debriefing, and follow-through. Awareness of specific signs that indicate when referral is appropriate can ensure that those referrals are made in a timely manner; this awareness can also assist school staff in interfacing with district psychologists and outside mental health consultants for the student's benefit. Finally, such a proactive posture helps school personnel deal with the children's families, who are likely to be in very real pain. In recent years, school Crisis Response Teams have developed to deal with the impact of critical incidents on students, staff, and the school. As these teams generate new strategies and approaches, they will add to the response options of educators and therapists seeking to alleviate children's suffering.

CHAPTER 4

What Therapists Can Do

We had all been believers, believers in ourselves
and hence the future. But events have driven a
barrier between the past and the present, and we
are now all refugees in our own country.

Peter Shrag, *Out of Place in America*

Extreme remedies are very appropriate for
extreme diseases.

Hippocrates, *Aphorisms*

Who, doomed to go in company with Pain,
And Fear; and Bloodshed, miserable train!
Turns his necessity to glorious gain . . .

William Wordsworth,
"Character of the Happy Warrior"

OVERVIEW

For most school personnel, what goes on in psychotherapy remains a mystery. Without a basic understanding of the direction and process of therapy, educators often feel unable to work with therapists. In addition, many therapists who do not regularly work with traumatized children do not feel comfortable in dealing with either the children or their families. This chapter distinguishes between crisis intervention and psychological treatment, defines the central task of therapy, and describes methods of child and adolescent treatment. In addition, it specifies information from natural settings that therapists can use, opening the door to the therapeutic process for nonclinicians.

Chapter Contents

Traumatized children are seen in a clinical setting for a variety of reasons. Central to their successful treatment is the management of their posttraumatic reaction, whether as the focus or as a component of treatment. Understanding the reaction is the first necessary part of treatment. Then, the work of reexperiencing, releasing, and integrating the experience must begin. The various treatment modalities employed with traumatized children, such as art and play therapy, aim at reexperience/release/integration. This chapter explores this process, starting with general considerations regarding course of treatment.

The purpose of such a discussion is twofold. First, clinicians typically have broad-based training in doing therapy and have developed skills in particular methods. In addition, detailed literature and training abound in specific treatment approaches. Less attention is paid, however, to articulating a clear statement of clinical directions and overall treatment progress with traumatized children. This chapter seeks to provide such a statement irrespective of treatment approach.

Second, nonclinicians such as educators, clergy, and others working with children are often faced with traumatized children. They need more than simply a few signs when contemplating referring a child or family for therapy. A basic understanding of what goes on—or should go on—in therapy will provide a better basis for decisions regarding referral. A clear statement of clinical directions will help as well.

Therapists deal with posttraumatic children in three contexts:

1. just after the trauma, upon referral

2. months later, for trauma-specific symptoms such as nightmares, phobias, and adjustment problems

3. much later, during developmental transition periods, when coping patterns have become problematic

Most of the cases of delayed reaction to traumas manifest indirect symptoms. The real value of a firm understanding of posttraumatic stress is heuristic. For those cases in which client symptomatology *could be* indicative of prior trauma, inquiry into background experiences is *likely* to turn up such experiences. This, in turn, may indicate that dealing with the trauma may be an essential part of treatment.

Posttraumatic Stress Disorder provides a direction for investigation when approaching critical incidents as well as maladaptive behaviors. By recognizing the possible developmental outcomes of trauma, clinicians and other adults can better plan comprehensive intervention approaches with traumatized children. Similarly, by recognizing the likelihood of prior trauma in the lives of adolescents whose behavior is maladaptive and problematic, clinicians and others can plan interventions that better address underlying causative factors.

This chapter offers an outline of the overall task of the clinician in providing treatment. As such, it provides nontherapists an accessible explanation of what therapists do when they treat posttrauma children and adolescents who have been referred to them. Teachers, social workers, and church or other youth service workers frequently feel that all therapists do is sit and talk or, conversely, that they work some sort of magic. This discussion is intended to provide nontherapists with a basic understanding of the optimal therapeutic process so that they may have a clearer sense of when to refer a child for treatment and what to expect when they do so.

The Therapeutic Task

When approaching these questions, an understanding of the normative process of trauma adjustment is important. Horowitz (1976) describes an "ideal course" for the adjustment to a critical incident: Recovery is maximized if the person

1. perceives the event correctly

2. translates the perceptions into a clear meaning

3. relates the meaning to an enduring attitude

4. decides on an appropriate action, and

5. revises memories, attitudes, and belief systems to fit a new developmental line made necessary by the experience (cited in Donaldson & Gardner, 1985)

This model was developed by Horowitz from his work with Vietnam veterans. As such, it is framed for adults within a specific developmental context (for more on this subject, see the discussion of Wilson's work in Chapter 2). While the developmental context differs for children, the model applies equally to them and provides a concise statement of treatment goals.

Donaldson and Gardner (1985) further expand upon Horowitz's model to generate the following treatment implications:

1. After a traumatic event, the afflicted person is less bothered in later life if he or she undergoes an ideal psychological processing (Horowitz's "ideal course").

2. This ideal course is interfered with by overly powerful memories persisting in "active memory storage" when "processing" does not occur.

3. Therapeutic information breaks the cyclical alternating of denial and numbing and intrusive repetitious thoughts by providing a safe environment in which one can experience the emotional response without automatic denial and numbing of the emotions.

4. Simple conscious recollections, emotional catharses, or reviews of one's thoughts and beliefs are not enough by

themselves but must proceed simultaneously and repeatedly for the best working-through process. (p. 368)

The posttraumatic reaction does not occur in a social or developmental vacuum. Treatment of trauma-specific symptoms usually takes place along with treatment of other problems secondary to the trauma, such as behavior problems, school difficulties, and family interaction. Attempts by the individual at coping with the trauma over time have a detrimental effect upon all aspects of development. The clinician is rarely presented with posttrauma cases that are simple (simple, that is, in the sense that there is an absence of complicating factors).

Memory Research

Current work in memory shows great promise in understanding the complex phenomenon of memory itself, how current behavior is influenced by traumatic memory, and how the treatment of posttrauma symptoms can progress.

For example, we are learning that memories seem to be stored initially as "implicit" memory (in visual, olfactory, auditory, kinesthetic, and affective fragments), and only later emerge as a personal narrative, or "explicit" whole memory (Van der Kolk, 1995). This later form seems to be associated with language development. Terr (1994) reports that children traumatized prior to language development tend to express implicit memories of abuse through their actions, attitudes, and emotions.

Lately the validity of recovered memories has been called into question as admissible court evidence in trials against alleged perpetrators of child sexual abuse. This is often considered by the lay public as an indication that such memories, revealed in therapy or spontaneously, are not to be taken seriously.

Some authors feel that memories of trauma are related more to suggestion by well-meaning therapists than to events that actually occurred (Loftus et al., 1994). Others (e.g., Williams, 1994) feel that some sort of amnesia or "repression" results in a special type of forgetting, which may be followed later by recall of events that did, in fact, happen.

Recent developments in memory research, however, are beginning to shed light on the process in which memories are stored and
retrieved. These processes account for much of the seeming inconsistency in memory recall after long periods of amnesia.

In describing their studies and reviewing those of others regarding the neurology of memory, Bremner et al. (1995) conclude that
stress-induced changes occur in the several brain regions and systems
involved in memory. Especially impacted is the hippocampal region
in the limbic system, which has two central functions: the encoding,
storing, and retrieving of memories, as well as the moderating of the
body's biochemical response to stress. This structure is vulnerable to
alterations by chemical changes during extreme stress and then is
rendered extrasensitive to further stressors. This can result in faulty
memory encoding and retrieval and in over- or underresponsiveness
to stress. Many posttrauma symptoms such as intrusive imagery, dissociated memories and reactions, delayed recall and distorted memories, and sensitization to certain stimuli—all signs of posttraumatic
stress—can be accounted for in terms of such neuroanatomical
changes. Thus some writers consider posttraumatic reactions to be
"disorders of arousal."

Similarly, longitudinal studies by Cameron (1996), based upon
data gathered over a ten-year period, of reactions of (formerly)
amnesic and nonamnesic victims of childhood sexual abuse shed
light on the long-term reactions to abuse, and the gradual process of
emergence of recovered memory. Recovered memories tend to return
gradually and in fragments, and the process of piecing together and
making sense of emerging memories can be distressing to both the
rememberers and their families.

Whether families should be confronted, or alleged perpetrators
blamed or even prosecuted, is a complex question with many legal
and psychological dimensions. Yet it is clear that the psychological
truth of emergent memories for the victim must be dealt with therapeutically. The clinic is not the court. Legal admissibility as court
evidence requires stringent conditions of factuality. The criteria is
whether or not the facticity of a proposed piece of evidence can be
reasonably doubted. Memories, by their nature, are subject to all
manner of questions. During the process of recovery they often
emerge in distorted, symbolic, dissociated, and partial form, and

change with the process of assimilation. Yet legal inadmissability does not detract from the psychological importance or usefulness of memory as critical to the process of understanding personal history and current behavior.

As we learn more about memory function, we will be able to sharpen our clinical and legal approaches to address both individual needs and the demands of justice.

Treatment Considerations with Traumatized Children

Clinicians working with traumatized children should adapt the general model of trauma processing to children's developmental levels and needs. This includes a sensitivity to the differences between various age groups and the exigencies of particular situations. The need for delicate assessment of the child's needs, strengths, and situation is apparent. This section will consider several factors to be taken into account by therapists assessing cases of trauma. Following a discussion of child-specific symptoms, various approaches to clinical assessment will be considered. At this point, some approaches to treatment can be described.

Children who have experienced critical incidents are at risk for subsequent maladaptive behavior as well as for various situational symptoms. Terr (1981) lists some of these child-specific symptoms:

- fear of death, separation, and further trauma

- misidentification of perpetrators and/or hallucinations of perpetrators

- no disavowal or traumatic amnesia

- absent vegetative or nervous effects

These symptoms are "child-specific" in the sense that they frequently occur with children and manifest in a manner consistent with developmental level, although they also occur normally with adults due to the regressive nature of response to trauma.

Interestingly, Terr (1985) and Nir (1985) differ as to the presence of intrusive imagery. As mentioned in Chapter 2, Terr (1985) has reported that children do not experience intrusive imagery or flashbacks. Nir (1985), reporting upon observations of childhood postcancer patients, indicates that intrusive recollections, repetitious dreams, and nightmares definitely occur. Perhaps Terr does not consider memories or dreams intrusive imagery, or perhaps Nir does not refer to flashbacks, but there seems to be a discrepancy in their reports. One possible explanation for this might be the differences in type of trauma experienced by the subjects studied by these two authors. Terr studied victims of high-intensity, single-incident trauma, while Nir observed cancer victims—children exposed to a long-duration, chronic stressor. It may be that chronic stressors result in intrusive imagery in ways that single-incident stressors do not. This issue warrants empirical resolution, as it is of some importance whether intrusive images are a function of developmental level or type of incident.

It must be stated again that the clinical understanding of posttraumatic reactions with children is barely past its infancy. Much of the major empirical research regarding child-specific posttraumatic symptomatology is fairly recent. Controversy exists regarding various issues. The intrusive imagery issue is one; another is the extent to which natural disasters are traumatic. As the clinical debates mount, it can be expected that research directions and methodology will sharpen and that more light will be shed upon the clinical picture. As research, funding, and treatment innovations intensify, practitioners will have clearer guidelines for making decisions regarding appropriateness of treatment modalities and indications for referral.

ASSESSMENT

The fact that there exist no universally accepted standards for assessment protocol is a reflection of the relative infancy of the discipline. Clinicians frequently have difficulty determining just what behaviors are symptomatic of trauma and indicative of specific treatment needs and what behaviors are part of other clinical pictures. In discussing treatment considerations, then, adequate assessment is paramount. Scurfield (1985) outlines four elements in a comprehensive assessment of posttraumatic stress reaction. Designed for adults, in principle they provide a framework for child assessment as well:

1. **Pretrauma history.** Parental and peer relationships, behavior patterns at home and school, preexisting behavioral disorders, social context, and stressors should be explored, with particular focus upon pre- and posttrauma differences.

2. **Immediate pretrauma psychosocial context.** Age and developmental level, as well as particular familial, social, or developmental issues, bear heavily on the meaning of the event, means of coping, and resources available.

3. **Traumatic events and immediate (emergency) coping attempts.** Objective factors such as the frequency, intensity, and nature of the event can each have different ramifications. The role (active or passive) played by the individual and the meaning of the event to the individual must be assessed, as well as immediate reactions to the event.

4. **Posttraumatic psychosocial context and reactions.** The effects of the environment (as supportive or problematic) must be explored in terms of specific resources and liabilities. Posttraumatic symptomatology must be considered.

Eth and Pynoos (1985a), in a study based upon their clinical experience and literature review, list a range of features manifested by children who have undergone acute posttraumatic stress:

1. exhibition of paralysis and immobilization, ranging from numbness to emotional storms; disorganized feelings, thoughts, and behavior; physical symptoms reflecting autonomic dysfunction

2. frozen, pale, or submissive appearance, or frenzied and panicked behavior

3. aimless, frenzied overactivity, sometimes culminating in tantrums or rage, or a shocklike, stunned reaction, presenting various degrees of unresponsiveness, inactivity, or torpor (p. 39)

4. predifferentiation (disorganization and primitivization of thoughts), deverbalization, and resomatization of affect (p. 46)

To assess such features adequately and make sense of them within the context of the child's experiences, Eth and Pynoos (1985b) utilize the following assessment protocol. Prior to the interview proper, information is gathered from the referral source. Then the child is asked to draw a picture of his or her choice. Sometimes the content of the trauma emerges directly; frequently, coping and defense maneuvers to minimize anxiety are evident. Second, the interviewer explores the child's perception of the traumatic event, with particular focus upon the child's perceptual and affective experiences, issues of accountability and impulse control, and past traumas. Drawings or reenactments of the event, fantasies of revenge, or other issues are sometimes employed. During the third and closing phase, present and future life concerns are reviewed, mourning is supported, and the interview is reviewed. Follow-up contacts are made available.

It should be noted that the referral source is only one means of obtaining background information. Parents, siblings, grandparents, and friends can provide detailed information regarding past history, individual characteristics, interests and issues, and recent changes. They can also provide—directly and indirectly—perspective on the family context. Other background resources include school personnel and records, church contacts, and social agencies.

Fredrick (1985b) points out five nonverbal signs of posttraumatic stress that are of special note in assessment, particularly among younger children:

1. sleep disturbances continuing more than several days, wherein actual dreams of the trauma may or may not appear

2. separation anxiety or clinging behavior, such as a reluctance to return to school

3. phobias about distressing stimuli (e.g., school building, TV scenes, or persons) that remind the victim of the traumatic event

4. conduct disturbances, including problems that occur at home or school that serve as responses to anxiety and frustration

5. doubts about the self, including comments about body confusion, self-worth, and desire for withdrawal (p. 88)

These indicators were specified by Fredrick to refer to young children, but they are not age-exclusive. This author's experience with acting-out adolescents shows that these behaviors serve both as indicators of prior trauma among adolescents and as normal responses to retraumatization.

Fredrick includes both structured (directed) and unstructured drawings in his assessment protocol as well as a traumatic-theme coloring book, which invites written comments about associated feelings and events. The use of such props underscores the need for innovative methods in both assessing and treating posttrauma children.

SHORT-TERM TREATMENT

Therapy is not a mechanical process. While some approaches are more obviously suited to some clients or problems, ultimately there are no formulas. Effective therapy is a function of the interaction between therapist and client. Just as clients have particular needs, therapists have individual strengths and styles. A therapeutic approach that works well between a particular therapist and client may be ineffective between the client and a different therapist. The best choice of therapy takes such differences into consideration. Therapeutic strategies, methods, and procedures cannot be chosen without reference to the individual situation.

Within these parameters, however, some treatment considerations may be generalized. Treatment of traumatized children follows and facilitates the general process of adjustment to trauma spelled out in Chapter 2 in the discussion of work by Horowitz and Solomon (1975, 1978). The initial factors in determining treatment approach are the length of time since the trauma and the severity of symptoms. This section will elaborate on this approach.

Treatment intervention considerations for children must differentiate between immediate, acute-stage interventions and longer-term interventions. In general, treatment during the acute stage with children should follow a crisis intervention model (Aguilera & Messick, 1982). The object of crisis intervention is to restore the victim to previous levels of functioning. Reorganization normally takes place after traumatic stress, and significant maladaptive reorganization can be precluded by effective intervention (Golan, 1981).

Also, emphasis should be placed upon mobilization of the individual's resources. In the case of traumatized children, this may include family intervention and assessment of the family's capability to provide the supportive environment the child needs at the time.

The goal of crisis intervention is the cessation of emergency reactions. Following a shared assessment of the personal situation, initial feelings and reactions are allowed and emotional support is provided, such as the opportunity to talk, cry, express anger, or whatever else. The initial desired outcome is the mobilization of the individual's personal, familial, and social resources for coping with the event. The emphasis is upon short-term goals, practical considerations, and concrete plans of action.

Crisis intervention with children offers an opportunity for children to make public their distress. Unlike crisis intervention with adults, this work with children requires extensive family involvement. A good conceptualization might be to apply the same sort of initial defusing of emotional content and reorganization of functions of daily living used with individuals to the family as a functioning unit. The child's dependence upon the family makes continued family functioning essential to the well-being of the child. The family is negatively affected by the crisis affecting the child, and restoration of family functioning provides the support the child requires.

Jeffrey Mitchell of the University of Maryland Department of Emergency Health Services uses Critical Incident Stress Debriefing (CISD), a group crisis intervention model designed for traumatized emergency teams, that holds promise as a structured intervention approach with other traumatized groups, such as families. CISD follows a structured format and is employed as soon after the crisis event as possible (optimally within 24 to 72 hours). This process is described in Chapter 3.

Not only do treatment situations arise in which individuals, children, and families are involved, but occasionally clinicians are faced with situations involving whole groups of people traumatized together. In long-term posttrauma groups, the basic dynamics of group management and process apply, with the commonality of theme and need for movement through the posttrauma assimilation process. With acute cases and cases following soon after the trauma, however, the clinical picture is different. In these contexts, the immediate need is for crisis intervention done within the group environment, using the same techniques as applied in individual crisis intervention. The focus is upon sharing reactions, understanding the event that has transpired, restoring prior levels of functioning, and mobilizing traumas.

As mentioned earlier, the basic steps of Critical Incident Stress Debriefing and the usefulness of CISD in classroom traumatic incidents are discussed in Chapter 3. The point to be made here is the importance of Mitchell's emphasis on a structural format to facilitate the group's transition through a shared process. Through implementation of group intervention for those traumatized, the cohesiveness of the group is maintained through the high-risk months following the incident.

While many have reported that a crisis "brought the group together," more often than not that is not the case. Groups tend to lose organization and cohesiveness when members have been traumatized together. The group process that Mitchell employs is instrumental on two counts. First, the effects of the trauma are moderated for the individuals involved. Second, the ability of the group to maintain its organizational functioning is increased.

Mitchell's Critical Incident Stress Debriefing model is applicable to the treatment of groups of children who have been through traumatic experiences together. Sibling groups of children who play together or children participating in activity groups are examples of natural groups who may undergo a shared traumatic experience. A more obvious and prevalent group would be the ordinary school classroom. The structure and trauma-appropriate format of Mitchell's model make it ideal for clinicians working with whole classes or other natural groups of children who were together prior to a critical incident and will remain together after it is over.

Crisis-intervention approaches focus upon function restoration and initial work in understanding and expressing feelings about trauma. The aim is primarily crisis management; as such, while it is an integral part of posttraumatic care, crisis intervention is not intended to provide comprehensive treatment. More in-depth, long-term, posttraumatic intervention is required in assisting the process of assimilation and accommodation to trauma.

LONG-TERM TREATMENT

Long-term treatment refers to the purpose and intensity of the therapeutic endeavor as much as to duration. Long-term treatment focuses upon productive resolutions of psychological and behavioral issues and complications following traumatic experiences.

The purposes of treatment include symptom reduction (reduction of phobic reactions, sleep disorders, behavior problems, and so on), but ultimately involve dealing with the experience of the trauma itself. Thus the clinical picture is generally complex and involves sorting through a number of intertwined issues. Some issues and complications, such as addiction, must be dealt with prior to approaching the trauma, while others, such as prolonged grieving, will not be resolved until the trauma is assimilated. In addition, some issues such as family relationships must be handled concurrently.

The central differences between acute and long-term intervention are associated symptomatology and resulting maladaptive coping patterns. Long-term posttraumatic interventions are discussed by Scurfield (1985), who outlines the following five treatment principles of PTSD. These principles are adaptable to child therapy, particularly in dealing with the family of a traumatized child.

1. Therapeutic trust relationship. Children and their families need to feel a trusting relationship with the therapist. Countertransference and authority issues can be particularly difficult with older children and adolescents. The therapist must be prepared to handle difficult information and emotions, and clinical skills in dealing with anger and grief are essential. The experience of trauma leaves difficult, painful memories and feelings of fear and low self-esteem. Frequently, traumatized persons do not feel good about how they handled themselves during the incident and afterward. Sharing memories and feelings about the event entails great risk and intimacy. Recounting the personal dimensions of the event opens the person to possible disapproval, rejection, or humiliation. Trust in the integrity, acceptance, and skill of the therapist is essential.

2. Education regarding the stress-recovery process. Because post-trauma situations requiring referral are often chaotic and seemingly out of control, children and their families need to gain a conceptual foothold. This includes learning facts and perspectives about what to expect during recovery. Especially crucial with children is that any concepts presented for educational purposes be understandable. The child's developmental level, conceptual processing style, and language skills must be considered when educational presentations are attempted. Readiness is a key issue, and timing is essential. Clinicians find themselves playing the role of teacher at various times during treatment. The use of stories, teaching tales, metaphors, suggestions, or handouts can augment direct answers to questions in presenting complex and detailed concepts.

3. Stress management/reduction. PTSD symptomatology can be mixed and functional difficulties varied. A hierarchy of treatment steps should be established, and the child assured that all symptoms will be dealt with in due course. The therapist should focus upon coping strategies that the child has used in the past and use those outcomes to assist the child to avoid maladaptive coping strategies. Specific problematic symptoms (such as intrusive imagery or loss of control) require specific techniques to alleviate the secondary anxiety and debilitation they can create. Various behavioral interventions can prove useful. Particularly useful in stress reduction is the approach utilized by Donald Meichenbaum (1983), called stress inoculation training (SIT), which provides a structural approach whereby the client is engaged as a participant in his or her own stress management. This, or a number of other stress management models, can be useful in teaching the client to monitor and control trauma-related stress problems.

4. Regression to or reexperience of the trauma. Basic in working through the traumatic experience is reexperiencing the event and uncovering associated submerged feelings. This process frequently involves moving back and forth between grief/sadness and anger/fear. The images and associations indelibly etched in the minds of those who have been traumatized are powerful. During crisis, people are highly suggestible, and the visual, auditory, tactile, and kinesthetic sensations received during the incident become associated with the emotional experience. As time passes, some specific memories are naturally defused of emotional content, while others intensify. To the extent the feelings and images become submerged, working through them becomes more difficult and more important. Until the event is "reexperienced," that is, until memories are brought to the surface and the emotional associations understood and put in perspective, progress toward assimilation and accommodation is stalled. Reexperiencing the event is central to the process of posttraumatic therapy. With children this process is moderated by developmental and conceptual variables; younger children tend to be less affected by "submerged feelings" and have difficulty conceptualizing subtle emotional differences, tending instead to evidence distress through somatic and behavioral means. Art and play therapy approaches tend to be useful with younger children, while role-play and Gestalt techniques can be added to the armamentarium of the older child's therapy.

5. Integration of the trauma experience. The event must be understood, its meanings explored, implications and changes caused by the event accepted, and acceptance of self accomplished (Scurfield, 1985, p. 241). Trauma precipitates a revaluation of the world. Given the event and subsequent life-situational changes, basic assumptions are sometimes felt to be no longer valid. These include assumptions about the extent to which the world is safe, what can be expected, whether or not to attach, who—if anyone—can be trusted, and whether or not life is worth living. Fundamental decisions are necessary regarding these and many other issues. Resolution of these issues is an involved process, but it is essential for the further optimal growth of the individual. The successful completion of future developmental tasks depends upon having a firm foundation. Fear or ambivalence in matters of attachment or value can undermine further attachment, commitment, or ability to risk.

The overall goal of therapy is to integrate traumatic experience so that the individual is free to develop in an optimal manner. This involves a basic restructuring of conceptual and perceptual functions to accommodate the event itself and the subsequent changes caused by the event. This integration and reorganization cannot take place until the emotional overload and oversensitivity surrounding memories of the event are released. Counterproductive coping strategies must be replaced by more effective stress management techniques; the individual must also understand the posttraumatic reaction in order to gain perspective and self-acceptance. Each of these tasks depends upon the establishment of a relationship of trust between therapist and client. When children are the clients this is of particular importance because of their limited conceptual development, lack of life experience, and fragile concept of self.

Eth and Pynoos (1985c) discuss four common psychological methods children use to limit traumatic anxiety following a critical incident. These affect not only future functioning, but also the content of experiences worked through in treatment:

1. denial-in-fantasy (reversing the outcome to mitigate pain)

2. inhibition of spontaneous thought (to avoid reminders)

3. fixation to the trauma (unemotional, often incomplete, journalistic reiteration of the event in order to make it more tolerable)

4. fantasies of future harm (to avoid pain, memories are supplanted by new fears) (p. 25)

In addition, Lifton (1979) reports that where actions have been perceived as ineffectual, children engage in "inner plans of action" in order to undo harm or gain revenge. Again, it should be noted that these methods are not unique to children; due to the regressive nature of the posttraumatic reaction they may be evident in adults as well.

Finally, Eth and Pynoos (1985d), in their study of child witnesses to their parents' homicide, discuss the interaction of trauma and grief in childhood. When grief has not been processed because of a defensive coping maneuver that does not allow the withdrawal of attachment from the lost object, maladaptive behavior often occurs. The strategies designed to deal with the intensity of grief become symptomatic themselves. In order to overcome symptoms, the individual must accept the loss. This entails the following process:

> The child must first accept the loss through reality testing and then tolerate the experience of the pain of grief. The child may feel sad, angry, guilty, lonely, tired, confused, preoccupied, and perhaps even ill. The deceased will be remembered as the child

struggles to adjust to the new environment. There follows the slow withdrawal of attachment to the deceased, increasing availability of psychic energy for forging new or stronger relations. (Eth & Pynoos, 1985d, p. 172)

When visual memories of the deceased cannot be reviewed and resorted, and when feelings toward the deceased cannot be explored, the grief process is blocked.

Trauma involves several elements that preclude grief processing. Eth and Pynoos (1985d) list five such elements:

1. Reminiscing may be inhibited because images of the trauma associated with memories of the person may interfere. The funeral, photographs, or compensatory play often assist in repairing the image of the deceased.

2. Feelings of guilt over conflicts in loyalty, accountability, and survival may inhibit grief processing. Inner plans of action to offset feelings of helplessness may result in self-blame.

3. Trauma can cause ego constriction when the child shuns intense emotion, narrows life choices, and develops cognitive difficulties. A cognitive style of forgetting may evolve.

4. Social stigma from the event may cause the family to respond by prohibiting reference to the person lost, which forces silence and blocks processing.

5. The traumatic memories can intensify fantasies of reunion and confound them with images of violence. This can make normal loss and related depression overwhelming and can result in helplessness (p. 175).

In the case of grief compounded by trauma, the traumatic anxiety and other symptoms must be dealt with first in order to allow grief processing to commence.

Because of the complexity of the therapeutic task and developmental considerations that require delicate therapeutic intervention, several approaches to posttraumatic therapy with children have evolved. The next section explores some of these approaches. This discussion is not intended to be definitive or comprehensive; it does not represent a "how-to" guide to therapy with children. Rather, it provides a general outline of the main features of each of several major treatment strategies.

Therapeutic Methods

What happens when a child is referred to a therapist? Different clinicians work with posttrauma children in different ways, mainly because clinicians differ widely in background skills and in preferences. Differences are also due to the unique characteristics of each client and each situation. But a third factor exists; simply put, a wide variety of therapeutic options will work. A thorough review of the variety of approaches and the efficiency and limitations of each would be beyond the scope of this volume, but some discussion about the variations in choices of therapies is helpful. Beyond indicating diversity, this discussion can indicate the manner in which each variation focuses upon some particular aspect of the assimilation/accommodation process. Thus several major clinical approaches to the treatment of posttraumatic symptoms in children will be briefly outlined, and some of the salient features of each will be highlighted.

BIBLIOTHERAPY AND WRITING THERAPY

The use of bibliographic material to address children's personal issues is not new (Wilson, 1951). Stories, poetry, and other writing are rich in human themes and drama, and identification with characters and situations is what writers aim for to "hook" their readers. It has often been said that literature, more than religion, philosophy, or even psychology, deals with the realities of human existence.

Bibliotherapy usually involves the discussion of a piece of literature, using one-on-one discussion or peer group interaction, individual writing, art, or other techniques for involving the child with the meaning of the work and the application of its themes, dilemmas, and resolutions to the child's own life. Books for children focusing upon life issues are available at all developmental levels. Materials should be selected that focus upon subject matter relevant to the issue faced by the child, be it loss, change, trauma, or difficult choices. The format of the work must be appropriate as well, taking into account the child's reading and maturity level and interests. Consideration should be given to illustrations and overall themes of the readings. Finally, what is read is less important than the manner in which it is processed between child and adult, and between the child and other children.

Children, particularly older ones, are often reached through individual writing exercises designed to allow personal expression in a private setting. While the resulting writing can be processed with a group, it can also be used solely between the helping adult and the child. Guided journals, and recovery and posttrauma workbook series, are now becoming available (e.g., Deaton & Johnson, 1994). Some of these materials are to be used by the child with no support, while some are to be used only in conjunction with a therapist or other trained helping professional.

The case for utilizing writing-only intervention was explored by Pennebaker (1985; Pennebaker & Beal, 1986) in comparisons of writing and talking psychotherapy. Apart from a temporary residual negative mood, Pennebaker reported long-term positive effects upon health following simply writing about traumatic experiences. These findings were supported in a follow-up study (Pennebaker et al., 1988), which also showed increase in immune function.

Skeptical of such reports, Murray et al. (1989) and Donnelly and Murray (1991) directly compared psychotherapy and written expression in terms of outcome, which—apart from the transient negative mood following writing—resulted in comparable effects. Speculating about the cause of negative feelings, Murray and Segal (1994) tested for the effects of vocalizing distress alone with a tape recorder in order to control for the social effect of listener response. They utilized both writing and speaking into a tape recorder, and found that both reduced the painfulness of recalling traumatic effects over a four-day period, resulting in a moderate increase in positive thinking and feeling about the topic and self. The negative mood initially increased for the writing intervention, but then collapsed after the four-day treatment. Murray and Segal concluded that the social context of psychotherapy probably accounts for the more positive mood among those treated by therapy. On the basis of other measures, the authors suggest that some individual differences, such as difficulty expressing feelings, may dispose some individuals to either spoken or written expression.

Exploring just what it is that makes writing therapeutic, Harber and Pennebaker (1992) concluded that the referential links of sensory concreteness, specificity, clarity, and imagery not only allow writers to communicate their private experiences effectively to others, but also allow them to bring their undisclosed material to consciousness. To the extent that readers find writing compelling and lucid, the writers themselves are likely to discover the mental reorganization that constitutes helpful insight. Writing, as reconstruction, assists the task of assimilating traumatic experience.

These studies, in which all of the subjects were college students, show therapeutic value in writing about traumatic experiences. However, generalization to children at lower developmental levels was not addressed, nor were the necessary adaptations of writing assignments. Obviously, writing can only be used by children old enough to be writing-fluent, which can be expected somewhere between the ages of 8 and 10. Because children are sometimes reluctant to share their feelings with others in discussion, the opportunity to write about problems in a private and quiet setting provides a safe environment for self-expression and discovery. Realizing the effects of writing upon mood, and the beneficial effects of interpersonal communication during the process of writing about difficult subjects, it seems clear that children would benefit from a close, supportive relationship in which their writing was given guidance and sympathetic review.

Using either bibliographic or writing exercises requires an appropriate choice of activity. Material must be selected to relate to the troubling issues, keeping in mind the child's age, reading, interest, and maturity levels, and the format of the reading material. Suggestions and prompts must provide sufficient structure to give direction, but leave the way open for personal response. The resulting discussion and written materials can be used as prompts for further work, but must be kept as confidential as possible. The child's responses must always be assessed for signs of distress and emerging needs.

NARRATIVE THERAPY

The effects of trauma are less dependent upon the nature of the incident than upon the perception of it on the part of the traumatized individual. The meaning of the event, and the manner in which it is experienced, are in part personal interpretations. Similarly, the sense made of the long-lasting effects of the event is also at least in part a product of interpretation.

As Van der Kolk (1996) has pointed out, the creation of narrative memory—a linguistic, and hence interpersonal, construction—involves the translation from nonverbal, purely personal, sensory based experience into linguistically communicable, hence interpersonally constructed, form.

Narrative therapy (White & Epston, 1991; Monk et al., 1996) employs this intrinsically language-based nature of constructed memory and meaning to assist clients in "reauthoring" their lives. Following the postmodern concept of the "deconstruction" of limiting assumptions and world views that bind the person to the problem, narrative therapists help clients recognize options and strengths they have "lost." More useful and productive descriptions of problems and personal resources are jointly explored to facilitate empowerment and choice.

The governing metaphor of narrative therapy is the story. The story of one's past and present is seen as a working definition of one's world view, including the delineation of possibilities and resources available. The story serves as a personal mythos, guiding both the meaning of past experience and the interpretation of new experience. One's accepted story embodies goals and values, struggles and limitations. The adoption of new, alternative stories amounts to a reevaluation of the world and oneself.

White and Epston make extensive use of written communications to clients between sessions to reinforce engagement in new ways of interpreting experience, and to witness and document progress toward therapeutic ends. Letters follow the session, may involve written response, and are engineered to actively continue the work beyond the clinic.

The emerging narrative therapy literature provides great insight to child therapists using writing and storytelling approaches with children. However, while narrative therapy utilizes writing, it is by no means limited to those contexts. Monk et al. (1996), who are all faculty or graduate students at the University of Waikato, Hamilton, New Zealand, describe the application of narrative concepts to work beyond the psychotherapeutic clinic, including school counseling, mediation, and community activism with indigenous and nondominant groups.

PLAY THERAPY

Play therapy was originally developed to provide release of difficult emotions such as fear, pain, and aggression through the child's participation in play in the presence of a therapist. Its goal was insight and interpretation of experience. Originally quite structured, play therapy today is relatively unstructured and allows the child to set the limits of the play situation. Currently, play therapists vary in the extent to which the child defines the process, the types of toys used, the extent of adult involvement, and the extent to which play is utilized in the overall therapeutic approach. Further, many play therapists use psychoanalytic principles of defense mechanisms, the unconscious, resistance, transference, and countertransference to explain play.

Toys that can encourage communication may be used in several ways and are capable of eliciting aggressive responses. As the child plays with the toys in his or her own way, the therapist can respond to the feelings expressed, build an interactive relationship with the child, and gradually help the child understand and restructure behaviors around a particular problem.

Play can be structured by the therapist into a set of sequences encouraging the child to face and master areas of conflict in real life. The therapist must establish considerable rapport with the child prior to initiating such directive leadership, and must work at maintaining rapport by encouraging verbal elaboration and using the child's pacing as cues.

Gradually the trends and problems reflected in the play become the explicit focus of discussion, expression, and problem solving. Play therapy can be utilized for general, developmental issue-oriented counseling, or it can focus upon trauma- and posttrauma-specific issues. Myrich and Holdin (1971) describe this play process in therapy with three stages:

Stage 1. The therapist creates an open atmosphere without attempting to force specific themes, types of play, or types of toys. The goal is to build rapport between child and therapist and to give the child permission in freely exploring forms of play. The secondary goal during this stage is the assessment of the child's problems, characteristics, and strengths. The therapist develops hypotheses regarding the specific problem formation.

Stage 2. This stage begins when a relationship of rapport, caring, and trust exists between therapist and child. At this point, the therapist introduces toys and activities that he or she believes (according to the hypothesis formulated) will elicit feelings, concepts, and communication related to the apparent problem area. The therapist notes reactions to these toys, and either considers the hypothesis supported or generates alternative hypotheses. Therapist and child discuss feelings, perceptions, and behaviors related to these toys and to the problem.

Stage 3. This stage is begun once the problem area is crystallized in the therapist's mind. It consists of a series of graduated play experiences designed to focus the child's activity directly upon the issues at hand. This stage employs a desensitization process and brings the child's expressions of feelings and development of conceptual perspective to bear on the problem. Through the facilitation of expression, clarification of behaviors and situations, and assistance in problem solving, the child's ability to deal with the traumatic experience and changed life situation is enhanced.

Play therapy utilizes the natural medium of play to build a helping relationship between child and therapist and to explore the cognitive and affective dimensions of the child's experience.

SAND PLAY

Sandtray work and sandplay have emerged as important applications of play therapy technique (Mitchell & Friedman, 1994). Originating with Margaret Lowenfield's *World Technique* (1979), sandtray work involves trays filled with sand and dozens of miniature toys, including figures, animals, fences, and blocks. In Lowenfield's approach, clients—many of them children—were invited to create "worlds" or scenes in any manner they wished. The therapist played an observational, or at most collaborative, role, while the client created a scene of his or her own construction. The sandtray toys created a symbolic world that could bridge the child's inner experience with outer reality. The therapist refrained from verbal interpretation until the work with sandtrays was completed.

Dora Maria Kalff, a Jungian by orientation, saw sandtray work as a way in which the child could connect the ego—essentially a social construct—with the deeper Self (Kalff, 1991). During the normal process of a child's development, the Self increasingly manifests in the life of the child, unless blocked by unfortunate experience. If the Self becomes blocked, the ego develops in an unhealthy, symptomatic manner. Kalff saw sandplay provide a safe and nurturing milieu in which a child could allow expression of the unconscious Self, and facilitate integration of that Self and the developing ego through a series of "trays" in which psychodynamic elements symbolized by the toys were arranged and rearranged into stories. This resulted in a balanced, more actualized state wherein the ego was reunited with and infused by the Self, releasing healing energy and allowing normal development to proceed.

In surveying current literature for criteria for sandtray researchers and clinicians to use to make sense of and guide a client's work, Mitchell and Friedman (1994) find five main considerations dominating the field:

1. The child's method of making the tray (scenes), including the child's motivation, how sand and water are used, the miniatures chosen and their placement, the changes within the child as he or she works, and any verbal or nonverbal expression of feeling during the experience

2. The use of objects and elements in the tray, including the meaning of the objects chosen, their placement and positioning, emergent shapes and themes, use of the elements (earth, air, fire, water), overall organization (use of space, barriers, balance, arrangement), and developmental level represented

3. The evolutional qualities of a series of trays, including changes of organization, themes, and content

4. The sandtray story itself, including content, process, emotions, themes, and resolution

5. The affective response of the therapist

Mitchell and Friedman point out that the history of sandplay reflects a traditional conflict between those focused upon its usefulness as a diagnostic instrument and those whose primary interest is on sandplay as a clinical technique. Sandtray therapists' main professional association, the International Society for Sandplay Therapy, was founded in 1985 by Kalff and retains her Jungian orientation and clinical focus.

One of sandplay therapy's major strengths is its primarily nonverbal procedures. As such, it can be used with young children and in multicultural and multilingual groups without being much hampered by linguistic limitations. Sandplay also is not limited to children's inability to draw representationally, and so can be used earlier in development. In addition, the manner in which sandplay therapy works, progressing through a series of client-initiated trays with little interpretation, makes it useful as an adjunct to other approaches. One such approach is the new Eye Movement Desensitization and Reprocessing. The interface between sandplay and EMDR will be discussed later.

ART THERAPY

The oldest of the new "expressive therapies," including writing, dance, music, and movement, is art therapy. Originally stemming from the psychoanalytic tradition, art therapy as an independent discipline utilizes the process of making artworks and the psychological disclosure provided by the content of those works to open windows to the client's inner world. From its inception to the present, the relative emphasis upon the art versus the therapy have shaped art therapy's different forms and purposes.

Art therapists vary in both techniques and purposes of art therapy activity. While all use art materials in service of personal expression, some focus upon assessment and interpretation, others upon creativity and interaction. Art therapists, while originally springing from the psychoanalytic tradition, now represent family systems, object relations, existential, Jungian, and a range of other theoretical positions. Art therapists function as adjuncts to multidisciplinary treatment teams, or as primary therapists. Art therapy may be limited to a discrete role within a different approach, or may be used as the total treatment modality.

Art therapies vary as widely as play therapies and can be said to have in common only the fact that visual and graphic materials are used to accomplish therapeutic ends. Art therapists have advocated the use of art as a total therapeutic treatment, as an adjunct treatment with limited objectives, or as an activity aimed only at "enrichment." Art therapy is used individually with patients, with groups of patients, and with families. Because of the intrinsic attraction artistic expression holds for children, it is well suited for use with children who have been traumatized.

Through artistic expression, therapists can establish accelerated rapport with children, gain access to complex conscious and unconscious material with minimum defensiveness, and provide opportunities for the expression of "unacceptable" feelings or truths. In addition, the content and process of artistic endeavor are useful diagnostically and provide corroborative evidence to substantiate information gained directly or indirectly elsewhere. Therapists need to have an understanding of children's developmental stages in drawing as well as some of the background of the child in order to make sense of the child's drawing diagnostically.

Kramer (1971) categorized five basic ways in which art materials can be used in therapy:

1. precursory activities: scribbling, smearing, exploring physical properties of the material in ways that do not lead to the creation of symbolic configurations but are experienced as positive and egosyntonic

2. chaotic discharge: spilling, splashing, pounding, and other destructive behaviors leading to loss of control

3. art in the service of defense: copying, tracing, banal conventional production, and stereotyped repetition

4. pictographs: pictorial communications that replace or
    supplement words (such communications occur as the
    therapeutic relationship grows)

5. formed expression: art in the full sense of the word—the
    production of symbolic configurations that successfully serve
    both self-expression and communication

The selection of materials, as well as activities, must take several
factors into account. The age, developmental level, and dexterity of
the child must be considered. Further, individuals vary as to the
emotional reactions different media evoke.

Art therapists differ as to the basis for and importance of interpretation of form and content, and the art therapy literature provides a variety of interpretive schemes. As with any procedure that
reveals partial information about the client, however, all such information must be treated as hypothetical until adequate corroborative
evidence is available to justify working assumptions or conclusions.

The art therapist uses artistic media and activities to establish
rapport, encourage communication, elicit themes, facilitate understanding, and promote the cognitive and emotional processing of
children who have been disturbed by traumatic events. As in play
therapy, the projection of and working with traumatic themes in the
nondirective, supportive, and intrinsically attractive context offered
by art therapy is useful in the treatment of traumatized children.

A major contemporary force in art therapy is Helen Lindengarten,
newly retired head of Loyola Marymount College's Art Therapy
Department. Helen was one of the first new wave of art therapists
who functioned as a primary practitioner, instead of simply acting as
an adjunct to a psychiatrist. As director of art therapy at Cedars-
Sinai Hospital in Los Angeles, she provided direct services to clients
and started the master's program in Clinical Art Therapy at
Immaculate Heart College, which later moved to Loyola.

Integrating psychodynamic theories with a family systems
approach, she uses art as a destabilizing strategy to assist individuals
and families to reorganize and balance in more functional ways. The
work of art becomes a metaphor for the inner and interpersonal
workings of the client. Accordingly, the therapist uses the client's
process of creating the work as a fulcrum for discussion, feedback,

and exploration. The work—as product of the clinical activity—provides a record of the process, and the therapist uses the activity to assist the client in understanding and shaping experiences of both the inner and outer world.

Nontraditional Art Therapy

Not all therapeutic programs incorporating art approaches are traditional. An exciting example is the Harlem Horizon Art Studio located on the seventeenth floor of Harlem Hospital, New York City. Funded as a part of the hospital's department of pediatric surgery's Injury Prevention Program, the studio provides a very different approach to a very different clientele. Initiating the Injury Prevention Program (which includes dance, in-school street first aid, schoolyard and playground safety and cleanup, sports, gun safety, and political action coalition programs), Chief of Pediatric Surgery Barbara Barlow cited the simple logic that it is easier and less expensive to prevent injuries than to repair them.

In seeking to stem the ever-growing injuries to Harlem children, Barlow hired artist Bill Richards to set up a studio in the hospital, and she invited neighborhood children to study under Bill's tutelage. The program serves in-patients and out-patients as well as interested community children. Within the first two years, it had served over 400 Harlem children, and from within this nontraditional setting has emerged a unique style of work that has drawn critical acclaim, as well as sales, from downtown galleries and shows in other cities—totaling some eleven major exhibits between 1989 and 1991. Proceeds are split between the emerging artists and purchase of art materials for the program.

Through this program, children and young adults have discovered personal talents and positive projects. They push themselves further than they ever expected, and they learn to see the world with a fresher and more open vision than one might expect from their surroundings.

Art Therapy in Disaster Intervention

David Wee, mental health program supervisor and disaster coordinator for the city of Berkeley, California (see page 113), organized an extensive intervention with children who were displaced by the

East Bay firestorm of 1991. Combining the principles of crisis intervention with art therapeutic techniques, Wee assisted child victims to deal with their feelings and emerging problems of adjusting to both troubling images of the disaster and difficulties of living in the postfire environment.

Wee used a method of intervention called Draw and Talk, which employs art materials. The approach begins with preliminary work with school administrators and teachers, explaining the classroom procedure and the role of the teacher. The teacher is then interviewed concerning significant events and traumas among the children so that the intervener will be sensitized to special issues that may arise in the course of the intervention. Parents are notified prior to the intervention, and they are given the opportunity to ask questions and to stipulate that their child not attend if they prefer.

During the classroom Draw and Talk session, children are invited to draw a picture about their experiences during the incident, or anything else they choose. The interveners spend time going from table to table discussing the emerging drawings with the children. Children are given time to complete their drawings. Next, the children gather in a circle with the facilitator. Those who want to share their drawings are invited to describe their experiences as depicted in their pictures. Thoughts, feelings, and reactions are reflected and acknowledged. Comments from the other children are welcomed. The facilitator aims at clarifying the child's thoughts and feelings, and encourages supportive interactions from other students. In addition, the facilitator validates the normalcy of reactions and can provide needed information to students. At the end of the intervention, the children are invited to take their art or to leave it for eventual use in a commemorative art show. The interveners and school personnel have a postintervention meeting to discuss follow-up and any referrals for further services needed by particular students.

BEHAVIORAL THERAPIES

A number of techniques are included in the broad category of behavioral therapies. Generally, while art and play therapies use a projective and interactive approach in helping the child deal with traumatic memories and changed circumstances, behavioral therapies have traditionally focused upon treatment of specific symptomatology. Thus behavioral techniques might be used to treat posttraumatic behavioral disturbances, such as bed-wetting, phobic reactions, and school avoidance.

Behavioral therapies have been used extensively in the treatment of hyperactivity, phobias, low self-esteem, shyness, test and school anxiety, uncontrolled anger, disruptive and combative behavior, and sleep disturbances. A wide range of treatment options exists, including behavior modification, covert conditioning, relaxation and guided fantasy, hypnosis, shaping, modeling, behavioral contracts, and assertiveness training. Because the focus of behavioral therapy has traditionally been one or another of a variety of techniques to treat a particular symptom, a global behavioral approach to postcrisis treatment is not clearly defined.

Typically, behavioral strategies are employed by therapists in treating specific problematic symptoms within a more comprehensive approach for dealing with the overall effects of the trauma. Thus a therapist may use a play therapy approach in dealing with memories of the trauma, grief issues, and posttraumatic adjustment problems, but use relaxation, guided imagery, and systematic desensitization to treat specific trauma-related phobic reactions. The major value of this balance is that it combines and directs the effective techniques of behavioral therapy in an orchestrated approach that takes causal and underlying conditions into account.

A behavioral approach for working with younger and latency-age children is Cognitive/Behavioral Play Therapy. CBPT (Knell, 1995) combines play therapy with a cognitive behavioral approach. While play provides the context and medium for child-therapist interaction, behavioral and cognitive strategies infuse the process of guided play. As opposed to more traditional nondirective play, CBPT utilizes therapist-directed goals and teaching. While therapist and child together select materials and activities, the therapist guides the child by reinforcement and interpretation. Knell describes CBPT as being structured, directive, and goal-oriented, using empirically demonstrated techniques such as modeling and shaping to teach adaptive strategies such as self-monitoring, thought structuring, coping-skill development, and more symptom-specific change. CBPT is typically used with young children to those in midchildhood.

THE THERAPEUTIC USE OF STORYTELLING

Historically, storytelling preceded written literature and provided for the intergenerational transmission of culture through the ages. Stories speak to us in deep and lasting ways. Numerous therapeutic uses of storytelling have developed, ranging from the use of universal themes from folk tales and fairy tales to the intentional use of multidimensional healing metaphors. Kopp (1971) defines three modes of "knowing," including metaphor in addition to empirical and rational knowledge. He characterizes metaphoric knowledge as intuitive, symbolic, and multilevel. A single metaphor may carry several separate meanings, each adding dimensions to the others. Milton Erickson (Erickson & Rossi, 1976) used metaphoric communication to engage subsurface strengths and knowledge as well as the symptom itself— which he considered to be an indirect form of communication—to assist the client in solving his or her problem. Therapeutic metaphors then can be imbedded in teaching tales that convey to children the means to transform their symptoms into growth (Mills & Crowley, 1986).

Storytelling therapy has recently become more interactive. Richard Gardner (1976) uses a storytelling method called Mutual Storytelling Technique, which he finds circumvents resistance as well as the conceptual limitations of children. By the therapist directly engaging in storytelling exchange with the child, he or she can enter into real dialogue in the child's own language about the child's own issues. At this level, the therapist can introduce healthier perspectives, adaptations, and resolutions to dilemmas and conflicts revealed in the stories. With some structured prompts to elicit the story, Gardner looks for the symbolization, mood, and themes expressed. He is also concerned with the emotionality inherent in the story, or presented upon delivery, and alert for atypical, non-age-stereotypic elements that can give clues to the child's circumstances and perceptions. By incorporating these various elements into an initially parallel story to share back to the child, the therapist can then engineer alternative, creative, and instructive outcomes that empower the child.

A recent use of interactive storytelling is that developed by Joan Lovett, using parent-authored stories that frame events leading up to a traumatic event, the event itself, the current situation, and the anticipated future in terms of the child's well-being and recovery. Lovett's combining storytelling with EMDR is discussed further in Chapter 5.

FAMILY THERAPY

Play therapy and art therapy approaches to working with children were developed primarily for individual therapy, as were many behavioral techniques. These approaches have also been used within a problem-centered group format. In general, the same goals and techniques are utilized, albeit within the constraints of group interaction and relationships. Family therapy, however, presents a departure in focus.

Family therapists emphasize different aspects of family experience. Some use a psychoanalytic orientation, interpreting family behavior from an individual psychodynamic and object relations framework. Communications therapists analyze and intervene in the ways family members communicate with one another. Structuralists look at the power, distance, boundary, and coalition relations existing in the family and attempt to change family functioning in those areas. Whatever their differences, however, family therapists deal with the posttrauma child within the context of the family.

Family therapy does more than deal with family members individually or all together. Rather, the inspiration of family therapy lies in its ability to allow the therapist to perceive, interpret, conceptualize, and intervene with the individual, taking the family experience as fundamental to the life of the individual. Thus, while working with the family as a group is not only possible but preferable, working with the child individually takes family functioning into account as the child's primary shaping force.

The family of a traumatized child is in crisis. Whether the crisis occurred outside of the family or within it, the family itself is affected, and family experience and interactions will change as a result. A detailed analysis of how families react to crises and ways that therapists can best interact with those families is presented in Chapter 6.

Family therapists deal with patterns of behavior within the family and between the family and the larger community. The therapist first learns to appreciate the realities and dynamics of family interaction, becoming a part of the life of the family. After conceptualizing how the family interacts in self-destructive ways, the therapist is able to initiate dysfunctional interactions, draw attention to them, and then present alternatives. Challenging such patterns, providing feedback about them, and initiating new forms of behavior allow the family to develop and practice options. Unbalancing rigid and limiting patterns of behavior, the therapist alternates between direct and indirect interventions. The therapist directly alters family interactions and regulates the emotional reactions of individuals as a result of those interactions. The therapist intervenes indirectly by providing feedback, interpretation, and conceptualization.

The goals of family intervention with the families of children in crisis are to restore family functioning to a level at which the child's needs for stability and security are being met and to assist the family in finding constructive ways to meet the challenge of conditions changed by the crisis event.

Psychiatric Treatment

Psychiatrists are medical doctors specially trained in the treatment of mental illness. Their training places them in a position to provide several services other therapists cannot. Psychiatrists frequently practice in hospital settings and often provide consultation to other therapists.

First, as medical doctors, psychiatrists can prescribe and supervise the use of medication. One argument for treatment that includes psychotropic drugs for symptom management is that trauma results in neurotransmitter changes in the brain, and medication can assist in rebalancing the neurochemical environment and relieve some of the overwhelming distress of the symptoms. This allows other therapeutic strategies to work. Psychiatric uses of medication include managing symptoms that are blocking therapeutic progress. For example, benzodiazepines have been prescribed for fear and insomnia, beta adrenergic blockers for physical symptoms of anxiety, tricyclic and monamine oxidase inhibitor (MAOI) antidepressants for major symptoms of PTSD. These medications have specific applicability and sometimes appreciable side effects (Eth,

Randolf, & Brown, 1988). The use of medication in psychiatric treatment requires careful diagnosis, prescription, and monitoring.

Recent studies (Davidson & Van der Kolk, 1996) indicate several promising areas of pharmacological treatment. They point to dysregulation of the catecholaminergic system being amenable to treatment with MAOIs and tricyclic antidepressants, as well as clonadine, benzodiazapines, and beta andregenic blockers. Davidson and Van der Kolk discuss more recent data pointing to fluoxetine and other selective seratonin uptake inhibitors (e.g., Prozac) as being useful in managing PTSD symptoms such as numbing and arousal, as well as depression. Posttrauma "kindling" effects, in which lowered activation thresholds produce over-arousal responses to the slightest stimuli, seem to be responsive to carbamazepine. Finally, they indicate that anxiolytic drugs such as clonazepam and buspirone can be helpful with increased startle responsiveness. The application of these findings to drug prescription with posttraumatic children, however, remains a medical consideration, especially with the newer drugs, given the need for and difficulty in testing for use with pediatric patients. In any case, the purpose of psychotropic medication remains focused upon symptom relief, so that clients are able to participate more effectively in programs of therapy.

Second, psychiatrists are highly trained in differential diagnosis and can be especially helpful in complex cases, distinguishing between symptoms specific to the trauma and those connected with other psychiatric conditions. These distinctions, often subtle, can provide critical directions for treatment. For instance, preexisting psychopathological conditions can predispose people to posttrauma symptoms, and can be exacerbated by psychosocial stressors (Eth et al., 1988). In addition, anxiety disorders, depressive disorders, or organic conditions can develop following and in addition to a trauma, further complicating the clinical picture (American Psychiatric Association, 1994).

Finally, psychiatrists can provide case management, orchestrating the efforts of several treatment disciplines for maximum effectiveness. This is particularly important in hospital settings, where the patient may be seeing psychologists for testing, art therapists, vocational rehabilitation counselors, physical therapists, and social workers in addition to being under medical supervision. This may occur outside the hospital as well. For example, a client may self-refer to a family therapist for a family problem. Observing some serious personal symptoms, the family therapist might begin family treatment and then make an additional referral to a psychiatrist for closer diagnosis, consideration of medication, and treatment consultation.

Adolescent Treatment Considerations

It is little more than an axiom in the therapy business that "what you see is rarely what you get." Presenting symptoms are not the whole problem, and even with suicidal behavior or drug addiction, treating the symptom is only the beginning. Most behavioral symptoms that generate referrals to mental health professionals are secondary to other deep-seated problems. This is particularly true with adolescents. Very few adolescents refer themselves to therapists; most are referred by school authorities, parents, or law enforcement agencies. Most are referred for school problems, substance abuse, depression, self-destructive behavior, or running away. And, as the research discussed in Chapter 1 and Appendix II clearly indicates, a large majority of these young people have histories of psychologically traumatic events. Effective treatment of their presenting symptoms requires addressing, and at least partially resolving, posttraumatic issues in most adolescents referred to therapists for nontrauma reasons.

As mentioned before, reactions to critical incidents often involve regressive features. For that reason, dealing with posttraumatic adolescents requires familiarity with all the child treatment considerations outlined above. In addition, treatment plans must consider the developmental implications of trauma discussed earlier. The remainder of this chapter discusses issues unique to adolescents, although much is applicable to adults as well.

The research reported in Appendix II shows that posttraumatic symptoms are manifested in adolescence primarily through maladaptive behaviors, such as substance abuse, running away from home, and serious school attendance problems. These behaviors are self-rewarding—at least in the short run—in terms of relief of anxiety, depression, and interpersonal conflict. For this reason they tend to become entrenched as psychologically addictive habits, as part of the social self, as a component of a complex of gradually restricted life options, and often as chemical dependencies. Treatment for these maladaptive behaviors must begin by controlling the immediate situation, whatever the etiological factors.

The results of this study show, however, that in establishing the likelihood of traumatic precursors to maladaptive adolescent behaviors, a comprehensive treatment plan must address possible underlying issues related to prior trauma. To the extent the maladaptive behavior is founded upon developmental issues raised by a traumatic experience in childhood, or upon associated factors, successful treatment of the problem behavior depends in part upon successful resolution and integration of the trauma.

Thus treatment of trauma-related maladaptive adolescent behavior must include trauma-specific intervention. Apart from other treatment aspects such as family or network intervention, the appropriate use of hospitalization, and psychopharmacological intervention, and apart from the specific treatment modality chosen, a comprehensive treatment program should include the following three elements: reliving, releasing, and reorganizing.

Reliving

The client must relive the traumatic experience (in the sense of revisiting memories in as full detail as possible), paying particular attention to specific visual, auditory, olfactory, tactile, and kinesthetic memories. The client's memories of circumstances leading up to the event and just subsequent to the event are useful in filling out the context of the experience. Associated cognitive and emotional states need to be explored. What the client perceived must be seen in terms of his or her interpretations, understandings, and conclusions concerning what transpired. The meaning the child has subsequently made of the event will be, in part, a function of the child's cognitive experience during the event. Emotional states during the event also become associated with the perceptual experience. Recalling particular sensory data will likely call up emotions that have been bound up in the psychological representation. Perceptual memories are very powerful means of gaining access to the cognitive and emotional realities that must be processed in overcoming trauma-related behavioral problems. Thus reliving the event provides the material for therapeutic gain.

Once trust is established with a particular therapist, adolescents are often anxious to share their experiences. They may willingly relate events that have happened to them, frequently with enthusiasm. Their interpretations tend to attribute responsibility for their own behavior—however contributive—to the situation or to other individuals. Self-structure is frequently tenuous during adolescence, and responsibility or culpability can be overwhelming. The therapist's use of indirect statements ("Situations like that can be really tough") or statements embedded in generalizations ("I've known a lot of people in this sort of situation who have ended up angry at . . .") can often facilitate ownership of memories or feelings.

Releasing

It is normal for feelings associated with the event to be "bound up" in complex specific memories of perceptions, interpretations, and sensory data. People resist experiencing pain, and memories of traumas are usually painful. Once the client recalls sensory data, his or her memories of feelings as well as current feelings regarding his or her posttrauma behavior, changed circumstances, and relationships will begin to surface. The client may see the therapist as an irritant, someone who is rocking the boat and "causing" the painful reopening of old wounds. The feelings, once tapped, may be released in an overwhelming flood or may come out painfully, in small spurts. The client may have to relive the event several times to achieve the release necessary for integration.

Adolescents are reluctant to show feelings that may erode another's estimation of them. Because they frequently are self-centered, adolescents have difficulty perceiving therapists as functionaries whose roles are simply to help them with these varying feelings. While adolescents may suffer great pain from behaviors that get them referred for therapy, their resistance to treatment is high because of their fear of the underlying feelings.

Reorganizing

As indicated before, the goal of posttrauma therapy is too often the assimilation of the traumatic experience and accommodation to the circumstances that have changed as a result of the event. This involves considerable personal reorganizing (or resorting). This process can involve changes in

— basic cognitive sets used for interpreting the world and anticipating what can be expected from it

— emotional reactions that were experienced during and following the event

— attributions of responsibility and personal control over events, and

— attitudes toward various persons, places, and events

This resorting process may be profound and may manifest itself in depressive behaviors. Further, this process takes on a developmental dimension, since it involves reconstructing the present based upon changed perceptions regarding the past.

Adolescents are particularly affected by this reorganization. They are in the natural developmental stage of letting go of their dependency upon the family, and are attempting to establish themselves as autonomous adults. As with toddlers, the issue of dependency looms large for adolescents and creates inner and interpersonal conflict. At the root of this conflict is a fundamental ambivalence: the drive toward independence violates the desire for protection within the context of the child's role within the family. Since the security of the past is forsaken, each attempt at independent decision making triggers an anxiety reaction. Conversely, any relaxation into old family role patterns triggers a sense of self-violation and is interpreted as retreat. Always difficult, even under "normal" circumstances, this developmental task is compounded by unresolved issues surrounding prior trauma.

Much of what adolescents must deal with concerns the process of gaining independence from the family. This creates a difficulty because the issues evolving from the family are often of paramount importance, yet the adolescent frequently needs to engage in therapeutic growth apart from the family. With adolescents, treatment strategies must be utilized that allow for indirect focus upon family dynamics. These might include the use of Gestalt techniques, psychodrama, role play, or other more active techniques. In any case, as the study reported in Appendix I has shown, the family structure compounds the effects of critical incidents, including those occurring outside the family. One technique for dealing with the family context—family mediation—is particularly useful when the family situation prevents work on trauma-specific symptoms. Posttraumatic intervention with adolescents proceeds in a patchwork fashion initially, presenting such conditions as self-destructive behaviors, running away or being thrown out of the home, or violence within the family. These conditions must be dealt with immediately in order to stabilize the situation. Once some stability is established, time can be gained to deal with underlying, trauma-specific issues.

FAMILY MEDIATION

One useful strategy for stabilizing chaotic home situations involves the therapist assuming the role of mediator within the family. Mediation is a form of family therapy best described as a family system crisis intervention. For mediation to be effective, several conditions about the purpose and manner in which it is conducted must be made clear to all parties. These include the following:

1. The therapist must shift from playing advocate to playing a more balanced, and unbiased, role.

2. The therapist's advance work with each party should include a clear problem statement, spelled out in specifics. Clear goal statements are necessary, and various possible trade-offs and contingencies should be explored. This not only assists the adolescent and parents in generating a more flexible set of options, it also allows the therapist to introduce an element of reality into each party's expectations. In addition, mediation provides the therapist with an opportunity to assess what each of the parties is up against in terms of attributes, emotional reactivity, and interaction patterns.

3. Mediation sessions should be issue-focused. The expression of anger, hurt, or resentment, for example, must be managed carefully. The point of mediation is not to work through feelings, but rather to make decisions regarding rules and arrangements of living. Often feelings must be expressed in

order for movement to occur, but the focus must always be task-oriented.

4. In their fight against themselves for independence, adolescents allow closeness with the therapist only when they perceive the therapist is on "their side" against the parents. The therapist's impartial role in mediation may appear to be a breach in the relationship between therapist and adolescent, making advance preparation necessary. Thorough discussion beforehand of this important role and debriefing afterward can prevent rupture of the therapeutic alliance. The same difficulty exists in gaining the trust of the parents. The adolescent's attempts at seeking independence can strain family ties to their limits. Parents often seek a therapist as a further ally in their desperate bid to reestablish control over the adolescent. If they feel the therapist is siding with the adolescent, they may be quick to discontinue therapy. Before the therapist attempts mediation, this issue must be raised and a thorough understanding of the implications of the unbiased role of the mediator reached.

5. Each session should begin with a definition of specific problems to be addressed and with a clear statement of decisions made. All decisions should be action-specific, with criteria of success indicated clearly and written down. Subsequent sessions should assess how well previous agreements are working, with particular attention paid to the specificity of agreement.

6. During the sessions the mediator plays a directive role:

   a. stopping and commenting upon the process

   b. restating rules when necessary

   c. feeding back impressions regarding the way in which each party is facilitating or blocking progress toward agreement

   d. providing relevant information, resources, or alternatives

   e. terminating and rescheduling the session if it becomes counterproductive

7. In addition, the mediator separates the parties for individual conferences regarding both content and process of the session. This might be done to clarify issues, suggest strategies, or enforce rules of procedures. Timely separation can also defuse rising tempers or provide time for an overinvolved party to regain composure.

8. The mediator, upon agreement of all parties, can include in the session other individuals who could provide helpful information, such as police officers, social workers, school officials, or other relatives. These people should be informed about the purpose of the meeting, their role, and the meeting format and procedures.

One of the results of initial mediation should be a decision about the circumstances under which additional mediation sessions can be called, and procedures set up to accomplish that. After the desired results are reached, mediation sessions are terminated. If the family so desires, family therapy can continue, but it will be under restructured conditions. Periodic follow-up sessions can be scheduled, and they should maintain the mediation format. The agreements reached should be monitored and adjustments made as needed.

Family mediation is a short-term intervention used to stabilize the family situation long enough for more traditional interventions to be used. While results can be revitalizing and transforming, the focus is upon stabilization. Treatment of the adolescent can proceed when the situation is stabilized, and the material presented during the mediation can figure heavily in subsequent work.

Conclusion

Therapists working with traumatized children draw upon two sources of specialized knowledge within their overall treatment strategy. First, they need to have a clear understanding not only of post-trauma reaction patterns, but also of the central tasks of posttrauma treatment. This perspective provides the direction and goals of therapy irrespective of clinical style or modality. The therapeutic "kernel" of reexperience, release, and reorganization focuses the basic task of posttraumatic therapy regardless of age. This task is accomplished in different ways by different therapists, and, of course, the choice of clinical approach is affected by therapist background, client needs, client developmental level, and the specifics of the situation.

Second, therapists draw upon certain specialized techniques within the context of their treatment plans. Formal approaches such as play or art therapy or family intervention may be used. Specific techniques such as the use of puppets, Gestalt techniques, hypnosis, or family mediation may be utilized within a particular approach. In this regard, the treatment of posttraumatic children does not differ all that much from other clinical pictures.

Other clinical factors may complicate treatment of trauma-specific symptoms. Family difficulties, running away, self-destructive behavior, substance addictions, and many other difficulties may require preliminary therapist-family interaction to stabilize the situation in order to make trauma-specific treatment possible. This is particularly the case with adolescents, whose resistance to therapy and reliance upon maladaptive coping patterns frequently create chaotic or life-threatening situations. Thus the therapist must be flexible and adept at designing multifaceted or even multiphased treatment plans with posttraumatic children.

This chapter, more a road map than a cookbook, has attempted to present these elements in a cohesive manner for the use of clinical professionals in order to provide a clear statement of clinical direction and an overview of therapeutic applications. Interested clinicians may consult Appendix II and the bibliography for further reference sources.

CHAPTER 5

Eye Movement Desensitization and Reprocessing (EMDR) with Children

"... not until a person goes through the process of reassociating and reorganizing his (her) inner life can results occur."

Milton Erickson, *Hypnotic Psychotherapy*

"You don't believe it when you read about it . . . but when you *use* it, you see there is something working here unlike anything you've ever seen before."

psychologist and veteran Steven Silver, reported in *The American Legion*

OVERVIEW

Therapies develop over time, originating with one person and gaining support from others in form of anecdotal evidence and case studies. Support leads to further reporting, and eventually controlled outcome studies seek to verify claims of treatment effectiveness. Due to the difficulties of clinical test design, ethical considerations, and time constraints, newer therapies often present exciting approaches and teach us much about recovery from trauma for years before adequate controlled studies accumulate. For the practitioner seeking to relieve the suffering of those in his or her care, the call to try new approaches is great. It is useful, therefore, to profile one of the newer approaches to therapy with traumatized children and explore what it has to offer. Eye Movement Desensitization and Reprocessing (Shapiro, 1995) is such an approach, new enough to attract controlled studies, but with enough completed cases established to have amassed a substantial record of anecdotal case reports that support EMDR's effectiveness. Chapter 5 will explore EMDR and its applications to child therapy and discuss its connections with other, more established approaches. The purpose of including an in-depth review of a single treatment modality is to illustrate the interplay between theory and practice, unique approach and general clinical issues, simplicity of approach and complexity of application.

Chapter Contents

Development of EMDR

Clinical Studies

EMDR and Children

Interface with Other Therapies

Conclusion

This chapter highlights a relatively new therapeutic approach in the treatment of childhood trauma, Eye Movement Desensitization and Reprocessing. EMDR was developed by Francine Shapiro in 1989 as a means of desensitizing traumatic memories and was reformulated in 1991 into a broader, more sophisticated format. Robbie Dunton was the first to apply it to children. In order to illustrate both the central features of EMDR as well as the flexibility and range of approach possible in using this method, the work of certain practitioners has been selected as representative. This chapter does not offer a comprehensive review of the discipline, nor is it meant to imply that those profiled are the only or the best practitioners. It must be stressed that EMDR is an organized, clinical approach and not a simple technique. Because EMDR should not be attempted without adequate training, no attempt will be made in this chapter to describe the movements or EMDR protocol. Instead, this chapter discusses the development, application, and variations of EMDR as an overall therapeutic approach.

Development of EMDR

Francine Shapiro, senior research fellow at the Mental Research Institute in Palo Alto, California, noticed that certain rhythmic side-to-side eye movements tend to break up the repetitious recurrence of troublesome thoughts and to render those thoughts less distressing. After some refinement, Shapiro utilized the eye movements with several traumatized individuals, resulting in symptom reduction. This was followed by a series of controlled studies, research reports, and clinical developments that have culminated in a virtual tidal wave of therapist advocates trained in Shapiro's method. In 1995 she published the book *Eye Movement Desensitization and Reprocessing: Basic Principles, Protocols, and Procedures.*

Shapiro (1995) cites recent work (e.g., Resick & Schnicke, 1992) indicating that the most successful method of posttrauma treatment includes both exposure to traumatic cues as well as cognitive restructuring. It is not enough to desensitize one to the things that trigger stress reactions; the underlying irrational and self-defeating thoughts and self-blame that accompany stress reactions remain. Shapiro postulates an innate "information processing" system that strives to integrate trauma memories and reactions into a positive, adaptive resolution. If this system can be activated, bothersome memories can be reassessed in such a way as to redefine the event, find meaning in it, alleviate the paralyzing self-blame, and relieve other facets of emotional distress.

While the neurological basis for the method's success is as yet unclear, Shapiro believes that when the client is led through the proper protocol, neurological memory and associative networks are cleared of intensive negative affects and cognitions by accelerated affective, kinesthetic, and cognitive processing. Eye movements, as well as auditory and tactile cueing that causes rapid alterations of awareness from side to side, can stimulate this rapid processing.

Clinical Studies

While EMDR is still emerging as a therapeutic modality, its effectiveness is well documented. Empirical validation is growing, and its applications in addressing different types of psychological problems are under development. At the time of this writing, approximately one hundred reports had been published. According to the EMDR Institute, from 1993 to 1995 nine controlled studies were reported, as well as an additional four that were nonrandomized. Four other have been published in 1996. In addition, Bessel Van der Kolk is currently conducting studies at Harvard University exploring brain changes following EMDR treatment, and while the studies are not yet complete, they appear to be showing positive changes at the neurological level.

In addition, clinical reports regarding applications with children are available, including use with traumatized children (Greenwald, 1994; Shapiro, 1995; Shapiro & Forrest, 1997), as a treatment for nightmares (Pellicer, 1993), in conjunction with artwork (Cohn, 1993), and auditory variants for use with childhood PTSD (Cocco & Sharpe, 1993). Uncontrolled (e.g. Puffer et al., in press) and controlled studies with children are fewer, mostly conference reports. Current studies in process include one following the treatment of victims of Hurricane Iniki by J. Carlson presented at the 1997 annual meeting of the International Society of Traumatic Stress Studies, and on traumatized adolescents (Scheck et al., in press).

EMDR and Children

Shapiro herself (1995) discusses the adaptation of EMDR for work with traumatized children in her comprehensive book outlining the basic principles, protocols, and procedures of EMDR. She stresses that EMDR should be used with children only if the clinician feels comfortable with children, is trained in working with children therapeutically, and is able to create a safe therapeutic environment. She also points out that EMDR is a powerful procedure that should not be used by clinicians who are not properly trained in the approach. The following comments are made for those who are concerned about the appropriateness of referral to an EMDR specialist, or for clinicians contemplating adding EMDR training to their own professional development in order to better treat children.

In discussing the application of EMDR treatment with children, Shapiro (1995) notes the following:

1. Children generally appear to be well adapted to EMDR and show rapid progress.

2. It is necessary to ensure that the therapist-child relationship is comfortable and that the child feels safe in the setting.

3. EMDR sessions with children tend to be shorter than with adults and may benefit from being interspersed with alternate activities.

4. The standard EMDR procedures need to be adapted in several key ways:

   a. Reports of feeling states must use concrete, easily understood definitions.

   b. Because younger children may have difficulty crossing the midline, nonvisual means of stimulating left-right focus, such as touch or sound, can be utilized.

   c. Special effort must be made to hold the child's attention.

   d. Positive cognitions should be phrased in child-appropriate terms.

   e. Clinicians should take their lead from the child's own cognitions, and not attempt to force more clinically appropriate but adult-based cognitions upon the child.

   f. Children can readily generate images of the source of the trauma, and those can be desensitized using EMDR procedures. This effect will generalize to the associated events, which themselves may be poorly understood.

   g. Reports of alleviated distress should be corroborated with changes in behaviorally observable symptoms such as bed-wetting and clinging.

   h. Targets for desensitization can include those identified through creative approaches such as play therapy, sandtray work, and art therapy activities.

Ricky Greenwald, currently a psychologist in Trumansville, New York, employs EMDR in his practice with children. In 1993 he published the first handbook (available through the EMDR Institute) for using EMDR with children. Building upon Shapiro's and Dunton's material, Greenwald compiles his own observations and those of Robbie Dunton and an original group of thirty or so EMDR practitioners across the United States who work with children. Entitled *Using EMDR with Children,* this handbook is planned to be released as a trade publication.

Robert Tinker, Ph.D., P.C., a psychologist from Colorado Springs, Colorado, uses EMDR extensively with his child clients and is a trainer at Shapiro's EMDR Institute. Tinker trained UNICEF trauma workers in Nairobi to use EMDR with Rwandan refugee children who witnessed their family members' bloody deaths during the civil war. He also trained therapists to work with child victims of Hurricane Iniki in Hawaii, has himself used EMDR with child victims of the Oklahoma City bombing, and has incorporated EMDR with children in his own practice. Tinker has recently trained clinicians in Scandinavia and others in Scotland who work with children traumatized in the Dunblane shootings.

Tinker (1996) underscores Shapiro's concern about establishing a "safe place" (a means for clients to regain self-control in the face of overwhelming feelings of distress) prior to using any method of treatment that involves recalling traumatic memories. Both advise therapists to proceed only after clients of any age learn self-relaxation procedures. That said, Tinker notes that children tend to be less overtly emotionally reactive to EMDR treatment than adults, and that treatment is generally more rapid. He also agrees with Shapiro that, developmentally, children have poorer eye-tracking skills than adults, and are assisted toward lateralized focus using hand tapping and/or auditory stimuli.

Tinker points out that a major key to assessing children's trauma reactions are reactive behavioral patterns in the face of external or situational stress. Such patterns give direction as to which specific emotions and events should be targeted for treatment. While adults often have long histories of traumas with complex associated memories and feelings, children's distress seems to be more emotionally event-specific. Once events and feelings are targeted and the best mode of approach determined, desensitization can proceed fairly quickly.

He has also found that children respond quickly to EMDR procedures. He generally uses the adult treatment protocol from age 8 up. For children between 5 and 8 years, he de-emphasizes the normal cognitive aspects of treatment, finding that targeting image, feeling, and body reactions for desensitization is often enough if cognitions cannot be elicited. Nightmares are wonderfully productive targets. Tinker agrees with Shapiro that creative approaches can generate useful targets for desensitization. Neither he nor Shapiro feels that a child must be able to cognitively link his or her feelings about the object to the cause of the trauma; the trauma and reactions to the trauma provide sufficient material with which to effect change.

With even younger children, Tinker uses alternate stimulation such as touch (for example, patty-cake games) and auditory cueing. He has determined a hierarchy of effectiveness, with eye movement the most powerful, hand-cueing second, and auditory the least effective with children.

Children react differently than do adults to EMDR desensitization, and this governs the role of the therapist. Adults have a rich backlog of experience; the therapist can allow the adult to follow his or her memory associations to see where they lead, trusting that those associations have their own unique interconnections. Children have a more limited range of experience; the specific troubling images, feelings, thoughts, and sensations must be discerned with the assistance of the therapist, and desensitized and processed separately. Tinker reports that he can best facilitate this by following a process of theme development using such prompts as "Think of another time in which you . . . ." In working with children, the EMDR therapist's leadership role becomes more important. This approach more closely follows Shapiro's protocol (1995, p. 219) for working with adults who have experienced recent trauma, and involves desensitizing each emerging target (image, feeling, kinesthetic discomfort, memory, and so on).

Tinker underscores Shapiro's assertion that the results of EMDR must be corroborated with parental observations of change in the child's posttrauma behavior at home and school, stressing that a child's feedback in the clinic is usually less obvious than that of an adult's, while the child's subsequent behavioral change in the natu-ralistic setting is often dramatic.

Tinker's 1995 study with Wilson and Becker, the first major controlled study documenting EMDR effectiveness to be published in a major scientific journal, exemplifies an exciting new trend. Breaking the iron grip of the university and journal editorial boards on research, scientist-practitioners are increasingly playing a promi-nent role in conducting and publishing empirical studies. Tinker is now compiling his clinical experiences using EMDR with children along with his research currently in progress to produce a text for clinicians. This material, supplementing the references already cited and other material in press, is much anticipated and will provide additional direction to many therapists who are already trained in EMDR treatment with adults, but who wish to apply the basic tech-niques to traumatized children in their care.

Interface with Other Therapies

EMDR has been used in conjunction with other, more traditional child therapies. Outlining several of these applications is helpful for understanding the depth and strategic usefulness of the approach.

STORYTELLING, SANDPLAY, AND EMDR

Children's stories and play are wonderfully metaphoric and projec-tive. Joan Lovett, a pediatrician in Berkeley, California, specializes in behavioral pediatrics and adolescent medicine. Offering a variety of short-term problem-solving strategies for behavioral problems and trauma, she integrates EMDR into her practice for reducing anxiety and treating childhood trauma. Lovett combines storytelling, sand-tray therapy, play therapy, and other approaches with her EMDR work (Lovett, 1996).

Lovett finds that EMDR can be woven into storytelling to help children and their parents recover from traumatic incidents. She uses a storytelling approach that includes parents in helping their child recover from a traumatic incident. Lovett invites the parents to write a story for their child, instructing them to start the story by describing the child as safe and loved, and then the events leading up to the traumatic incident, the critical incident itself and its after-math, and ending with the resolution of the trauma. While the parents read the story to their child, Lovett uses EMDR techniques to desensitize and reprocess the scary parts of the story. This storytelling approach is especially helpful for children who are younger than 6 and for older children who were traumatized before the age of 6.

Lovett finds that sandtray work is also well suited to interfacing with EMDR. She uses her collection of sandtray figures in a variety of ways to help children using EMDR. There are three main ways she incorporates sandtray figures into the process:

1. She invites children to choose a figure that could help them make their own imaginative power stronger. This figure can be used as a focal point for eye movement. It can also be used to lend its power to the child or to be a sort of guardian for the child who goes through the EMDR process.

2. She asks the child to create a "safe place" in the sandtray. A chosen figure is then used to conduct EMDR while the child imagines being in a safe place and experiences the feeling of safety being "grounded" in the body.

3. She uses the sandtray to weave EMDR into ongoing sandplay process. When figures are "stuck" or in danger, EMDR can be used to give them what they need for rescue. EMDR can facilitate the sandtray process by decreasing anxiety and reinforcing positive cognitions as they emerge.

In describing her use of EMDR with other approaches, Lovett indicates that the blending of different styles allows her to do things that she otherwise could not, often with excellent results. Combining EMDR with play, artwork, puppet play, or storytelling allows children an opportunity to express themselves in a way that is natural to them, while EMDR techniques catalyze the deep healing process. Young children often need to have educational information provided in order to successfully resolve traumatic experiences. Lovett uses EMDR to enhance children's abilities to learn ways to take care of themselves, to assess situations, and to feel safe and confident.

She has found that EMDR especially appeals to adolescents who want to improve their performance at school, decrease test-taking anxiety, enhance their self-confidence, increase their ability to deal with social situations calmly, and make life feel easier. Some adolescents choose to reprocess traumatic memories in a way similar to that used by adults. Other adolescents prefer to do EMDR in conjunction with sandtray work or even puppet play. In *Small Wonders* (Lovett, in press), a book written about children's trauma and the role of EMDR in facilitating the resolution of trauma, Lovett describes how EMDR can help children recover from trauma and regain their ability to sleep, eat, play, and develop healthy relationships. Her book presents case histories of children successfully treated with EMDR, and contains methods for integrating EMDR with storytelling, artwork, play, and sandtray therapy.

EMDR and Art Therapy

One approach to working with traumatized children is art therapy, discussed in Chapter 4. Art therapy allows children to open communication with the therapist via constructed artworks, which form the basis for assessment, interaction, and further activity. Art is a natural medium for children and allows access to inner content that is otherwise blocked by fear, limitations in language, and lack of narrative understanding. The child has control over the material surface and the tools used to communicate the affective aspects of his or her experience, and the properties of various art materials can be adapted individually. By manipulating the materials and process of the artwork expressing traumatic experience, the child can gain mastery over it. Art activities are a natural complement to EMDR.

San Francisco art therapist Linda Cohn, MFCC, ATR, has reported her integration of art therapy and EMDR to produce rapid, lasting success in meeting therapeutic goals with traumatized children (Cohn, 1993, 1996). She considers the two to be a powerful combination, bringing together the targeting and integrative capabilities of art with the desensitization and reprocessing of EMDR.

Cohn finds that the two approaches share important similarities and complementary differences. Both rely upon the utilization and processing of images to produce change. The creation and use of images helps children to consolidate fragmented memories and relate them to current situations. Both methods help integrate right- and left-hemisphere functions, thus combining the various processes for accelerated recovery. Finally, both methods tend to work more rapidly than verbal therapy alone.

The two approaches can be especially powerful when used in combination. While both systems employ imagery, they differ in the way in which images are expressed. With EMDR, accessing and describing images is limited to verbal description, and nuance and subtlety may be lost in articulation. The use of art activity allows for such dimensions, as well as nonverbal, preconscious, and unconscious material to become accessible. Unlike EMDR, art therapy results in concrete productions, which can be more effectively used diagnostically and to track progress. This process provides rich material for EMDR processing, which then accelerates integration and problem resolution.

Particularly for children, it is true that "a picture is worth a thousand words." In one picture the therapist and child can see the child's world unfold; aspects of the situation that are important are portrayed in relationship to one another. Closeness, distance, bonds, divisions, similarities, differences, investments, energy—all can be portrayed in simple, concrete form. A multitude of directions for EMDR work can come from one picture.

In EMDR work with children, drawings and other artwork can be interwoven throughout the procedure. Children encode information largely in visual terms, and they readily use drawings where words fail them. This substituting of images for words facilitates the use of EMDR treatment with those who have less sophisticated verbal skills or limited ability to abstract experience.

EMDR can work quickly to release and desensitize otherwise overwhelming affects if the child is able to proceed with it. If not, artwork can facilitate preparation for EMDR by sublimating affective energy into creative channels. This serves several functions. Not only can commonly shared artistic images become another way of communicating and deepening the child-therapist relationship, but the distance provided by the "objectification of affect" into artworks allows the child emotional room to work with those feelings. The child can try on, test, and "see" behavioral options, and thus cognitively explore the uncertain ground between subjective feeling and objective reality, which has been rendered unsafe by trauma.

Cohn feels that the movement from the subjective, inner work of EMDR processing to the detached, neutral projection into art helps the child increase flexibility in psychological functioning. All of the child's systems are more fully reinforced and integrated. Perceptual, semantic, emotional, and cognitive processes can be integrated on multiple levels: verbal and nonverbal, active and passive, conscious and unconscious.

Cohn has found the combination of art therapy and EMDR gains effectiveness from several factors:

1. Artworks are projective. The art object is a symbolic projection, and as such it is often easier to relate to, allowing the child to gain distance, lessen the emotional charge, and neutralize the intensity of unconscious material. The projected artwork can be a diagnostic tool for the therapist, and can help articulate the negative thoughts and beliefs that underlie the disorder. Since artworks can indicate and clarify memories of incidents and current emotions, they can also be used to determine targets for direct EMDR work.

The use of art produced during treatment can be as instructive to the child as it is to the therapist. In discussing one case example, Cohn (1996) told how one child, an 8-year-old girl who was abused by her mother and treated with EMDR, had progressed to the point at which she reported no more anger: "I feel happy and energetic, now." A subsequent drawing showed obvious elements of anger and hostility. When asked about the drawing, the child replied, "The girl looks mad. I guess I am mad at my Mom." A child may not be aware of other feelings, or might not wish to reveal them verbally. Seeing the anger still in the picture was a discovery for the child, and further sets of eye movements finally resulted in a drawing that was clearly without anger.

2. Artworks provide a permanent record of the therapy process. Drawings, collages, and other works produced in the session are concrete images providing a tangible record not subject to alteration by memory. These images help the therapist to see what the child is experiencing, and they help the child to confront the reality emerging from his or her own hand. Review of a series of works can provide documentation of significant issues that were dealt with during the process of therapy. This is of particular importance in the treatment of children using EMDR, as a child may have difficulty recalling the intensity of the pretreatment images and experiences without such a record.

3. The process of creating artworks is a metaphor for the client's life process. Artwork requires the child to set limits, create boundaries, explore choices, and take risks. By observing this process, the therapist can detect reaction patterns, problem-solving blocks, and belief systems that might be appropriate for future processing with EMDR. Artwork can contain emotions safely, allow the child to experiment with possible alternatives, and provide a place to articulate positive cognitions that can then be reinforced using EMDR.

4. Art provides a pacing advantage in conjunction with EMDR. The art-making process has a unique movement and flow. Using art in conjunction with EMDR gives the therapist greater options to pace the course of therapy within and between sessions. Verbal therapeutic processing tends to be slower and EMDR more rapid. The middle pace of art therapy may be less threatening at times to "jump-start" blocked processing or to make the child more comfortable, encouraging continued processing. Art is particularly useful at the beginning of treatment when the child needs to feel more in control, or later, when the child needs to take more time to integrate EMDR-generated material. Client balance and movement is maintained in the pacing or "dance" among verbal, art, and EMDR therapies.

5. Art can be used to ground the EMDR process. Art activities can serve as a grounding device because of their concreteness and spatial matrix; the EMDR immersion in memory, thoughts, and reflection is brought back to earth. The child experiences the art content as "just a drawing" rather than as something that is happening currently. Reviewing a series of artworks can aid in termination of therapy by providing documentation of significant issues throughout the therapeutic process.

In a typical session, Cohn alternates between the two approaches to maximize the effects of each. Her case studies (1993) present a fascinating study of timing and technique, which effectively assist clients in accessing and integrating perceptual, somatic, emotional, and cognitive systems in order to effect rapid change. Both art and

EMDR activate all children's systems of processing, yet children encode in a visual and kinesthetic way. When Cohn works with children, she modifies the EMDR process to use art activity as an avenue of communication. This allows children to report on their EMDR experience, circumventing many children's limited use of language, and also allows the therapist to more accurately interpret the child's message. The child, in turn, is helped to perceive his or her own thoughts, feelings, and changes.

EMDR and Family Systems Therapy

EMDR has been successfully integrated with family systems approaches to therapy. Two family therapists in private practice have done much in the way of articulating their interweave of these approaches, Craig Penner of Santa Barbara, California, and Chad Glang of Colorado Springs, Colorado (Penner, 1996; Glang, 1996). Both echo previous observations that children tend to resolve disturbances quickly with EMDR, often with little apparent awareness of doing so. The therapist may not know in the session that significant change has occurred, and must be in continual contact with the family to assess the effects of therapy on an ongoing basis. The family is also in the position to advise therapists of salient aspects of the traumatic experience or context of behavior that the child is unable to articulate, and can also provide observations of the child's behavior at home or school that bear upon treatment. Thus, assessment necessarily involves ongoing interaction with the family system.

EMDR work can benefit from a family systems perspective in other ways. Penner points out that assessing the family for using EMDR with a member is similar to any clinical situation involving observation of families. He considers issues of safety, trust, structure, flexibility, openness, and honesty. While more individually oriented therapists emphasize the establishment of a "safe place," or accessible state of mind that allows the child to deal with challenging feelings and ideas without fear of losing him or herself, Penner and Glang both consider the family environment critical in determining whether the child will receive the support and comfort necessary to process traumatic material and cope with the uncertainty therapy entails.

The EMDR work itself can be diagnostic. Craig cites cases in which he has found it necessary to do more traditional family therapy before using EMDR with a child. Whereas he thought EMDR would support the child's changes, he discovered that the system worked only to a certain point, at which the child no longer wanted to proceed with treatment even though resolution was not apparent. After going back to the family to explore the impasse, he found problems that the family needed to address. "Going back to the family" refers to the strategy of dealing with therapeutic roadblocks by taking the issue to the family and looking for interpersonal factors that may be inhibiting progress. The key factor indicating a need to return to the family seems to be important shifts in the child's processing that are accompanied by a withdrawal from the process.

Penner cites a case in which a boy who had been abused by a teacher was suffering from nightmares and acting aggressively. After assessing that the family was healthy and supportive, Penner felt that EMDR would be helpful and that the family could support the boy's changes. For a time the EMDR work progressed normally, and the boy seemed to be resolving the issues in typical fashion. While working on forgiveness issues, however, things became stuck. Going back to the family, Craig found the mother herself unable to forgive the teacher, and she was giving the boy mixed messages. Because the child had the idea that forgiveness entailed forgetting, he felt some pressure not to forgive, as well as a fear that forgetting would increase his vulnerability to future abuse. Direct work with the family on clarifying that forgiving does not mean forgetting allowed the boy to return to EMDR work and take it to completion.

Similarly, Penner has noted certain types of impasse in EMDR processing that indicate a bind caused by the power of the family. Loyalty to rules and people can be incredibly strong, and gaining an objective view in order to loosen the bind can be like a fish trying to describe the water in which it swims. Backing out to the systems level can create a crack in the story that enables processing to proceed.

Central to Penner and Glang's approach is a distinction between blocking beliefs and current systemic blocks. A *blocking belief* is a negative cognition about the situation, oneself, or one's participation in the situation that prevents successful processing. Blocking beliefs can be about the self (for example, "I am worthless" or "I am inadequate") or about the world ("Forgiving means forgetting" or "People can't change").

Systemic blocks are mutually held beliefs or patterns of interaction in the family that cannot be addressed or questioned unless there is a change within the entire family, beginning with the parents. If the treatment involves the child implicitly challenging those beliefs or blocks, progress is unsupported and unlikely. The child must somehow be given permission by the family to go ahead and think, talk, and act openly, and this permission can result from family intervention.

Glang cites a case in which a 10-year-old boy refused to let his older brother play with his video game. Shortly thereafter, the older boy attempted to strangle his sister. The 10-year-old blamed himself, and that response was targeted for desensitization in EMDR therapy. Progress was stymied until the client reported that his irrational belief of being at fault was enthusiastically supported by both the perpetrator and victim of the violence. Until the block within the family system was dealt with, EMDR could not help with the belief about responsibility. His father was called in from the waiting room, and reassured the boy that his brother had full responsibility for his own violent behavior. The boy breathed a sigh of relief, and plans were made to continue EMDR the following week.

Glang asked the father to summarize the session for the boy's mother that evening so that she could add her assurance. This directive uncovered another systemic block, however, as her response to the child was to question him angrily: "How could you blame yourself?" In the following session, Glang helped the mother see that her anger was driven by a fear that she was failing as a mother. She was then able to deal with her guilt around this and other issues, which were preventing her from being emotionally present to her son. The boy was then free to tell his mother the many ways in which he experienced her emotional absence. She was coached to welcome this difficult feedback and to make appropriate changes. With these systemic blocks cleared, the boy experienced enough safety in his family to continue and complete his EMDR work.

While family therapy is seen to remove obstacles to the EMDR treatment of individual children's trauma, the converse is also true. Penner and Glang report that EMDR is useful in complementing and expediting family therapy. This can include cases in which one family member has an issue that isn't caused by the current system, but that interferes with family functioning. In one case a daughter was brought in for tantrums, and Penner began working with the whole family. In so doing he uncovered some problems in parenting that were creating ongoing tension for the children. The mother appeared overly reactive to her daughter's tantrums, and Penner did some individual EMDR work with her. It became clear that the mother resented and felt guilty about becoming pregnant out of wedlock and having to get married; she had been playing out these resentments toward her daughter without realizing it. Once she had identified, processed, and resolved these issues through EMDR, she was able to return to work on the current family issues from a much calmer position. As Gland points out, EMDR has the special power of taking the person to the truth. The truth is sometimes an original trauma, but often not.

One of the great advantages that EMDR offers to the individual/ systems interface is that individual issues can be dealt with rapidly and effectively so that the person can return to the systems work without a great deal of time lost from the group process. Penner also points out that individual members reporting and integrating their gains from EMDR has a contagion effect: others see the changes and see that change is indeed possible.

Penner and Glang report treating a variety of children's problems by interweaving family systems strategies with EMDR, including anxiety, compulsive behaviors, depression, phobias, bedwetting, night-mares, sleepwalking, sleep disturbances, poor self-image, defiance, and addictions (with teens). Penner reports tracking school behavior problems back to events or self-limiting beliefs that set those prob-lems in motion, targeting the self-image problems that grow out of poor school performance.

EMDR AND EDUCATIONAL THERAPY

Prior to assuming the position of administrative director of the EMDR Institute in Pacific Grove, California, Robbie Dunton practiced pri-vately as an educational consultant. Discovering EMDR, she put the approach to work in solving learning and school-related problems with her young clients. Tapped by Shapiro to teach advanced EMDR clinical trainees about applying EMDR strategies with children, Dunton pioneered much of the work in this area.

Much has been written about the connection between trauma and learning difficulties and attention deficit hyperactivity disorder, or ADHD (see Chapter 2), and EMDR appears to show great promise as a means to address those underlying psychological problems. As success in school is critical to children's development both cognitively and emotionally, the application of EMDR to school difficulties is very exciting.

Working with school problems presents certain advantages; Dunton points to the availability and applicability of school testing and observational report data and academic history. This sort of information is not always accessible in clinical work, and is sometimes not applicable; yet within the context of treating school difficulties it is both accessible and germane. In this regard, those bringing the child for treatment can usually be counted upon to provide a rich set of behavioral targets for therapy. Sources of information regarding targets include the reason for the referral, family and teacher observations, and the child's own concerns.

Dunton has successfully treated learning problems directly with EMDR. She cites (1996) the case of a 14-year-old boy who was working at the second grade level in mathematics and was placed in a special class. Dunton found that utilizing EMDR with the boy in working with math facts allowed him to process information impossible until that time. Within one session, multiplication tables through 12 were learned and retained.

In addition, EMDR can facilitate a stronger and more positive sense of self-esteem. The connection between self-esteem and learning is well established, both being in part dependent upon the other. Dunton feels that self-esteem can both lead to and be undermined by school failure, and she has had good results using EMDR to address esteem issues with children. She has found children's school success thwarted by emotional problems such as depression and anxiety, and she has used EMDR with clients to deal not only with the underlying issues, but also with the resulting attitudes toward learning.

In her clinical work, Dunton developed several techniques for applying EMDR procedures and protocols to work with children. For instance, EMDR employs the Wolpe numbered scale to help clients report subjective distress. Realizing that children's developmental limitations make such a scale useless, she developed the Calibration of Movement chart, which allows the child's pointing to be translated by the therapist into a numeric level.

The standard EMDR approach utilizes eye movements crossing the midline. Yet this is difficult for younger children and for those with developmental and ocular motor difficulties. ADHD students often cannot tolerate near-point focus and are sometimes tactile-defensive. Dunton devised several alternative approaches for such children, including the use of colored paper on a wall, auditory stimuli, and therapist/child handclapping. In addition, she developed a set of powerful, vivid images that can be used by the child to understand and retain otherwise unclear perspectives. These images can open expectations of new alternatives. One such image is a "chest of drawers," useful to assist children in accessing personal resources that they otherwise do not associate with current problems.

Working with children, Dunton found that EMDR was sometimes more effective than the child realized or could report on. She found that symptom reduction occurred of which she was unaware, unless she found someone who could observe changes in the natural setting. Dunton discovered that feedback regarding treatment effectiveness is likely to be behavioral, and hence depends upon ongoing communication among therapist, parents, teachers, and other professionals in the school context who see the child regularly.

The potential for EMDR's application to learning situations is exciting. Difficulties in cognitive and emotional processing have long been addressed in the school and clinic, with sporadic success. The development of EMDR as a method of removing blocks to learning, and restructuring declines in self-esteem related to school failure, will take time, but it will be time well spent.

In 1997 Shapiro published a second book, co-authored by Margot Silk Forrest (Basic Books). *EMDR: The Breakthrough Therapy for Overcoming Anxiety, Stress, and Trauma* is written toward a general audience of parents, clinicians, and other adults who work or live with traumatized individuals. Its purpose is to show, through case studies, the dramatic way EMDR has been used to bring about therapeutic healing. Anyone interested in the dynamics of change cannot help but be fascinated by the way in which these cases are discussed in fresh detail and in nonclinical language.

Two of the case studies are children. *EMDR* follows the treatments of Ashley, a five-year-old girl with a severe attachment disorder, and Davy, only 14 months old, who was severely traumatized when he woke from anesthetic in the middle of cleft palate surgery. Davy's case is remarkable in that his presenting symptoms are profound and defeating—he (and his grandparents) suffered from night terrors several times a night, as well as extreme fears and headbanging—and that these symptoms ceased after only two sessions of EMDR. Ashley's case is equally remarkable in that her disorder was more pervasive and she did not have the strong family resources Davy had to fall back upon. Ashley's therapy had to address her mother's own attachment difficulties, phobias, and her violent behavior toward her younger brother. EMDR worked in a situation where any therapeutic progress was unlikely.

These cases make compelling reading, not only because of the young age of the clients and surprising effectiveness of treatment, but also because of the comprehensive way in which the interweaving betweeen EMDR and more conventional therapeutic modalities is revealed. *EMDR* bridges the gap between the emphasis upon clinical protocol of her first book, and the drama of actual practice. Shapiro has provided a helpful means for the uninitiated to find out much about how EMDR is used.

EMDR appears to present an attractive and promising therapeutic option for those who would help alleviate the suffering of traumatized children and forestall the debilitating effects of posttraumatic symptoms in later development. It must be stressed that EMDR's usefulness is determined by the skill, perceptiveness, and wise judgment of the clinician. It is a complex method dovetailing with an overall clinical program, not a quick-fix technique. Shapiro and Tinker, and others using EMDR with children, stress the need for therapists to be thoroughly trained in proper EMDR treatment protocols, aware of the limitations of the approach, and to use EMDR only within the context of a balanced clinical program.

A list of trained EMDR therapists and clinician trainings is available through the EMDR Institute, P.O. Box 51019, Pacific Grove, California 93950, (408) 372-3900.

In 1995, the Eye Movement Desensitization and Reprocessing International Association was formed. The EMDRIA has taken over many of the EMDR Institute's functions, including organizing the annual conference, publishing the EMDRIA newsletter, and setting EMDR training standards. Ricky Greenwald has recently formed a special interest group focusing upon children and adolescent issues within the EMDRIA. Lists of trained EMDR clinicians are available through the Association: P.O. Box 140824, Austin, Texas 78714-0824, (602) 912-5300.

CHAPTER 6

Families in Crisis: The Ecology of Change

The "intrapsychic" realm becomes meaningless
if it is taken out of the realm of the relational
context.

Ivan Boszormenyi-Nagy & Geraldine Sparks,
Invisible Loyalties

Accidents will happen in the best-regulated
families.

Charles Dickens, *David Copperfield*

The joys of parents are secret, as so are their
griefs and fears.

Francis Bacon, *Of Parents and Children*

OVERVIEW

All professionals who deal with the families of children in crisis deal with families in crisis. Whether the focus is upon the child, a group in which the child plays a part, or the family itself, the professional's effectiveness will be directly affected by the reaction of the family to the child's distress. This chapter provides a model for understanding and anticipating the impact of the crisis upon the family. The effects of crisis upon the central dynamics of family functioning are discussed, as are the resulting potential pitfalls for involved professionals. The chapter concludes by outlining troubleshooting strategies.

Chapter Contents

Hanging from the ceiling of the east wing of the National Gallery, the enormous but ethereally graceful Calder Mobile slowly swings around, constantly changing position. With its many parts linked together, the mobile nevertheless maintains a delicate balance, as movement is met by countermovement. Silently, this massive work of art reveals combination after combination of spatial interrelationships as it dances through time. Families, too, change gradually and continuously although not so silently.

As individuals change, other family members gradually adopt new roles and new forms of interaction; thus the family, like the Calder Mobile, adapts to the changing realities of individual movement and growth. The impact of crisis, however, can throw off the balance and smooth workings of even the strongest family.

Crisis can occur within the family itself. Some examples of internal crises are the disclosure of incest, the death of a family member, and an outside event that has affected all members together. On the other hand, crises may directly affect one member outside of the family; for example, a child may be victimized or may undergo a critical incident at school. In any case, the entire family will become involved. Educators, therapists, and other professionals dealing with either the whole family or children who have been through traumatic experiences outside will necessarily have to deal with the family on an ongoing basis. The professional's understanding of the dynamics of family functioning after a crisis will determine his or her ability to interact with the family in an effective, productive manner.

The Family's Response to Crisis

Crisis puts great stress upon the family, interrupting routines, making abrupt changes, and creating much anxiety. Whether the crisis occurs within the family or affects a single member outside the family, all members undergo change to a greater or lesser degree. Change creates stress for the system as well as for the individuals within the system. Communication patterns, role relationships, expectations for each other's behavior, trust that others will meet one's own needs as usual, and flexibility in tolerating individual needs are just some of the affected dimensions of the system.

Just as individuals react to the stress brought on by trauma, so do families. Family functioning adjusts in many ways to the changes within and between members. These changes can be for the better; often a family will respond to a crisis by drawing closer together, reassessing how it functions, and wanting positive changes for the enrichment of all concerned. Unfortunately, that is not always the case.

Often, crisis brings the opposite reaction. Families may become fragmented, with members becoming isolated and unable to reestablish a closeness they desire. Communication lines can become blocked and resentments can develop that are difficult to overcome. Crisis frequently brings long-standing conflicts into the open in such a way that they may seem impossible to resolve. Families sometimes lack the resources to manage the restructuring necessary to accommodate the changes brought about by crisis.

Inability to communicate supportively, a continuing climate of crisis and confusion, pervasive insecurity and lowered self-esteem among family members are all a part of post-crisis response and, contribute to the family dysfunction. Avoidance reactions discourage self-expression and disclosure, and so limit the capacity of the family to support its members.

Trauma to one of the adults in the family is likely to affect the entire family system. Krugman (1987) reports family symptoms of denial, minimization of, and avoidance in dealing with the traumatic memories, intrusive imagery, and intense feelings. To maintain its tenuous balance, the posttraumatic family becomes restrictive to changes in individual family members, avoids reminders of the trauma, and is impulsive in acting out its distress. These three trends can lead to more serious dysfunction.

While open family systems encourage growth and are reasonably flexible toward change, the posttraumatic family tends to draw in upon itself in search of safety and security. Members can become resistant to influence from outside the family and intolerant of expressions of personal distress from within. Personal growth and change become equated with abandonment. Thus the posttraumatic family can become enmeshed, constricting expression and restricting the use of outside resources, all of which preclude recovery.

Similarly, the family may attempt to avoid fearful traumatic memories or disturbing associations by disengaging emotionally from one another. As one or both parents become increasingly distant, inaccessible, and inattentive, children may be neglected or abused. And as parents become functionally impaired, children may be forced to adopt compensatory roles in the family in order to care for themselves. Finally, to the extent that traumatized family members impulsively act out their distress, family life becomes chaotic. The family becomes prone to repeated crises brought about by normal changes that appear catastrophic because of posttraumatic stress.

Krugman (1987) summarizes the pathogenic family adaptation to trauma as including the following pattern, which has an inter-generational transmission effect:

1. The trauma occurs, engendering intolerable thoughts and feelings

2. The family system responds by organizing itself defensively to control the intensity of experience

3. The interactional and emotional life of the family reorganizes itself to adjust to chronic reactions

4. Maladaptive behavior patterns become reinforced

5. Defensive adaptations are passed along to subsequent generations, increasing vulnerability to stressor

Family restructuring following crisis often occurs in three stages (illustrated on the facing page in Figure 1):

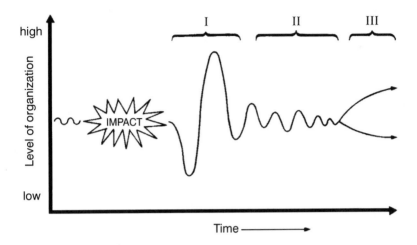

Figure 1. Stages of posttrauma restructuring.
I = Recoil. II = Reorganization. III = Restabilization.

I. Recoil. Following a critical incident, family members initially respond by allying themselves to meet the threat. During this time the family feels closer together than ever. Almost a second honeymoon for the family, this initial stage is characterized by increased intimacy, trust, and communication. Long-standing conflicts and resentments are typically held in temporary abeyance.

II. Reorganization. Later, when the situation has stabilized somewhat, old patterns of communication and old conflicts and role relationships reassert themselves in the face of the increased stress caused by the crisis. This may lead to increased polarization, differentiation, and fragmentation, felt doubly hard by family members who have not only been hurt by the trauma but also feel new levels of isolation highlighted by the recent increase in family solidarity.

III. Restabilization. Finally, if family members are unable to rebuild the relationships exactly as before, the system settles into a new period of stability characterized by deteriorated or increased levels of intimacy, affection, communication, and trust.

As indicated, the reorganization phase presents a challenge to the family. New levels of family strength can be gained, or existing strength can be lost. Each of the process and content functions of the family can be explored in terms of the postcrisis reactions. An understanding of the specific challenges faced by the family following a child's trauma provides the professional a focus for intervention with the traumatized child and his or her family. The challenges of reorganization also present potential pitfalls for intervening professionals.

Impact on Process Dynamics

Process dynamics refers to the ways in which the family gets things done. How the family makes decisions and communicates, the operational agreements and expectations, the emotional distance between family members, how the family handles changes—all of these are part of the family process dynamics. Many of these dimensions of family functioning can be affected by crisis and can provide challenges for professionals attempting to provide assistance. The most troubling of such dynamics can be contractual disputes, role rigidity, homeostatic resistance, and distance polarity.

CONTRACTUAL DISPUTES

Relationships are agreements. The contractual agreements holding within a healthy family provide efficiency, stability, and reliability in the ongoing coordination of family interaction. Confusion, resentment, and betrayal result from the unclear and dysfunctional contracts in a less healthy family. Crisis can focus family members' attention upon their contracted agreements, allowing them the chance to restructure their relationship for greater adaptability, coordination, and intimacy. On the other hand, the crisis situation can stress relational contracts to the breaking point.

Professionals are affected by family contracts in two ways. First, the professional is thrust into a web of reciprocal expectations that are both invisible and real. All necessary routines of family life are premised upon expectations regarding roles, rules, and standards. Most of these reciprocal expectations are unspoken, so the incoming professional must be alert for indirect signs of agreements and expectations among family members. Through the professional's involvement with the family, the family structure changes, and the balance requires readjustment. Children have certain expectations regarding adult behavior, boundaries, and territory, and the intrusion of an outside professional into the family system disturbs their expectations. The crisis situation probably has shaken family members, and each will be particularly sensitive regarding expectations for the future. This can be difficult for several reasons. In addition to the problem of a family not being willing to communicate "how things are," the family may not be aware that things could actually be different, or that the professional does not immediately understand all that needs to be known about the family.

Second, and potentially more troublesome, the professional may not be able to overcome his or her own particular family background and may proceed blindly, assuming that the client family functions just like the family back home. These perceptual "blinders" render the professional ineffective in dealing with new realities. Insensitive stumbling over personal territories, blundering into areas "not discussed," and violations of authority structures can cause great turmoil for the family seeking to reestablish order in their world.

ROLE RIGIDITY

A healthy family is characterized by functional roles. Each member has a certain amount of flexibility in changing role expectations and adopting new role functions when appropriate to changing situations or emerging personal needs. An unhealthy family is characterized by rigid, unbending role expectations. Under the increased stress of posttraumatic situations, some families attempt to cope with changes by controlling a family member's behavior. Limiting acceptable actions to established role-compatible behavior lends predictability and constancy to family interaction. This strategy creates difficulty, however, when the situation requires new means of coping or when individual needs have been changed by the traumatic experience. Role rigidity can be dysfunctional in the face of changing needs. The following case study is offered as illustration.

CASE STUDY: ROXANNE

Roxanne's mother had a certain amount of trouble with two things: men and alcohol. Roxanne's father was an alcoholic who left the family when Roxanne was very young. Her mother would go out drinking and pick up men to bring home, men who often became abusive and beat her and Roxanne. She finally found one she could beat up at least half the time, so Roxanne acquired a stepfather but retained the violence. Since Roxanne was the oldest child, she often found herself physically protecting her younger sister and brother.

Roxanne also did most of the cooking because her mother was frequently drunk or in the midst of conflicts. During her high school years, Roxanne worked after school and bought groceries with her paycheck. She cooked and washed clothes for her siblings and stepfather, and she broke up fights. Over time she became the family organizer, without whom the family would cease to run.

A crisis came when Roxanne decided that she could no longer keep up those responsibilities and still pursue a life of her own. Her mother and stepfather had separated and her mother had moved. Roxanne took advantage of an opportunity to attend a training program in another part of the country. The external pressure from all family members for her to stay was intense. Her mother did not want her to leave because of the increased workload it would mean for her. Her siblings were terrified that they would not be taken care of. Worse, Roxanne herself felt severe guilt over leaving them behind and almost abandoned her training program midway after receiving several frantic calls asking her to return.

She became worried later when she found out that her younger brother was starting to cook for the family and had just taken a part-time job after school. Roxanne had left the role, but the role remained.

Much of the conflict that occurs in a family following the intrusion of a professional can be traced to the process of modifying and restructuring role relationships.

Often, when such conflict occurs, the professional is blamed for the changes and is resented by those whose lives have been altered. The family members (however irrationally or unconsciously) may identify the professional as the one somehow responsible for the change. Thus establishing warm, working relationships with all family members can prove to be a lengthy process for the professional.

Some conflicts between individuals may be the product of role collision rather than personal differences. The professional can become entangled in these disputes, which involve the entire family system, not just the obvious participants. Sometimes, where divisions exist within the family, some family members assume that the role of the professional includes taking sides in a conflict. Other times, professionals encounter resistance from the family member who feels that his or her role as authority figure is threatened. When this occurs, other members may experience confusion about who will make decisions or whose judgment to trust.

Finally, the professional may have expectations regarding role distribution based upon his or her own family experience. In the client family, the gender, age, and sibling order may not yield the same role functions anticipated by the professional and may be experienced as somehow not feeling right. As a consequence, the professional may make assumptions and act upon expectations that are inappropriate.

HOMEOSTATIC RESISTANCE

Families have an innate tendency to resist change, and to a certain extent this is normal and healthy. It provides the stability needed to maintain family functioning through the inconsistencies of life. It can become a source of malfunctioning, however, if this homeostatic resistance sacrifices the family's flexibility and adaptability to changed conditions. Crisis situations are chaotic, and, in the family's attempt to continue functioning through the chaos, homeostatic resistance may become a problem rather than a solution. Like a rush of antibodies after exposure to an invading virus, various forms of homeostatic resistance can paralyze the family in the face of a need to change. Conversely, in other families, crisis will shake the family loose and allow homeostatic habits to be reexamined. New forms of adaptability can strengthen the family system.

Resistance to change is a normal and frequent aspect of family life. Homeostatic resistance tends to increase according to the degree of stress the family system is undergoing. Thus, therapists and other family consultants rarely deal with families in which major change is not occurring (or adjustments to a previous change being made), and they often experience the effects of homeostasis. Unnecessary conflicts, divided loyalties, contractual misunderstandings, role adjustment problems, and behavioral difficulties are all ways in which homeostatic resistance to change can surface.

CASE STUDY: THE WILLIAMS FAMILY

The Williams family came to the attention of the school counselor when the family began an anti-sex education campaign among parents at the school of their handicapped child. During an ensuing meeting, Don and Sarah Williams bitterly attacked the school's family life program on the grounds that it would "put ideas" into the head of their 15-year-old daughter, Cindy. They reasoned that, having been disabled following an accident and confined to a wheelchair, Cindy did not need such problems.

Like most couples, Don and Sarah had had fantasies of what their baby would be like. Those fantasies had not included a disability. When they discovered that Cindy was not the child that they had expected, they had to make changes. They accomplished these changes over the years, gradually developing a lifestyle to meet their own needs and their child's special needs. This family lifestyle was hard-won, and it was based upon Cindy being a perpetual child.

The Williamses were not ready for the major changes that lay ahead. In addition to her physical disabilities, Cindy was not ready to live without supervision, and the prospect of making a transition to meeting Cindy's adult needs was overwhelming to her parents. Sex education served as a rude reminder that Cindy was growing up, and the Williamses were not ready to accept that fact and all its implications.

Generally, resistance such as that shown by the Williamses is a response to fear of the unknown. Homeostasis can also be based upon unresolved loss and its denial; the attempt to sabotage change may be an attempt to resurrect the past. On the other hand, the origins of family resistance may not be emotional at all, but may simply be based in the family's lack of alternatives.

DISTANCE POLARITY

Distance is an ambiguous term when referring to affection, intimacy, and influence; it covers the wide range between isolation and fusion. Too much distance is experienced as abandonment, while too little is experienced as suffocation. Crises can serve to reawaken the bonds of affection and communication among family members; the threat of loss of things dear, whether routines, presence of significant members, or a way of life, can serve as a reminder to complacent family members, as can the reexperiencing of cooperation and shared goals. Conversely, where habits and routines have disguised the gradual eroding of affection and increased the conflict between individuals, upset and changes may serve to highlight the distance that has developed. Particularly in situations in which resentment already exists, this distance may never be bridged and may escalate family fragmentation.

Not only do families have pecking orders based upon power relationships, they also have a definite "social territory" system that regulates the distance between members. This territoriality serves to maintain appropriate distances between members, and it is enforced by the contracts, role relationships, and feedback systems of normal family interaction. Family structural changes (particularly the kind necessitating the aid of a professional) frequently alter the social territorial balance and distance relationships.

CASE STUDY: THE BROWNES

The Brownes first contacted a counselor in the middle of the night. Mrs. Browne, in a desperate call, reported that her five children were at that very moment fistfighting in the street.

Advised to order them in and to call the police if they refused, she agreed to bring in the family the next day for counseling.

Mr. Browne had died two years before, and Mrs. Browne was left with a 22-year-old (who was recently married), a 19-year-old (who would have gone to college had she not felt so needed at home), and a set of 15-year-old triplets. The triplets were treated as "the kids," while the 19-year-old was cast as a miniparent.

Mrs. Browne spent much time in the session (and evidently at home as well) complaining about how hard she worked and what little appreciation she received. Home life was chaotic, with cooking and cleaning sporadic, discipline overreactive or nonexistent, and much conflict and fighting.

In spite of the obvious need for assistance in regaining order in her home, Mrs. Browne managed to sabotage most of the therapist's attempts to reconcile family differences. She would start and restart arguments, use therapy time to spotlight herself as the victim, and contradict trivial details when her daughters were trying to speak. In addition, she would resist attempts to remove the 22-year-old (married and living elsewhere but still intervening in family arguments) from the problem situations.

Mrs. Browne needed to maintain an atmosphere of crisis in the house. She had continual fighting, arguments, and conflict to occupy her waking hours. She had to keep the triplets in the role of children so that her role as mother remained intact. She needed to have the older daughters invested in family roles to prevent them from leaving. She did all of these things because she needed to deny the profound feelings of grief she felt over the death of her husband, a loss she had not yet accepted. The family was held in the grip of homeostatic paralysis until she could resolve that loss.

Professionals may violate family distance patterns without being aware of doing so. Because regulation mechanisms differ from family to family, professionals may fail to perceive these patterns because they are used to the ways their own families, or families with whom they have worked, operate. Also, unaware professionals may find themselves "triangled" into a family conflict, and consequently their efforts are rendered less effective.

The previously discussed process dimensions of the family focused upon the manner in which crisis affects family functioning, particularly at the second stage of reaction. As the immediacy of the crisis is over and the normal family relationships confront the changed, postcrisis realities, the family system responds either positively or negatively in its coping strategies. Positive coping results in increasingly flexible and adaptive roles and contractual relationships, decreased homeostatic rigidity, and distance adjustments that are more nourishing for the development of the individuals within that family. If the system responds negatively, the family is pitched into role and contractual inflexibility and maladaptive retrenching. Homeostatic paralysis limits the family's adaptive capacity, and isolation and fragmentation ensue.

Impact on Content Dynamics

The content dimensions of family functioning reflect this vitalizing versus disintegrating effect of crisis on the family. The extent to which family members feel loved or unloved may be challenged by crisis reactions. Differences in perceptions of love and distinctions about which behaviors evidence love may become problematic as the process dimensions of family functioning reflect the stress of the crisis. Further, the bonds of love may be shown to be inadequate to counteract the debilitating effects of dysfunctional process—love may not be enough. Similarly, parenting style differences, likely minimized during the regular life of the family, may create serious conflict between the parents and confusion among the children in the chaotic postcrisis environment.

Like individuals, families differ from one another in the ways they show affection and the ways in which they expect affection to be shown to them. It is easy for a professional, caught in his or her own pattern of expectations, to misinterpret differences in family modes of loving as being lack of love. It may well be that in a particular family a child really is not loved or is not shown love appropriately, and the professional can help in that situation. However, the professional must take care to be sure that the problem is not simply his or her misunderstanding about a different mode of loving.

Parents often operate on several levels at once. When establishing goals, expectations, and standards regarding therapeutic services for their child, they function from a rational, problem-solving basis. Later, when observing or evaluating those services, they may operate from a very different mind-set, heavily influenced by family legacies and introjects that demand different standards from those previously agreed upon. The professional may then be surprised at the apparently inexplicable change in the parents' attitudes, as the professional's work is found unsatisfactory, inadequate, or unproductive. Worse, the professional may distrust his or her own abilities in such cases, believing messages implying incompetence from parents whose doubts originate in their own conflicts over values, styles, and expectations.

The intrafamily ledger of obligations and entitlements may be unbalanced by the events occurring during the crisis and by the changed situations following the crisis. This may be intensified by unspoken contractual differences between family members regarding just who is entitled to what and just what sorts of behaviors create what sorts of obligations. Also, the crisis situation may have created new pressures that cannot be tolerated by members who suddenly feel burdened by obligations created by the crisis situation. Such obligations may force that member to avoid dealing with the others to whom he or she feels indebted. Just as friendships are sometimes lost because of indebtedness, families can be similarly affected.

Finally, family legacies—the roles, scripts, and predictions assigned by the family to individual members—may be confirmed or challenged by the crisis experience. Take, for example, a family in which it is assumed that women are unable to handle emergencies. In such a family, the women may handle a crisis by falling apart simply because they are expected to do so. Also, the mere fact that an overwhelming crisis has occurred—a rape, for example—may confirm the legacy to the rest of the family. Conversely, if an emergency occurred to such a family and a woman turned out to play an indisputably strong role in resolving the crisis, the result might be confusion among other family members or within the woman herself. This confusion might cause family members to begin reassessing their basic fabric of legends, legacies, and scripts, and the sources of continuity and stability in family functioning. Again, the family may be challenged to grow and mature from this experience, or it may suffer a weakening of the bonds of family culture, leading to estrangement.

The professional does well to be aware of contradictory behavior that is an outgrowth of an interplay between past and future. Professionals should observe such confusing behavior when trying to differentiate when adults are acting from their rational, fully powered present from when they are acting from their allegiances to the past, attempting to re-create an at-home feeling by being true to values they learned long ago. Professionals also need to avoid being cast as a symbol of the present, because those who are allied with the past will then resist their most sincere efforts.

Troubleshooting Strategies for Professionals

The following troubleshooting questions are useful in assessing family functioning. When faced with a difficult family situation, the professional should ask him- or herself the following questions to assess posttraumatic family functioning:

1. What stage of posttraumatic adjustment—recoil, reorganization, or restabilization—is the family in?

2. Has the family passed from one stage to the next? Does that account for their changing relationships with each other and with me?

3. If conflicts between family members or between the family and me exist, could differences and errors in assumptions about mutual expectations create these misunderstandings? Would clarifying or making those assumptions explicit assist the family? [If appropriate to a professional role]

4. [If the professional works for an agency] Would misunderstandings about the role and intentions of the agency account for the conflict between me and the family?

5. Are there unspoken or indirectly spoken messages about expectations that I am missing or misinterpreting?

6. Could the conflicts, whether or not a result of faulty contracts, have their basis in role expectations that are incompatible, misunderstood, or different now than they were before?

7. Could my own conflicts be the result of misunderstood role expectations?

8. Are there differences between the roles I expected (as a result of my own background) and the roles particular family members play? Am I sure that such differences do not underlie the difficulties?

9. Could the family's demonstrating unnecessary conflicts, divided loyalties, contractual misunderstandings, role adjustment problems, or behavioral difficulties be a means of resisting needed change? (Consider how the problem could function to avoid family change.)

10. [If the professional suspects such homeostatic resistance to change] Is the resistance a result of emotional causes or based simply upon a lack of alternative skills?

11. [If the professional is experiencing conflicts with certain family members] Have I observed the closeness/distance relationships and how they are maintained through communication feedback? Am I transgressing distance limits? Am I unaware of distance messages that affect family members?

12. Am I making accurate assumptions about individuals' distance needs and patterns and about their distance regulation mechanisms? Have distracting patterns changed since the crisis? Does that create individual needs that are currently not being met?

13. [If the professional is becoming entangled in a family conflict] Is there any indication that I am being "triangled" in by one of the members?

14. To what extent has the crisis strained the bonds of affection, disrupted normal parenting functions, and challenged scripts within the family?

15. Have I looked closely at my own affectional and affiliational needs to make sure that I am not projecting those needs in my assessment of the family?

16. Am I clear about my own value structure so that I can avoid negative evaluation of the family on the basis of those values? Is my assessment of the family based upon the extent to which their values contribute to the development and well-being of each member, not on whether they match mine? Have their values shifted as a result of the crisis?

17. Could the crisis experience have created confusion or challenge to the family in the areas of value introjects, projections of belief systems, obligations, and entitlements? Could this confusion explain otherwise inexplicable behavior?

18. Might conflicts between me and family members be based upon those dimensions considered above?

19. In assessing parenting skills, am I basing the evaluation upon my own bias about parenting styles? To what extent has the parenting style in the family changed or deteriorated since the crisis?

20. Are my strategies planned with attention to their likely effects upon the whole family system?

Conclusion

This chapter has highlighted ways in which families respond to crisis. Knowledge of the outlined dynamics provides professionals who are dealing with posttrauma children some conceptual tools necessary for understanding the families and gives some direction in working constructively with them. Each of the process and content functions of the family has been explored in terms of the strengthening or disintegrating effects of crisis on the family system. Educators, therapists, and consultants coming in contact with families of traumatized children or with families who have been traumatized from within must be alert to signs of the family's particular stage in response to the crisis and the manner in which the family functions along these various dimensions toward strength or disintegration.

CHAPTER 7

Trauma Prevention Curricula

For every person who dies, there are at least two other people who are going to be hurt, be it a mother or father or just a person who was a best friend from when they were little kids.

14-year-old friend of a suicide victim

Death and Emptiness are the firm ground upon which life walks.

Alan Watts,
Cloud Hidden, Whereabouts Unknown

OVERVIEW

School personnel, as well as consultants dealing with schools, are called upon to provide prevention programs in many areas of student safety. While crises are often unavoidable, traumatic reactions may often be preventable. This chapter offers a prevention curriculum that provides an inoculation effect for children.

Chapter Contents

There will always be trauma in the lives of children. Death is a fact of life, as are myriad other losses. Regrettably, children will continue to be victimized, and families will continue to malfunction. While crises may not be eliminated altogether, proactive planning and preparation can reduce the damage they do. Crisis prevention prepares children for difficult events that may occur later. Learning experiences can be orchestrated within the child's home life and school curriculum to ready the child for challenges.

What facts and skills should children be taught now to protect them from the possible harm of unforeseen events that might occur later? How can we prepare children without teaching them to fear the future and to adopt defensive postures toward living? Which traumas should the child be prepared for and which ones left to chance? Although these questions are troublesome, they should not lead to paralysis. Children should be provided with two types of learning experiences. First, they need to develop a generic set of skills useful in coping with any sort of traumatic experience. Second, they need to know just what their own reactions to crisis might be and what reactions are normal.

The best way to determine which preparatory skills and learning experiences would be appropriate for a wide range of crisis experiences is to start with an analysis of children's needs during and shortly after critical events. This informal and summary analysis should focus upon children's reactions and the eventual outcome of the events as discussed in Chapter 2, "Children's Reactions to Trauma." Children's acute situational reactions to crisis are themselves frightening and upsetting, and children may be negatively affected in several ways.

Crises are typically experienced as a feeling of being out of control—a time when the individual's capabilities and resources are overshadowed by the situation. During such incidents, individuals are highly suggestible. The event overwhelms the child, who in turn experiences fear, personal inadequacy, vulnerability, and dependence upon others. Because the child is increasingly impressionable during these experiences, he or she risks the secondary reactions of lowered self-esteem, feelings of powerlessness, and heightened levels of anxiety. This erosion of the child's self-confidence and feelings of self-worth results in the need for greater coping efforts and increases the risk of maladaptive behaviors.

The posttrauma cycle is a stress cycle (see Figure 2). Reactions to the crisis create greater stress, leading to symptomatic behavior. Lowered self-esteem and pervasive anxiety lead finally to the development of maladaptive coping behaviors. Each stage is a response to the results of ineffective attempts to cope with stress. At each of the stages in the development of the cycle, however, effective stress management can interrupt the downward spiral. Stress management includes understanding not only the dynamics of the reactions, but also specific strategies useful in breaking the stress cycle. If a child learns to use several coping strategies for managing reactions in stressful situations, those strategies can be transferred to crisis events. More important, if the child has learned which reactions are stress related, he or she will be able to keep those reactions in perspective.

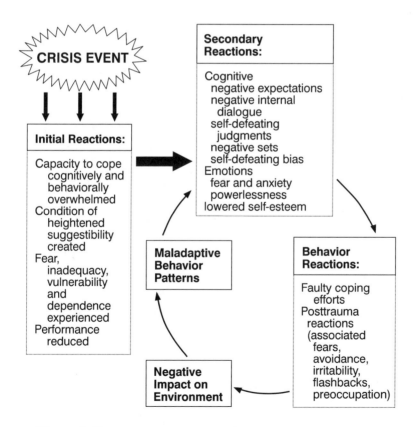

Figure 2. Posttrauma reaction cycle

Analyzing Needs

The crisis situation places intense demands upon the child's ability to communicate. Crisis creates personal and interpersonal chaos, overloading the child's capacity to organize perceptions, thoughts, and plans. This means that the child is frequently unable to determine *what* to communicate to others. The crisis situation is chaotic itself, with disruptions in routines, role relationships, and normal patterns of interaction. Adults are often as confused and disoriented as the children. Simple transactions and interactions become impossible, so the child is frequently unable to determine *how* to communicate to others. Yet while confusion and disorientation make communication difficult, the child's need to communicate is much greater than at normal times. Following a crisis, the child needs to share emotional reactions and disorientation with others to avoid isolation. He or she must ask questions to make sense of the situation. He or she must communicate basic needs. Most importantly, the ability of the child to work out successful coping strategies to deal with the posttraumatic reaction is dependent upon the child's ability to make needs known, to request assistance, and to stand up for his or her rights. This requires the ability to assert.

Times of crisis are times when people need each other. Emotional contact, understanding, sharing, passing information, and assistance of all types are just a few of the supports people in crisis need from those around them. The individual's total configuration of supportive people and the resources they can provide is called the support system.

During crisis, several factors conspire to render the individual's support system inadequate. First, people often limit their support groups to those resources they usually need; little thought is given to "what if" situations. Second, crisis sometimes involves the removal of a key person in the support system, whether through death or through the person's involvement with the crisis. Third, the ability to conceptualize the changed support system and to fulfill those needs is often lacking. While crisis creates increased reliance upon the support system for continued functioning, the system is often deficient. Children, especially, have problems assessing their own support needs and determining how to get them met.

As indicated in Chapter 2, many of the troublesome reactions to trauma are cognitive in nature. Children in crisis often appear overly calm because they are quietly struggling to make sense of the event. Reactions to difficult situations may include confusion and sensory overload, resulting in an inability to act effectively. Difficulty in distinguishing between trivial and important information, and problems in setting priorities, may lead people in crisis to behave in situationally inappropriate ways. Their time sense may be distorted; they may struggle to make sense of incoming sensory data. These various cognitive reactions to crisis may persist for hours and days after the event and may become a problem. A child reacting to trauma may have great difficulty in basic decision making and problem solving, a difficulty which will be compounded if the child is not skilled in either activity. This deficiency leaves the traumatized child without the necessary resources to regroup cognitively.

Finally, following the trauma, the child may be upset by his or her own reactions to the event. Cognitive disorientation, emotional upheaval, and physical symptomatology can be extremely frightening. The crisis situation is experienced as out of control, and then the child is confronted by experiencing him- or herself as out of control as well. This amounts to a retraumatization, and it often has as detrimental an effect upon the individual as did the original trauma. The child doesn't understand that these reactions are essentially normal. The feelings, memories, and troublesome reactions attached to critical incidents are often experienced by children in isolation. Whatever adults know about the frequency of critical incidents or about normal cognitive, emotional, and physical reactions to them, children rarely are privy to such knowledge. Adults rarely talk about trauma with children. As a result, children feel alone when experiencing a crisis, and after reacting to a crisis, they often don't understand their reactions.

This informal analysis indicates five postcrisis needs:

1. stress management skills

2. communication skills

3. skills in identifying and using support systems

4. problem-solving and decision-making skills

5. skill in understanding postcrisis reactions

Since prevention must consist of anticipating a crisis and then taking proactive steps to moderate the effects of the crisis, prevention efforts should focus upon these five areas. Taken together, the acquisition and understanding of these skills amount to a strengthening process, a development of inner resilience to stressors that cannot always be avoided. The first four areas are not trauma-specific. They are integral parts of any personal or character development program. They represent basic skills that facilitate attainment of personal life goals at any level. The fifth skill is trauma-specific. By avoiding the secondary response to crisis reactions, the damage done by the incident is minimized. A comprehensive prevention program includes concept and skills acquisition in each of these five areas. While it is beyond the scope and purpose of this chapter to provide a comprehensive discussion of each area, certain basic aspects of each can be outlined and salient directions defined.

Building Resilience

The informal analysis of children's needs during and shortly after incidents has indicated five areas that need to be addressed in a comprehensive prevention program. One of these areas concerns the understanding of crisis reactions and is specific to traumatic situations, but four non-trauma-specific skills are also important: stress management, communication, support system building, and decision making/problem solving.

A variety of materials and programs already exist that stress a combination of such skills; a few of these programs are listed in Appendix III. Some programs consist of a "cookbook" of group exercises, others are primarily conceptual and theoretical, leaving classroom or group implementation up to the leader. Finally, some programs blend a conceptual direction with structural activities. Leaders are cautioned to have cohesive directions as well as flexibility in choosing and adapting activities to fit the particular developmental, background, and sophistication levels of the group. Children do need a focus, explanatory system, and sense of cohesiveness for what they are asked to do, particularly when they are developing skills in interpersonal contexts. Seemingly random activities that ask them to risk, stretch, and grow with no apparent reason or direction invite resistance. Children also need to be respected as individuals, with their personal differences taken into account. Groups will be more interactive and productive if the activities fit them rather than vice versa.

A complete prevention curriculum would be beyond the scope of this chapter. However, some general considerations that govern the selection of curricula are important. These considerations will apply whether the selection includes supplementary material, general approaches, or complete programs in any of the four areas. Thus each of the four areas will be treated separately, with general directions set forth to provide leaders with an overall "set" useful in curriculum planning.

One issue remains, however: should prevention curricula be kept separate or be infused into the ongoing curricula in the school setting? Following the dramatic child sexual abuse allegations at the McMartin preschool in Manhattan Beach, California, former Richstone Family Center trainer Wendy Deaton advised teachers to take the following steps in incorporating resilience curriculum into the normal school curricula:

1. Use language and concepts that are age-appropriate. This ensures understanding and allows messages to be heard, not just stated.

2. Support children's positive sense of self. Self-esteem is fragile and often the first casualty of abusive situations.

3. Encourage children's freedom to question. This skill is essential to the prevention of abuse and other traumas. If the classroom process discourages the freedom to question, then the process invalidates its own content.

4. Recognize and label feelings. Feelings serve as indicators of inner and outer conditions. Children need to be able to identify and articulate their own feelings in order to understand what they are going through, to recognize when to take action, and to know what to communicate to those who can help.

5. Use games to develop problem-solving ability. Games provide a nonthreatening context in which confusion and difficulties can be encountered and solutions attempted. Talking about strategies does not aid learning as much as applying them under realistic conditions.

6. Reinforce positive ways of handling problems. Within the ongoing context of school projects and interaction, children should explore both positive and negative ways of handling problems. If positive approaches are rewarded, they tend to become part of the child's permanent repertoire.

7. Develop positive communication skills. Communication, the foundation of coping skills, is necessary for children to enlist aid and overcome isolation.

8. Reinforce children's view of the teacher as a trusted adult to whom they can turn. This is the beginning of a support system.

9. Dispel myths about people, the world, and certain experiences. Often children act upon limited or faulty information and in so doing constrict their own options or act in counterproductive ways.

10. Utilize positive prevention materials (as opposed to "Don't do this!" or "Avoid that!"). Positive materials promote strength and resilience rather than fear and defensiveness.

11. Incorporate entertainment and enjoyment to hold interest. Children learn from play. Play is the primary means by which children explore the world, attempt solutions, learn from mistakes, and attempt novel responses. Capitalize on this powerful force rather than fighting it.

12. Support assertiveness, independence, and autonomy.

PROBLEM SOLVING

Problem-solving and decision-making skills are essential for all children. Growth is rarely easy. A child is like a myopic person groping for his or her glasses in the morning; without vision, it is difficult to find the right answers. Yet vision is a product of experience. In crisis the difficulties of growth are even greater due to the abrupt changes, new and overwhelming information about the world, the psyche's natural shock reaction to calamity, and increased stressors. When children are trying to cope with the chaos of crisis or postcrisis situations, they need to have skills for solving problems and making decisions. Learning new skills in a crisis environment is extremely difficult, and the situation deteriorates for the child without those skills. When children have gained experience in making decisions under conditions of uncertainty and have learned a basic repertoire of problem-solving approaches, they are in a much better position to minimize crisis damage. This basic element of character development becomes the key in the prevention of unnecessary psychological and physical harm during crisis.

Most discussions of problem solving and decision making emphasize the rational steps involved with evaluating alternative courses of action. This typically involves some variation of the following six-step method:

1. Problem clarification. Problem clarification not only involves a definition of the problem, but also rules out aspects of the situation that are not a problem. Further, a clear understanding of how the problem maintains itself and why it is a problem for the individual is helpful, as is a statement of what sort of changes in the situation will constitute a solution.

2. Options and alternatives. At this stage, various alternative solutions are generated. To encourage creative thinking, options should be raised whether or not they seem immediately promising. Once several options have been generated more elaboration can take place, with emphasis upon proactive considerations. The goal at this stage is to generate several well-formed solutions for possible consideration.

3. Evaluation. Each of the alternative solutions must be evaluated. The likely outcomes of the available options are compared with the changes in the situation, as defined in Step 1. Each possible solution must be considered in terms of inherent problems, including difficulty in implementation and availability of resources. Any necessary preliminary testing should be undertaken and an open mind maintained in case new options present themselves.

4. Decision making. If the individual is making a solo decision, this amounts to selecting which alternative maximizes benefits and limits liabilities. If a group is deciding, then the problem of consensus must be addressed. This may turn into a political conflict, so procedures for group decision making must be made explicit.

5. Implementation. The elaboration of options undertaken in Step 2 provides the groundwork for implementation. After the decision has been made, an implementation plan must be detailed and accepted. Four of the journalist's W's (who, what, where, and when) must be answered. The "why" has already been established. If an individual has decided upon a course of action, the plan of implementation may not need to be formalized or even recorded. If a group has made a decision, the plan will probably need to be made explicit. Part of a formal plan will include a time line and a system to ensure completion.

6. Evaluation. After the solution is implemented, the results must be evaluated. Did the results meet the needs and expectations that prompted it? Was the problem solved? Were the criteria for solution articulated in Step 1 met? During this process, new alternatives or even new perspectives on the problem may have presented themselves. The final evaluation may have shown the chosen solution to be deficient. In this case, new options can be attempted using the same steps. On the other hand, the solution may prove adequate.

This rational model of problem solving/decision making is presented in fairly full form. It can be presented in alternative ways, however, for different age groups. Young children may not be presented with this model directly. Instead, stories might be read or told to them in which problems are encountered and the children asked in a natural and conversational manner:

1. What's going on here?

2. Why is that a problem?

3. What do you think he/she should do?

4. What do you think would happen if he/she did that?

5. What else could he/she do?

6. Which do you think would be best?

7. What did he/she do?

8. What would you have done? Why?

In individual conferencing this model does not need to be presented directly. Rather, the elaborating questions could be asked and directed in such a manner as to engage the speaker in a rational problem-solving course.

The rational dimension to decision making and problem solving is not the only dimension, however. *How* decision making/problem solving is taught is just as important as *what* is taught. Learning increased autonomy is the content message of problem solving, and that content message should not be violated by a teaching process that invalidates autonomy. Thus Deaton stresses a four-stage process with which the content can be taught in day-to-day classroom interaction. She presents this process for younger children, but it can be adapted for older children when appropriate.

In live problem-solving/decision-making situations, the adult moves through the following steps when the child is ready:

1. The adult makes decisions/solves problems, which the child observes.

2. The adult includes the child in decision-making and problem-solving responsibilities.

3. The child solves problems and makes decisions with observation and some guidance from the adult.

4. The child assumes decision-making and problem-solving responsibility, with an adult serving as a resource.

As Deaton points out, children learn best from modeling and experience; this format of gradual assumption of responsibility allows children the opportunity to evaluate information, recognize alternatives, and take action.

Another dimension of problem solving and decision making concerns the perception and evaluation of feelings. Because children often are taught to discount their feelings, they may confuse thoughts and feelings, ignore feelings as a valid source of inner information, and feel that their emotional reactions are of no importance. This leads to increased isolation and inability to communicate pain. As a *part* of the problem-solving and decision-making curriculum, the following steps should be taken:

1. validate and affirm the child's expression of feelings

2. assist the child in recognizing, identifying, and naming feelings

3. validate intuitive awareness

4. help the child to differentiate between thoughts and feelings

Decision making and problem solving, then, can be taught as a separate curriculum or infused as a supplement to in-place curriculum. In either case, not only should a concise problem-solving method be introduced, but the process dimensions of learning by doing and feelings as information should be stressed.

SUPPORT SYSTEMS

Our normal life routines are carried out within a web of interdependence. People need support from other people—emotional support, nurture, financial support, guidance, correction. People in crisis need more support. Crises deplete resources, alter the balance, create new needs. They can even change the available supports. Whether the crisis comes from within the group or family or from outside sources, existing interpersonal supports may be pushed to their limits and the supports themselves found to be inadequate. Children are especially vulnerable to crises, in part because they may lack the conceptual and emotional wherewithal to build, maintain, and restructure a support system.

There are two keys to an adequate support system. The first is the anticipation of need. Supports cannot be limited to present needs, and they cannot be limited to one's partner, parents, or family. When crises occur the personal situation changes and new needs arise, and this means that new supports must be sought. Yet during crisis the individual is usually the least able to assess personal needs, evaluate the types of support available, and embark upon a project to enlist the appropriate support. Crisis creates change; chaos creates vulnerability and helplessness. The time to engineer an adequate support system is before anything happens. This means assessing not only current needs but also anticipated needs during possible crises.

The second key to adequate support is an external system. This means that supports for one's family life need to include people outside the family. By the same token, supports for one's work life should include supports outside the workplace. Thus if the family or the workplace becomes the problem, the individual is not bereft of support. This is of particular importance for children, because the crises they experience frequently come from within the family, and the family is usually their primary source of support.

No one person or family can do all or be all for anyone else. The world is complex, and so are individual needs. The major content of a support system curriculum lies in anticipating needs, locating people to meet those needs, clarifying what can be expected from those people, and learning how to access them.

Following are eight possible categories of support persons:

1. *Leaders:* These people can help by providing structure and direction. They can be especially important in the chaos following a trauma.

2. *Guides:* Although guides do not set structure, they do help define goals, consider possibilities, and think through positive and negative aspects of alternative courses of action.

3. *Similar Souls:* Such people share common interests, mindsets, and concerns. They can help solve problems and motivate.

4. *Close Friends:* Close friends can provide nurturing, shared intimacy, and emotional support.

5. *References:* Often we need someone to vouch for our character or skills.

6. *Referral Agents:* Agents can provide connections with other human resources.

7. *Mentors:* Mentors provide inside information, performance feedback, and motivation for a novice to explore new

approaches and capabilities. Mentors may be abrasive or demanding.

8. *Other Helpers:* Other helpers can meet more specific needs, such as providing money, shelter, equipment, and safety.

With children, emphasis can be placed upon such institutional supports as police, medical personnel, teachers, and recreational leaders, and upon extended family care providers such as grandparents, aunts and uncles, and family friends.

The use and maintenance of a support system entails drawing upon people selectively as they are needed. This requires skill in choosing and in asking particular persons for assistance. Accessing support involves communicating needs and making requests (see the next section). Enlisting support also entails preventing those persons who are not helpful from getting in the way. In crisis, unhelpful social contacts are not supports. Finally, a formalized list of those in the support system and how to reach them is useful in assessing its completeness. Several operational rules are helpful in maintaining a support system:

1. *Keep it simple:* An attempt should be made to keep the system as simple as possible to minimize the energy necessary to maintain it.

2. *Keep it current:* The relationships should be kept up-to-date so that when support is needed, the resources are informed and appreciative of the need for their assistance.

3. *Keep it equal:* The relationship should be one that both parties feel is fair, whether this is accomplished by returning help, payment of money, a joint sense of accomplishment, or whatever else makes sense. Otherwise resentment and guilt may build up and cloud things.

4. *Keep it external to the job or family:* The relationship should allow the person to engage in conflict or reorganization if necessary without undermining the needed support.

5. *Keep it flexible and open:* The relationship should provide backup support and feedback for the supporter so that he or she can do a more efficient job.

The process of teaching about support systems may be presented in a group problem-solving mode. The group can brainstorm a great deal of the necessary information. One good approach is to begin by presenting a situational problem, then asking what needs a person in that situation might have. Once a set of categories is derived, then the question, "Where might the person go to meet those needs?" can be asked. Discussions may include maintenance questions and methods for requesting support. Finally, a rudimentary chart of each student's personal system may be made. The sophistication of the categories will depend upon the developmental level of the students, and the group discussions will generate an appropriately leveled chart. Such a chart should include phone numbers or locations if possible.

COMMUNICATION

In crisis, communication is the means through which solutions are suggested, decisions implemented, stressors changed, and support enlisted. Not an inborn gift or something that can be learned during crisis events, good communication requires skills, patterns, and intentional actions learned through practice.

Communication skills are taught daily in schools; organized communication skill activities and curricular material abound, and formal and informal instruction go on constantly. This is only in part intentional, because the majority of what parents, teachers, and other trainers teach children is what they do, not what they say. *How* adults communicate with children is much more important than *what* they communicate about. Some 75% of what adults need to teach children about communication is conveyed through how teachers look, dress, move, gesture, speak, and listen.

What the communication teacher *does* is most important. Teachers must model good communication by controlling nonverbal messages, saying what they mean, listening actively, asserting themselves, and letting others in on what they are thinking and feeling. Students learn to communicate by being taken seriously, by being drawn out, and by having their communications reinforced. Communication is two-way, especially in classroom situations; communicative teachers must interact in a real way.

Obvious ways in which communication teachers may block communication and model blocking behaviors include the following:

1. Providing solutions. Despite the efficiency of having the right answers, the act of providing a solution preempts the cognitive process of the solver, implies incompetence, and is an affront to the individual's dignity. Solutions should be provided only when the situational requirements for the answer outweigh the cost in terms of human autonomy.

2. Giving advice. Related to providing solutions, giving advice implies a relationship of partial dependency and should be used only when adequate preparation has been made, ensuring that the individual is "ready" to hear the advice. Giving advice usually generates more resistance than compliance.

3. Preaching. Preaching and moralizing send an indirect message about the student implying a lack of trust in the individual's responsibility, moral sense, or ability to make personal decisions.

4. Warning or commanding. Warning causes resentment, resistance, and rebellion, inviting testing of consequences and polarization.

5. Arguing. Arguing, or even attempts at persuasion through logic, provokes defensive positioning and counterargument. Again, the content of the message is lost to the process dimension.

6. Criticizing. Criticism, however well intended, is experienced as personal assault. Further communication is discouraged because attempts at communication expose the individual to social risk.

Since many of these blocks are practiced unconsciously, feedback regarding communication skills is essential to skill development. One very powerful format for teaching communication skills is triad grouping. Countless exercises can be carried out in groups of three. For most exercises, the three participants assume the roles of speaker, listener, and observer.

The speaker, who is following the directions of the exercise, is the active person, while the listener is the passive participant. This varies, of course, given the nature of the interaction required. For example, in tasks stressing active listening with a reluctant speaker, the listener may do more actual speaking than the speaker yet still be considered the listener because the focus of the exchange is to determine what the speaker is trying to say. The presence of an observer serves two functions. First, when exercises are conducted with large groups, pairs of participants can easily distract each other from the task at hand. The presence of an observer serves to reduce this tendency and to keep the triad focused on the exercise. Second, the observer can give valuable feedback to both speaker and listener as well as sharpen his or her own level of awareness.

Three areas that should always be covered when teaching communication are nonverbal communication, listening skills, and assertion. In teaching adults nonverbal communication skills, the focus is upon controlling the messages sent nonverbally by the speaker, striving for congruity between the message and posture, gestures, and facial expressions. With children, however, the emphasis should be upon learning to "read" another's nonverbal messages. This provides the child with increased awareness and may help him or her in responding to adults during crisis situations.

This leads naturally to listening. During crises, children need to hear what they are told, particularly since their own ability to focus and understand is probably impaired. If children are taught to establish habits of checking out their understanding, asking questions for clarification, and eliciting elaboration until they feel satisfied that they really understand, they will be better able to seek the information they need when they need it. Once again, teachers can teach listening behavior best by modeling and reinforcing.

Listening includes focused inquiry. Table 3 (see page 216) illustrates the subtle differences in questioning strategies that can be modeled by communication teachers. They are grouped along two dimensions. The first dimension concerns the directness of the question, ranging from suggestive comments through facilitative questions to direct questions. The more direct the questions, the more confrontational they are.

The second dimension concerns the particular type of question and is divided between probes for content and probes for process. Content probes include the who, what, why, where, when, and how questions, focusing upon clarification, specification, and elaboration of detail. Process probes explore the implications of the content and

Table 3: Focused Inquiry

	Suggestive	Facilitative	Directive
Probes for content			
Clarification	"Oh? . . ." ". . . it did [or whatever appropriate verb] . . . ?"	"In what way . . . ?" "How?"	"I don't understand . . ." ask directly for deleted information
Specification	". . . yes . . . [pause]" "this was . . ."	"Who [or what, when, where]?"	"Who [or what, when, where], specifically?"
Elaboration	pause, waiting expectantly . . . ". . . yes . . . ?"	". . . and . . . ?" ". . . then what happened?"	"Could you tell me more?" "Would you elaborate more about . . . ?"
Probes for process			
Feelings	convey empathy about expressions of feeling: "I think I might feel . . ."	"Sounds heavy [or sad, etc.]. Could you tell me more about how you feel?"	"How do you feel right now?" "Are you feeling . . . ?"
Relationships	"Sometimes these things change how it is at home, or with our friends . . ."	"Is everything OK with . . . ?" "How are things at home?"	"Do you feel OK about the two of us?" "Does . . . believe you?"
Impact	". . . wow! . . ." ". . . confusing? . . ."	". . . sounds difficult [tough, painful, serious, etc.] . . ." "I wonder what that means . . . ?"	"How important [serious, etc.] was that?" "What sense do you make of all this?"
Changes	"How are things going?" ". . . are other things OK?"	"Are things different for you now?" "Have you noticed other changes?"	"What about [mention changes you see and anticipate]?" "Any [specific changes you are looking for]?"
Transfer	"Sometimes there are similarities . . ." "Other things can get involved . . ."	"Are you seeing similarities?" "Is this affecting something else for you?"	"Sounds like . . . ; what do you think?" "Does this mean that . . . ?"
Choices	". . . thought about what you might be able to do?" "Thought yet about what's next?"	"Do you have any options?" "Any plans yet?"	"What options do you have at this point?" "What are you going to do?"

the interaction itself. These include the feelings, relationships, impacts, changes, transfers, and choices following from the content of the message. Table 3 provides sample questions for illustration.

Assertive communication is essential for children in crisis, who must make their needs known to adults around them. Because material is readily available for teaching assertion skills, assertiveness will not be discussed here except to comment upon congruity. As in other areas, the process of instruction cannot violate the principle or the content of instructions. Assertiveness cannot be taught without the child being allowed to assert him- or herself. Communication cannot be taught as a unit independent from the rest of the experience of schooling. If the classroom is managed so that children cannot practice assertiveness, character development requiring self-expression will be hampered.

Stress Management

The final area of non-trauma-specific prevention curriculum is stress management. An extended discussion of both chronic and situational stress is provided later in this chapter. In general, children do not need to know a great deal about the theory or physiology of stress other than to recognize stress reactions when they occur. More important, children need to be presented with a range of coping strategies and enough practice so that they are able to implement those strategies themselves when necessary. Strategies useful in crisis situations can be addressed in trauma-specific instruction.

Two types of stress affect the child in crisis: background stress and trauma-specific stress. With background stress, children who are experiencing high levels of chronic stress in their daily lives or who have recently experienced other serious situational stressors are at risk for traumatization. Conversely, children whose lives are in a state of balance and equanimity are likely to be less seriously affected by a crisis event. Their psychological reserves are full; they are not "barely hanging on"—they have extra psychic energy to cope with the event. All children have stressors in their lives, and the manner in which they cope with those stressors determines their coping efficiency. Children who are not coping well with their life stress will have great difficulties handling crisis. Prevention programs should include components that teach children how to manage normal life stress.

The second type of stress affecting the child during crisis is trauma-specific stress. An overload of stress may be created by abrupt changes in routines and life circumstances, the entry or departure of significant relationships, or the sudden debunking of cherished assumptions about security and future options. Perhaps worse still, coping strategies that were adequate in precrisis circumstances may be quite lacking in the postcrisis environment. The child needs not only adequate coping strategies, but a reserve of future strategies, flexibility in adapting them, and the ability to access current functioning and coping skills.

The subject of chronic and acute stress management from the point of view of the working professional is discussed later in this chapter. Before determining specifics in stress management training for children, the reader should review that section. The various programs available in elementary or secondary stress management curriculum can then be reviewed for appropriation.

Trauma-specific Instruction

The central focus of prevention is instruction in the structure of reactions to trauma. Stress management, communication, support system building, and decision-making and problem-solving skills are generalizable and transferable to almost any human endeavor. Noncrisis contexts such as social situations, school work, family interaction, and recreation draw heavily upon such skills. While essential to postcrisis stress management, they are not specific to these situations. Knowledge of posttrauma reactions, however, is specific to the posttrauma situation.

As indicated before, crises are compounded by the unanticipated emergence of postcrisis reactions. "Normal" reactions following crisis include various symptoms in each of four separate areas: cognitive, emotional, physical, and behavioral. In addition, reactions occurring during or shortly after a critical incident can differ from those occurring weeks, months, or years after the event.

Experiencing any of these symptoms can itself be disorienting, disturbing, and traumatic, particularly if the individual does not anticipate the experience. This retraumatization can be moderated and possibly altogether avoided if the individual knows in advance that such symptoms are a normal response to trauma. This can be accomplished through a structural preventive program stressing trauma-specific education. An adequate trauma-specific educational curriculum would include the concepts presented below, modified to fit the developmental levels and educational needs of the children involved.

BASIC CONCEPTS

1. Many experiences that could happen to anyone can be traumatic. These include accidents, death of parents or others who have been close, divorce, rape, bad drug experiences, assaults, abandonment, and natural disasters.

2. People differ in their vulnerability to trauma. Experiences not traumatic to some people may be traumatic to others.

3. Various background factors, such as those listed here, make some people more vulnerable than others to trauma:

   prior trauma
   psychological needs
   background stress
   physical fatigue
   family disruption
   recent changes or losses
   feelings of inadequacy
   overly optimistic or negative attitudes
   beliefs

4. Traumas may create various symptoms during or shortly after the crisis. These are, for the most part, normal; they include the following:

Cognitive	*Physical*
confusion	headaches
problem-solving	pounding heart
difficulties	muffled hearing
problems separating	nausea
trivial from more	cramps
important things	sweating
time distortions	rapid breathing
	feeling of faintness
	other signs of shock

Emotional	*Behavioral*
fear	slowness
anxiety	aimless wandering
anger	dejection
irritability	memory problems
frustration	hysteria
	hyperactivity

5. Traumas may also create various symptoms in the weeks, months, or years following the crisis:

Cognitive	*Physical*
fear of going crazy	fatigue
preoccupation with incident	increased illness
orientation toward past	physical concerns
denial of importance	
of incident	
confusion	

Emotional	*Behavioral*
depression	substance abuse
grief	self-destructive behavior
guilt	sleep problems
resentment	social withdrawal
fear of reoccurrence	compulsive talking
oversensitivity	about event
	avoidance of incident
	location
	school or work problems
	relationship or family
	problems
	flashbacks

6. Experiencing these symptoms means the event was serious, not that the person is crazy.

7. Normally, these symptoms initially get worse. It takes time before they get better. Talking about the incident and reacting with counselors, other adults, and even friends will help a great deal.

8. Some of these symptoms may never disappear, or long periods of time may go by and then suddenly symptoms may reappear. This is often related to stress or to developmental changes. When these symptoms are bothersome, it helps to let others know what is happening and to talk about reactions.

These basic messages, central to any trauma-specific prevention program, must be tailored to the group's developmental and experiential levels. The program must be flexible enough to allow for individuals to discuss their own experiences. Developmentally, some children are ready to deal with some subjects before others. For instance, 5-year-olds may talk about frightening experiences, accidents, or victimization, but they will not fully understand discussions regarding death, since their concepts of death are not yet comprehensive (see the discussion regarding loss in Chapter 1).

SENSITIVITY

Professionals who lead prevention sessions must be sensitive to the possibility of trauma-specific discussion eliciting responses in children who have "unfinished business." Children who are especially quiet or distracted during the session may be having difficulty coping with painful memories or feelings about past experiences. The "right to pass" during such discussions must be announced beforehand and respected throughout. Dealing with such material is good if handled sensitively, but callous treatment of posttraumatic reactions amounts to retraumatization. Although it is tempting to use a group member's experience as an example when the child seems to be willing to discuss his or her experience, great care must be taken not to violate the child's integrity. When posttrauma individuals decide to take advantage of what seems to be a supportive environment to share their feelings and experiences, they are often acting upon impulse to break a painful silence. It is almost a compulsive act. When an insensitive or thoughtless leader capitalizes upon such a moment for curricular purposes, it amounts to manipulation. It is likely to push the individual to more disclosure than he or she may later feel comfortable with. This compounds the damage, discourages future trust, and reinforces the child's sense of isolation.

CLASSROOM MANAGEMENT

Classroom management during trauma-specific discussion can be a problem. On one hand, some students may become distracting and disruptive because the traumas from their pasts make the discussion very uncomfortable for them. Frightening images and memories, disturbing feelings, and difficult themes may arise in response to the content of discussions. On the other hand, the distractions and disruptions caused by such children may prevent other students who need exposure to the information from benefiting from the session. Although discussing trauma may be similar in some ways to teaching math, the feelings and needs involved are likely to be more intense. Often such situations are best handled directly; for instance, the instructor may say, "Karen, you are doing [this] and [that], and that is disturbing others. Please don't." At other times an indirect approach is better: "A lot of people find that talk about [this subject] makes them nervous. Let's all take a deep breath and relax, and we'll try again."

Finally, when all else fails, the teacher may find it necessary to send the troublesome child on a special errand or task. In any case, professionals leading such sessions should always assume that disruptive behavior may be an indirect message, and should follow up with an individual conference. Chapter 3 discussed in depth how to handle such a conference.

CONFIDENTIALITY

Another sensitive issue is family privacy, an area that poses an unusual dilemma for which there are no easy answers. Children may need the opportunity to speak out about painful family experiences, but often families have informal and unspoken rules against divulging any information to others outside the family. This factor becomes extreme in pathological families, such as alcoholic, violent, or incestuous families. These families often actively enforce family secrets to prevent the children from disclosing to outsiders any details of the family's abusive behavior. If the prevention class reinforces this conspiracy of silence by not allowing children to speak about troublesome things, the isolation is compounded. However, no one wishes intimate facts regarding his or her life broadcast indiscriminately. Rules regarding group confidentiality are important but not foolproof. Such rules are only marginally enforceable. If a prevention session has 30 children participating, then 29 children from other families become privy to private information, as do their families, other children who are told, and the children's family friends, as well as the leader, colleagues of the leader, and their families and friends. Many parents become concerned when they feel that their child is being encouraged to tell family secrets during class or group sessions.

Thus the leader is again in something of a dilemma. If sharing personal stories is encouraged, the family's privacy may be violated. If sharing is discouraged, children's needs are neglected. While no simple answers exist, a few general guidelines may be helpful:

- Clear rules that address the right to pass, confidentiality, and ownership of feelings and perceptions can help set the structure and a positive tone.

- A clear statement of the leader's own responsibility for reporting abuse or danger can establish parameters for discussion.

- The leader can choose to make an explicit statement to the effect that students should respect their family's right to privacy. Students may be given alternative ways to discuss the issues, such as "I once knew of someone who . . ." or "I have a friend who feels . . . ."

- The leader can model responsible ways to discuss personal experiences.

- The leader should make certain that administrators affected are aware of the nature and process of the discussion, and should ask for their input on setting limits. Their support is essential in case of community repercussions.

- The leader should be clear about personal comfort zones.

DISCLOSURE

In situations where traumas are discussed, the possibility of disclosure of child abuse increases. Children may say things in discussion that cause the leader to suspect abuse. Children may ask to speak with the leader after the session or the leader may wish to inquire further. In any case, where professionals have grounds to suspect child abuse, they probably have a legal responsibility to report their suspicions to proper authorities. Each state varies on liability in these cases, and it is essential for professionals to familiarize themselves with their legal responsibilities. Such liability can create anxiety and hesitancy on the part of professionals regarding their willingness to teach crisis prevention; such anxiety is normal and rational. However, those who work with children should keep in mind that they have a moral responsibility, as helping professionals and as human beings, to do what they can to alleviate children's suffering. Therapists, school personnel, and others who work with children are often the only adults in a position to identify abused or neglected children and to begin the process of social intervention. The best hope of such children is in the hands of those helping professionals with whom they come in regular contact.

Trauma-specific instruction, then, consists of both information and group affirmation, which function as inoculation against secondary reactions to crisis. Trauma creates isolation and the experience of being out of control. These feelings tend to undermine self-confidence and compound the effects of the trauma. Learning about the wide range of normal reactions to critical incidents is powerful affirmation to those children who have experienced crisis.

Conclusion

Building resilience and addressing the confusion created by the chaos of crisis assists children in developing coping strategies. These provide a conceptual set that assist children in making sense of their reactions and the reactions of those around them. In addition to offering children aid and understanding, it is also helpful to give them tools with which to assist their peers. And, to the extent the helping adults in their lives also possess these tools, the more stable children's lives will be.

Raphael et al. (1996) suggest teaching "psychological first aid" skills to parents, teachers, and other helpers. These include the basic

responses of comforting and consoling; protecting; furnishing immediate, practical assistance; providing goal orientation and support for
reality-based tasks; facilitating reunion with loved ones; facilitating
retelling of the individual's own story; allowing expression of feelings; connecting with support and assistance systems; facilitating a
beginning sense of mastery over the situation; and screening for further counseling or intervention.

The next chapter presents a different perspective for the adult
who deals with children's crises. As previously pointed out, the
actions taken by an intervening adult with the child during or
shortly after critical incidents can either compound the harm done
or prevent further harm. One factor directly affecting an adult's ability to intervene effectively is the level of serious stress in his or her
own life. Stress limits the emotional reserves available to the professional asked to cope with children's crises. In addition, dealing with
children's critical incidents can be highly stressful. Long term prevention must address the issues of chronic staff stress and staff
response to crisis intervention.

CHAPTER 8

Managing
Professional Stress

Our work calls on us to confront, with our
patients and within ourselves, extraordinary
human experiences. This confrontation is profoundly humbling in that at all times these experiences try our view of the world we live in and
challenge the limits of our humanity.

Yael Danieli (1994)

OVERVIEW

*Recognizing that professionals dealing with crises are themselves at risk for
burnout and trauma, this chapter addresses the issues of acute and chronic
helper stress management. A brief section discusses special problems regarding
suspicion and reporting of child sexual abuse. The concepts of vicarious traumatic stress and countertransference are explored, and the necessity for self-
care is argued.*

Chapter Contents

While stress is no new topic, much has been learned over the past few years about the unique stressors of, and their effects upon, professionals who work closely with traumatized children. This chapter explores the various dimensions of stress among those who would help children in distress, and draws implications for self-care for professionals. Despite the uniqueness of professional stress, it does come in two types, chronic and acute. Work with traumatized children is often carried out in difficult settings, and this discussion must begin with a look at the workplace itself. Then the special ways the work itself affects the professional can be explored.

Stress is the result of personal investment in difficult situations. If no investment exists, there is no basis for stress. Most professionals decide to work with children for all the right reasons. For the most part they like children, and they work with them because they feel it is important. Professionals who deal with children want to do the right things because they believe that what they do counts. They care, they are motivated, and they are set up for serious stress because of their motivation. Teachers, therapists, and other such professionals are expected to be the do-alls of society. Parents expect them to handle any situation and, worse yet, the professionals expect it of themselves. When stressful situations worsen, professionals often respond by increasing their own standards of performance. Thus the stress cycle escalates.

It is normal to assume that stressful situations directly cause our stress reactions. Yet investigations of the dynamics of stress-related problems show that they are best understood as unsuccessful coping cycles (Meichenbaum, 1985). Each stage is a reaction to the overall situation but also serves to set up the next stage. Because each stage represents an escalation of stress, adversely affecting the total situation, this process is cyclical in nature, as illustrated in this chapter.

The first stage consists of a situation and the individual's *expectations*. If the expectations are reasonable and realistic, there is a better chance of successful coping than if expectations are unrealistic and unreasonable.

The second stage consists of *appraisal:* the situation is evaluated for type and projected outcome. Three styles of appraisal can destine that situation to success or failure. First, certain types of judgments are self-defeating. Black-and-white thinking, preoccupation, categorical and absolutist judgments, overgeneralizations, and "looking for the negative" can place the entire situation in an unworkable, pessimistic light. Second, a self-fulfilling bias may cause a person to concentrate on information that confirms preexisting beliefs and ignore information that contradicts those beliefs. The result is obvious—the person's subsequent experiences confirm the preexisting beliefs. Third, the appraisal stage may create stress due to a person's negative sets. Habitual beliefs, assumptions, and commitments influence the way one interprets situations. Past experiences and emotional vulnerabilities can lock people into negative ways of viewing and responding to the world.

An *internal dialogue* can serve to reinforce the negative appraisal and expectational set, compounding a person's reaction to perceived stressors. This is the third stage of the stress cycle. Not only does the person experience the world in a needlessly negative way, but he or she may repeat such self-messages as "Nothing ever goes right," "You blew it again," "You stupid fool," or "Oh no, here we go again" over and over. Such thoughts happen almost spontaneously and influence the way a person interprets and predicts events. Negative thoughts automatically affect how individuals feel about situations and may create further negative situations.

The fourth stage of the stress cycle is *emotional response,* not only to the external events, but also to the expectations, appraisals, and automatic thoughts accompanying the events. When a person has perceived and appraised a situation as threatening and has listened to automatic thoughts giving negative messages, he or she tends to react emotionally, to get upset. His or her nervous system goes into the "fight or flight" response. This starts the complex physiological arousal process that leads to emergency behavior and further emotional upset.

The key to dealing with the emotional response to a stressful situation is to become aware of it and manage it before it becomes unmanageable. Early awareness buys time to change thought patterns, leave the situation, take action to change the situation, or work at modifying the physiological response itself. Physiologically, the relaxation response is incompatible with the arousal response; hence techniques that increase relaxation decrease emotionality. Getting away, controlling breathing, exercising, and counting to ten are active ways to break the stress response cycle.

The fifth stage of the stress cycle is the actual *response* to the situation. How a person responds in turn affects the situation positively or negatively. Responses are shaped by the appraisal, expectational, cognitive, and emotional processes in the overall interpretation of the event. To the extent those processes have been negative, a person is set up for a negative response. The resulting behaviors then contribute to a disintegrating situation.

A thorough assessment of stress reactions would need to include an assessment of each of the stress cycle stages discussed above.

Stressors in the Lives of Professionals

Professionals working with traumatized children do so in a variety of settings, filling a variety of roles. Some are clinicians in private practice, others social caseworkers in agencies, and still others teachers in the classroom. Some stressors are unique to specific settings, yet there is a common set of difficulties faced by all. These reflect funding constraints, demands from the public and legislators, the intensity of the clientele, and the motivation to serve.

Many stress symptoms are the same as those found in highly demanding jobs in any sector and can be physiological, emotional, or relational. They can affect professional performance and one's ability to carry out team functions. Some occupational manifestations of stress include the following:

work overload
feelings of being overwhelmed by responsibilities
inability to detach from work emotionally
impaired performance
withdrawal from or dehumanization of those served
role strain
decreased satisfaction

Teachers, therapists, caseworkers, and their managers will benefit by closely inspecting how stress is manifested in these ways and learning specific preventive measures to counteract and manage that stress.

Classroom teachers seem to be one of the most highly stressed professional groups. In some ways their tasks are impossible. They must function at the intersection of a matrix of conflicting demands, and everything they do is a compromise between competing needs. At any given time they are expected to meet the widely diverse needs of a class of some 25 to 30 individuals. They are subject to the changing whims of parents, community groups, administrators, and legislators, and they are expected to remedy not only educational but also emotional and social deficiencies. Moreover, teachers as a professional group seem to be more prone to self-criticism, perfectionistic self-demands, and sensitivity to criticism than other groups. As a result they tend to suffer from symptoms of chronic stress. Because of the paradigmatic nature of teacher stress, much of the rest of the discussion in this section will draw upon the stress dimensions of teacher job performance.

Clinicians and other professionals each have their own stressors. Caseworkers, for instance, have the crushing responsibility for the well-being of children in dire circumstances, yet have been given impossible caseloads and overwhelming procedural limitations. Private clinicians must work very closely emotionally with traumatized children, yet they face constant pressure from managed care organizations to limit their treatment costs and constant risk of liability lawsuits, which could close their practices permanently.

Each of the occupational manifestations of stress listed above will be addressed in this chapter, with a focus upon how it affects the professional. Ways to approach the management of each will be outlined.

WORK OVERLOAD

Parkinson's law applies to file cabinets and professional agendas: they always expand to fit the space assigned to them. As if drawn by demons, professionals working with traumatized children work at making work. Clinicians fill their client load to a maximum, spend evenings doing billing and reports, and finish by reviewing professional literature and writing articles. Teachers are worse. If paper correcting is completed, then bulletin boards need revision. If that is done, then new assignments can be designed. If everything is in place and working fine, then a new system is necessary. While making professional salaries, most teachers take mountains of simple correcting home and do it themselves—a task that neighborhood junior high school talent could probably do faster for less than minimum wage.

Teachers often lose track of what they should reasonably expect of themselves. They often adopt an "$n + 1$" criterion of acceptability. If n represents a given level of productivity, $n + 1$ is the level they feel they need to attain to be able to relax and be satisfied. Whatever their output, more is necessary. Few teachers would expect from others what they expect from themselves. This may reflect a "need to be needed," guilt over past "failures," or a need to be beyond reproach. Teachers—and other professionals—need to follow their own advice and set behavioral objectives for themselves, thus limiting their self-expectations. In addition, all professionals rarely seek consultation, yet they need to seek out others whom they can trust to help them sort out reasonable professional expectations.

Overwhelming Responsibilities

Most of the same overload dynamics apply to feelings of being overwhelmed by responsibilities. The specific job responsibilities as outlined in job descriptions and contracts rarely approach those actually assumed by working professionals. Professionals working with children can choose to assume limitless responsibilities, and typically do. The professional context is frequently open-ended; professionals frequently take actions without knowing the results, and get little objective feedback about the outcome of efforts expended on behalf of children. As test scores rarely provide information on the most important kinds of client change, professionals are tempted to turn to newspapers, election results, and feedback from needy families to determine how their children are progressing in terms of recovery, development, and learning. A sense of community emergency exists surrounding services to children at national and regional levels, as journalists, politicians, and interest groups compete to address the latest perceived crises. Yet this agitation rarely serves any purpose other than increasing the number of bureaucratic speed bumps to be negotiated in the provision of service.

Professionals need to step back and set their own service priorities. They should review those priorities with others in the position to evaluate them. They should list the steps necessary to carry out their priorities and celebrate each step as it is taken, irrespective of what supervisors and critics would wish. All professionals, particularly those who work in relative isolation, such as private clinicians, should affiliate with a professional support system in order to keep their work in perspective.

DIFFICULTY DETACHING FROM PROFESSIONAL INVOLVEMENT

Work with children is draining because lives are involved. Troublesome cases and concern over crises can plague professionals during off-hours. The plight of an individual child or family can seem unsolvable. The weight of the pain encountered in clients can generalize to one's perception of the world. The burdens of overload and responsibility can weigh down professionals during the very time they should be recharging their batteries and revitalizing their lives. The helping professions are like the ministry; they are "on" 24 hours a day and lack the social latitude nonprofessionals enjoy. The psychological effect of working in a fishbowl environment reinforces the inability to detach. Professionals take their work home in their heads, if not in their arms, particularly when dealing with crisis situations. Rumination is a professional job hazard.

Overinvestment can produce anxiety or even cause the onset of a more serious stress reaction or burnout. A conscious effort to stop thinking about professional concerns at home; to leave preoccupation with students, clients, or cases at work; and to recognize when work life is intruding upon family life is critical to professionals' well-being. Creating and scheduling time for competing outside interests is not only valid but highly professional, and ensuring that family time gets priority is fundamental. Finally, if professional matters become increasingly difficult to separate from personal life, time off may be necessary.

OVERINVOLVEMENT WITH THOSE SERVED

Personal involvement and the dedicated life are extolled as virtues socially and morally, and particularly in graduate school. Yet overinvolvement compromises effectiveness. A therapist who becomes the social support system for a client, a teacher who spends evenings and weekends as a surrogate parent for a student, a caseworker who makes unnecessary home visits—all not only impair the developing independence of their clients, but undermine the value of the working relationship. Built-up resentments at nonreciprocal relationships and distorted judgments due to personal involvement may offset the gains that the extra assistance and rapport might bring.

Professionals should remember three important points. First, the problem belongs with the client or family, not with the professional. To the extent the professional becomes enmeshed in the problem, the client loses one of his or her major resources—the professional's perspective and objectivity. Second, the professional must acknowledge that human beings have complex problems. With the possible exceptions of cases involving very young children, some cases of victimization, and certain medical conditions, the solutions to those problems must be generated by the person with the problem. In the long run, the professional not only *should not,* but in truth *cannot,* fix anything. Third, depending upon the extent to which the professional's energies are sapped by overinvolvement with a certain few clients, other clients are deprived of his or her proper involvement.

IMPAIRED WORK PERFORMANCE

Professionals are sensitive about their work performance and will be the last to admit impaired performance, even to themselves. *Burnout* is a term referring to a lapse in interest and motivation, decline in performance, and lowered professionalism. Burnout is a result of chronic stress or overwhelming situational stress. A decline in work performance affects professional self-image and creates interpersonal difficulties on the job. Objective feedback is essential to professionals in monitoring their own work performance. This is true in many fields. For example, when asked about personal strategies for professional empowerment, one executive explained that he met every six months for professional feedback with another executive who had a similar placement in a complementary organization. The two men were in positions to observe each other's performance and were privy to gossip from the same professional community. Neither stood to gain or lose from the other's fortunes. Each benefited greatly from the informed, objective feedback. Professionals need to set up such sources of feedback for themselves.

DEHUMANIZATION OF THOSE SERVED

Just as a nurse may refer to a patient as "the coronary in room 310" or "the appendectomy in 218," psychologists often perceive and identify their clients in terms of their particular disorders or behavioral quirks. Teachers find themselves seeing some students in terms of the obstacles they represent. A class of 34 individual lives becomes 29 papers to grade, 5 make-ups to schedule, and one parent conference. Client crises become entanglements to avoid. Dehumanization of those served is a sign of burnout and frequently a precursor to performance decline.

Time away for reflection and replenishment often helps. Alternate avocational interests that enrich personal or professional lives work wonders. Also, getting in touch with "normal," nonneedful people can revive optimism. Exploring career redirection not only keeps professionals abreast of options, but relieves the feeling of being trapped in the work environment.

ROLE STRAIN

Roles are sets of expectations people hold about one another's behavior. When one individual fulfills several roles, different behaviors are expected of him or her. If incompatible or inconsistent behaviors occur, the resulting distress is called role strain. Among all the different service careers, teaching provides the clearest example of role strain. Teachers wear many hats (curriculum manager, disciplinarian, friend, team player, and more), and sometimes the role demands are ambiguous, conflicting, or ill-defined. Role strain can be stressful, depending upon the degree of conflict and the degree of investment the teacher has in meeting all role demands equally well. Clarifying and setting priorities regarding role demands and communicating openly with other team members about mutual responsibilities can help develop an initial understanding of the situation. Additional perspective may be gained by consulting with other individuals outside of the school setting about the reasonableness of the various sets of expectations. Professionals may also seek support and outside resources from other professionals. Teachers should keep abreast of changing expectations and revise their priorities accordingly.

DECREASED SATISFACTION

Too much drain for too long will dry up any well. A professional's energy and enthusiasm cannot be sustained in the face of a constant drain. When role strain, overinvolvement, inability to detach, and work overload begin to take the joy away from professional service, the result is dissatisfaction. Burned-out professionals do not gain a sense of satisfaction from their professional efforts or from themselves. When job roles become limiting due to specialization or increased role demands, new role responsibilities will usually revitalize flagging spirits. Doing research, joining an extra task team, or taking a leadership role may release energies that have been bottled up too long. Similarly, decreased job satisfaction may herald a need for outside sources of fulfillment or possibly reconsideration of present career directions.

Each of the manifestations of stress discussed above can surface independently, but usually they come in a package. Also, professionals can take several specific actions to lower stress levels significantly. As indicated before, each stage leads to the next in an escalating cycle that tends to maintain itself. An adequate assessment of stress-inducing personal traits should be organized that takes into account the major stages of the stress cycle. Similarly, a personal stress management plan should indicate at least one specific strategy for each of the major stages in the cycle.

HELPER STRESS

Dealing with children's crises can be an enormously stressful experience for professionals. As one disaster psychologist commented after consulting on-scene following an airline crash, "One cannot walk through the aftermath of a disaster and remain unaffected." In part, perhaps because we as adults feel we should be able to prevent trauma from befalling children, dealing with children's crises takes an emotional toll. Since this helpless feeling affects professional performance, part of the prevention of further damage to children entails management of personal situational stress. This final section explores the normal reactions for professionals in crisis situations.

While we would like to feel competent in all things, able to walk through turmoil and difficulty unscathed, this rarely is the case.

Most of us look back at our "finest hours" and either laugh or cry at how we felt at the time. It is normal to feel only marginally competent, only partly in control, and barely effective during a crisis. Usually only later do we decide that we really managed the situation fairly well.

Crises in the lives of children tend to engender certain types of unsettling feelings among professionals. Here are some common reactions to both individual and group crisis management situations.

Fear over liabilities. When confronted with catastrophic situations, staff members often feel that they can do little to "fix" the pain. The expectation that "I should be able to fix it" leads to feelings of helplessness. Crisis situations sometimes involve specific actions that can be taken by professionals to reverse conditions, alleviate pain, or set in motion procedures for resolving problems. More often, however, there is little that can be done in this sense. Professionals often feel that they should be doing something more dramatic than taking the supportive steps outlined in this book. In part, this reflects a deeper feeling of despair over the human condition. It is simply one of the hard facts of life that people who don't deserve it sometimes get badly hurt.

Anger. Dealing with children in crisis is disturbing. Feelings of anger and rage are often the result of dealing with children who have been victimized by adults. When managing a crisis situation, it is important for professionals to take two steps. First, when interacting with others during and shortly after the incident, they should make a conscious effort to avoid displacing anger on others. Second, they should find someone to talk to after the incident in order to vent feelings of anger and gain perspective on the incident.

Guilt. Commonly, professionals feel guilt for not seeing the signs of crisis sooner or not acting sooner than they did. Related to this guilt is the unsettling feeling that if only one's training had been better or if only one had read certain books or had handled the incident better, things might have been different. In the desire to protect children and act professionally there is a tendency to adopt perfectionistic standards in self-evaluation, often based upon the fear of being evaluated negatively. While it is important to review performances mentally, at some point it is equally important to let go of self-criticism. Professionals must remember that the past will not be reversed by dwelling on it.

Desire to protect. Listening to the pain and learning about unfortunate situations often creates a desire in professionals to provide 100% protection for the child 100% of the time. Obviously this cannot be, and usually the damage has already occurred. It may be helpful for those working with children in crisis to understand this feeling as a compensation for feelings of guilt, anger, or inadequacy.

Distrust. For the professional dealing with a traumatized child, feelings of distrust of the home situation, the law enforcement system, and the institutional helping system are natural. This distrust is further fed by the "what-ifs." What if the perpetrator gets out, what if the police can't catch him or her, what if he or she gets a light sentence, what if the parents take it out on the child? It is difficult to determine who and what can be trusted when circumstances are chaotic. This may be partly due to the disorienting effects of the personal stress reaction. A good policy is to begin inquiring among other professionals working in the same area— "Have you ever had difficulty with . . . ?" When such network investigations are not possible, direct confrontation with the agency representative or the person the professional doesn't trust is sometimes helpful—"There are some things that are worrying me, Mr. . . . ; frankly, I'm concerned that . . . ."

Old personal issues. Often the child's critical incident or life situation parallels the adult's own past or present. While this can create shared experience, rapport, and understanding, it can also create discomfort, pain, and significant distraction. The adult's unfinished business can interfere with focusing on the child and can drain needed energy. This occurs in several ways. The professional who is aware of the parallels and open to sharing them might become intrusive, spending more time and energy discussing his or her own situation than the child's. Such dialogue can be useful in building rapport, facilitating sharing, or illustrating structural dynamics or solutions; but the adult will likely be hurting more than helping. When the professional is unaware of the parallels, he or she may be influenced by the personal unfinished business in uncontrolled ways. Thus decisions regarding the gravity of the situation, estimates of the impact on the child, and choices regarding what next steps are appropriate may be determined more by the adult's past than by the child's present.

Overinvolvement, unfinished business, or the intensity of the situation can leave the professional in great emotional turmoil, need, and self-doubt. Crisis prevention includes self-care to avoid difficulties later. Following a crisis management intervention, professionals should seek out social supports to discuss the event and explore the feelings the situation has raised, old or new. The perspective provided by an objective, concerned third person can be essential in managing the impact and subsequent effects of the event. If, during the crisis, the professional is unable to focus upon the child because of personal emotional involvement, he or she should realize it and take care of him- or herself, finding someone else to take care of the child.

CHILD SEXUAL ABUSE

Of all the crises that can occur to children, child sexual abuse is often the most problematic to professionals. The situational stress reactions discussed above are intensified due to the nature of the offense. At the same time, there is an increased concern over professional liability, public exposure, and exaggerated media attention. These factors compound the already existing stress: the professional wants to help the child, but is afraid of the entanglement.

Sexual offenses perpetrated on children generate great animosity in adults. This is a deeply embedded reaction; most cultures have strong taboos against sex with children. This animosity is further compounded by recent revelations about the alarmingly high incidence of such contacts, further indicating that a great many professionals were themselves molested or abused as children. In turn, they are likely to experience intense feelings of their own when confronted with an abused child. The manipulative nature of the offense creates another source of intense reaction within professionals. Adults who molest children exert intolerable pressure upon those children to remain silent; they betray the trust children have a right to expect.

Professional liabilities regarding properly reporting cases of sexual abuse have become increasingly stressful. Most states and counties have very explicit laws requiring professionals to report cases of suspected child abuse to police or other law enforcement agencies, and professionals are legally liable if they do not do so. Yet, most professionals—even after specific training—feel confused about what does and does not constitute grounds for suspicion. Certainly direct disclosure counts, but the many possible indirect indicators are often baffling.

Against the legal and moral demands to report cases, some of which are not all that clear to begin with, is a set of threats to the professional who reports even clear cases. Professionals (sometimes justifiably) fear any or all of the following ramifications of reporting:

- having to testify in court

- lack of enforcement agency follow-up

- retribution to the child

- retribution to the professional, physical or otherwise

- inappropriate removal of the child from his or her home and placement in an inadequate, poorly managed facility

- lawsuits for improper reporting

- overreaction by the system

- disruption of school or therapy program for the child

- retraumatization of the child

The family is a strongly protected, quasi-sacred social institution. Even an obviously dysfunctional family may exert political pressure on the school through the community. A professional who questions the integrity of a family frequently ends up isolated. The stringent requirements of reporting may leave the professional feeling that he or she has betrayed the child's trust. The powerful, often vicious, defensive reaction of the family may create a situation in which higher-level administrators or governing bodies will not support the reporting professional and will actually bring organizational pressure to bear on him or her.

But professionals must keep the larger perspective in mind. It is through public disclosure of child sexual abuse and involvement of many social agents that the abusive cycle is broken and the healing cycle begun. While it is tempting for professionals to view themselves as saviors working as solitary agents for children's well-being, the abusive cycle is too pervasive, too subtle, and too tenacious to be broken by one individual. The stresses encountered in combating abuse are best met in the same manner as the abuse itself—through a public, systematic approach that involves a network of support.

MANAGING CRITICAL INCIDENT STRESS

Child sexual abuse is only one of a host of critical incidents that can confront professionals working with children. Parental death, disfiguring accidents, and terminal illness are examples of other problems that can be overwhelmingly stressful to the professional who is attempting to deal constructively with a child. Like chronic stress, critical incident stress must be managed, or the professional will be rendered ineffective. Books, articles, workshops, and training programs abound with stress management theory and technique, and it would be needless duplication to outline such treatment here. There are several strategies central to managing critical incident stress, however, that would be most helpful to mention.

The first and most important thing a professional can do following a crisis incident is to go through a personal debriefing. The importance of this cannot be stressed too highly. Professionals need the chance to share their own reactions with others who are safe, who understand, and who are capable of dealing with the intensity of feelings generated by crisis. Ideally this should take place shortly after the crisis, but can occur with optimal results up to five days later. Background factors that set the stage for vulnerability to the incident must be examined. Personal interpretations of the incident that may be unproductive must be examined. Implications and meanings of the event must be explored. Feelings surrounding the crisis and personal crisis performance must be vented. Alternative ways of handling the emotional fallout must be found. The severity of the incident must be validated and personal adequacy affirmed.

The most difficult part of this process for the professional is finding someone with the requisite skills whom he or she can trust. As a normal preventive step, any human services professional who deals with people should seek out such a person in advance and establish a working relationship with that person, so that he or she is available when necessary.

The second thing the professional must do after a crisis incident is find some other professional who knows of the situation and its context, someone who can provide perspective. This person can be approached for advice, clarification of perspectives, and presentation of options. This is a person with whom professional judgments can be verified and ideas considered. Such a relationship should not be contaminated with emotional overflow; consequently, this person should be different from the debriefer described above.

The third step is for the professional to determine the resources needed and available to handle the situation. These can include human, legal, material-informational, and political resources. The purpose of this assessment is to generate a plan for handling the emergency and for garnering the means necessary.

Finally, it is essential that the professional distance him- or herself from the situation. Professionals need to become involved in recreational, rejuvenating, and normalizing pursuits with people whose company they enjoy and who have nothing to do with the work situation in which the crisis occurred.

Combined with a rational, ongoing stress management program, following these four strategies in managing critical incident stress can do much toward diffusing the debilitating intensity of the experience. The most difficult part is overcoming the inertia and denial systems that bog down professionals following crisis. Having such a plan outlined and ready for personal use prior to crises can help the professional take the necessary steps.

The discussion thus far has been limited to sources and manifestations of chronic stress in the human service workplace. This is a unique workplace, however, involving the professional in ways different from, say, an insurance office or a bank. Work with traumatized children or children in crisis places unusual and highly personal demands upon service providers. To make this clearer, and to provide insight into the special sorts of self-care strategies important in this context, the concepts of vicarious trauma and countertransference must be explored.

Vicarious Traumatic Stress

David Wee, mental health program supervisor and disaster coordinator for the city of Berkeley, California (see pages 113 and 257), has consulted during the aftermath of many disasters around the United States. As part of his response he assists therapists, counselors, and community workers who provide crisis intervention and psychological assistance to victims.

Following the Northridge earthquake, a major earthquake in a large urban area, David Wee and Diane Myers, a disaster mental health consultant in the San Francisco area, assessed the stress reactions of crisis counselors and community workers providing psychological support for victims. Their paper can be found in Appendix II. The workers' reactions reflected the fact that most of them lived in the earthquake area and had been exposed to the same conditions their clients had lived through. Wee and Myers compared those reactions against stress reactions of a group of similar professionals who had also survived the earthquake but were not providing disaster counseling services.

Stress was measured by an adapted version of the Frederick Reaction Index. The crisis counselors reported significantly greater levels of stress than did the noncrisis counselor controls. While there was little difference between groups on the basis of demographic characteristics, disaster experience, disaster recovery, and empathy from others, there were significant differences on reaction index items including decision making, concentration, feeling detached, guilt, jumpiness, numbness, and problems with sleep. Over half of the crisis counselors reported symptoms indicating moderate to severe levels of PTSD. It can be assumed that the difference in levels reflects the involvement in crisis counseling with victims rather than simply exposure to the earthquake.

What was behind these professionals' reaction to their clients, and what does that, in turn tell us about the effects of work with traumatized children?

SECONDHAND TRAUMA

The term *vicarious traumatization* refers to the development of post-traumatic symptoms in a helper (or anyone exposed secondhand to trauma) that parallel symptoms manifested by those who are helped. In part, it is due to the helpers' empathic engagement with the clients, and the clients' graphic accounts of the traumatization. By listening closely and heartfully to the suffering of others, helpers are exposed to the sources of suffering at an intimate level. Therapists must engage their clients intensely; caseworkers and teachers must deal not only with whatever is revealed in the course of their work by their cases and students, but also with the posttraumatic acting out and behavioral manifestations of their pain. The more the helper connects with those helped, the greater the helper's vulnerability to vicarious traumatization.

Figley (1995) proposed a new diagnostic term, Secondary Traumatic Stress Disorder (STSD), to refer to his formulation of vicarious traumatization, Compassion Fatigue. STSD symptomology parallels that of PTSD, including reexperiencing, avoidance, and persistent arousal phenomenon. The difference lies in that the stressor event has occurred to a traumatized person with whom the subject has come into contact, the events reexperienced are images of the helpee's events experienced by the helper, and hypervigilance is experienced by the helper rather than the helpee.

In extending the definition of vicarious traumatization, McCann and Pearlman (1990) point out the cumulative nature of vicarious trauma, emphasizing the profound effects upon the helper's sense of meaning, identity, world view, and beliefs about self and others. Pearlman and Saakvitne (1995) differentiate trauma work from general psychotherapy. They feel that work with trauma forces helpers to

— acknowledge daily the reality of trauma in the world

— become aware of the potential for traumatic hurt and loss in their own lives

— confront reminders of personal past traumas

— deal with helpees who manifest powerful needs and mistrust, and who are reenacting painful, abusive, and denigrating relationships within the helping situation and

— deal with helpees who often cast the helper in malevolent, dangerous, or exploitative roles that may assault the helper's identity

These characteristics of helping relationships with trauma victims as opposed to other clientele groups place special strain upon trauma workers. Not only does the subject matter of the encounter create troubling images and knowledge for the helper, but the trauma-specific behavior and seeming intractability of symptoms make such work difficult and potentially injurious to the helper and his or her family.

Trauma, and exposure to others' trauma in the helping relationship, can bring about disruptions in the developing sense of self. In outlining guidelines for evaluating the possibility of vicarious traumatization, Pearlman and Saakvitne (1995) identify several areas of inquiry that give insight into the nature of the effect of the helping relationship:

Identity, world view, and spirituality. Helpers can come to question who they are in terms of their own histories and self-esteem, as well as who they are as persons and helpers. Their views of causality, life philosophy, and morality may be altered. Cynicism and jaded beliefs can develop.

Self-Capacities. Helpers can lose their capacity to maintain their positive sense of self, and with it their ability to manage strong moods and feelings. Avoiding disturbing stimuli, immersion in work, compulsions, addictive behavior, and loss of connections with others can indicate a diminished self-capacity.

Needs and beliefs. Helpers can suffer distortions in their basic needs and beliefs, as well as in their capacity for meeting those needs. In addition, the esteem in which one holds others can be diminished by exposure to traumatic events. Finally, the ability to perceive the world as a safe place can be unrealistically altered.

Interpersonal relationships. The capacity for engaging in sustained and sustaining relationships can be compromised by exposure to traumatized people. Doubts about self-worth and confusion about self, others, and the world; or withdrawal and other posttrauma symptoms can influence the way in which relationships are experienced: This, in turn, creates further doubt, which influences the helping relationship.

Ego resources. Judgment, the ability to maintain interpersonal boundaries, and the capacity for self-protection can all be affected negatively by work with victims of trauma. This not only decreases available personal resilience, but also decreases the ability to assist others to build their own resources.

Imagery. When memory is improperly encoded and stored, a common occurrence with traumatic experiences, intrusive imagery can follow. With helpers, this can take the form of intrusions of images received from those being helped, and can be distressing to the helper by virtue of their being out of control.

The extent to which those who work with traumatized individuals are affected by vicarious trauma is unclear, though in recent years research has begun to focus upon this problem. In a study of stress in counselors in the field of trauma, Arvay and Uhlemann (1996) found surprising levels of distress compared to counselors who did not work with trauma victims. Two findings in particular deserve note:

1. 14% of counselors working with trauma victims reported traumatic stress levels similar to those experienced by clients with PTSD. This is quite significant, as Arvay and Uhlemann cite other studies that report rates of only 7% to 11% of PTSD among victims exposed to violent crime, deaths, and accidents, and 5% to 8% rates of PTSD among victims of environmental trauma.

2. 16% of counselors working with trauma victims reported emotional exhaustion and burnout. This compares with studies cited showing 2% to 6% rates of burnout among psychotherapists not specializing in trauma.

Clearly, work with traumatized children is risky business. But what drives the indirect transmission of trauma from the helpee to the helper? What is it about the helping relationship that makes self-care so difficult?

COUNTERTRANSFERENCE

The way we perceive those with whom we work is shaped as much by our inner state as by our clients themselves. This was Freud's premise over a hundred years ago and it still stands. The classical interpretation of countertransference emphasizes the interplay between the inner experience of client and therapist. The client and his or her pain cause the therapist's own conscious and unconscious conflicts to surface. That in turn determines how the therapist perceives and reacts to the client, and the sense the therapist makes of his or her behavior. This perspective on the countertransference reaction stresses the subjectivity of the therapist's reactions and focuses upon the detrimental effects upon the client if it is not addressed.

Contemporary versions differ in emphasis (Wilson & Lindy, 1995). Wilson and Lindy describe the primary role of therapists (which can be extended, to a lesser degree, to the rest of the helping professions) as creating a protective context of *sustained empathic inquiry*, within which the trauma victim can integrate his or her traumatic experiences. The underlying premise is that hearing the client's pain and circumstances elicits reactions in the helper that most people would experience in the same situation. This is a more objective interpretation, and focuses less upon the therapist's inner conflicts and needs and more upon the universality of distress.

Both interpretations are valid. Countertransference reactions do arise in the helper, and can have a distorting and detrimental effect upon the helper and those helped. How, then, do we manifest these reactions in our experience and our behavior? According to Wilson and Lindy, countertransference reactions can take two general forms.

One type of countertransference reaction is a general underresponsiveness to the person. This may be experienced by a therapist who finds a particular client, student, or patient hard to like or boring. That person may fail to strike the helper as "interesting" or "important." When we are underresponsive, we dissociate ourselves from the speaker, objectifying and distancing ourselves from the other, and we may experience some or all of the following:

- Our feeling response becomes numb, and we lack the emotionality normally expected in such a situation.

- We deny and discount the reality and validity of our clients' experiences.

- We minimize the seriousness of our clients' situations, in our own mind and often out loud.

- We avoid thinking about our clients or their needs, often allowing ourselves to become distracted by our own thoughts and fantasies while they are speaking.

- We distort our clients' reality in the way in which we perceive or interpret their circumstances or reactions.

- We detach ourselves emotionally from our clients or their situations, withdrawing and intellectualizing.

- We become overly "clinical," joke about them, or become cynical about their motives or adequacy.

This is helper shutdown. Caring professionals who are burning out sometimes become underresponsive after a long period of over-responsiveness. They lose their original motivation for helping and suffer a slow decline of effectiveness toward their clients and feelings of diminished professional self-worth.

Wilson and Lindy's second general type of countertransference reaction is overresponsiveness to the client. When we have an overly responsive countertransference reaction, we lose our objectivity and involve ourselves too much, experiencing some or all of the following:

- We experience deep feelings, either sympathetic or antagonistic to the people we are helping. Sometimes these feelings are confused or even hidden.

- We see (or are sometimes blind to) our own drama and themes being played out in the lives of our clients.

- We feel drawn or even compelled to act, often seeing the situations as compelling and ourselves as a rescuer.

- We become overcommitted to the situations and have difficulty maintaining professional boundaries. We devote too much of our personal and professional time to the cases, compromise normal practices, have difficulty demanding and collecting appropriate fees, or allow ourselves to be intimidated or abused by acting-out clients.

- We allow ourselves to become emotionally or physically involved with the clients in ways that compromise the helping relationship.

- We rationalize our clients' inappropriate behavior and do not help them take responsibility for it.

- We find ourselves sharing our client-specific symptomology, and sometimes become oversensitive to trigger stimuli (sights, sounds, feeling tones, locations, and situations) germane to their circumstances.

- We experience intrusive imagery, such as preoccupation, dreams and nightmares, and flashbacks from the images generated by our listening to their stories.

- We reenact their stories and themes directly and indirectly in our own lives.

- We have a lowered response threshold, producing oversensitivity and irritability that we in turn bring home, producing difficulties in our own family life.

Very few professional training programs—even for psychotherapists—focus upon the effects of countertransference upon the professional. If it is discussed at all, the emphasis is on the way in which countertransference impacts care of the client. Yet the cost is staggering. For their efforts at helping others, caring professionals' lives often show the following results of countertransference reactions:

- We engage in maladaptive coping efforts such as overcompensation, drinking or smoking, other substance abuse, and gambling.

- We often develop difficulties maintaining professional boundaries between ourselves and our clients, coworkers, and work itself.

- Our reactions to the stress of our work spills over into our personal and home life, contaminating our relationships.

- We come to distrust others and the world, seeing them as flawed at best, and sometimes even malicious.

- We experience the world from a victim's eyes, becoming fearful for our own safety and the safety of those whom we love.

- Our ability to experience pleasure and joy becomes muted.

This is a high cost to pay for helping others. These reactions impact our lives, be we psychotherapists, teachers, nurses, social workers, or mothers and fathers. Whenever we enter a helping relationship, countertransference may occur, sabotaging our relationship with the one we are helping, as well as with our family and ourselves.

STRATEGIES FOR SELF-CARE

As discussed above, much of the symptomology of vicarious traumatization parallels that of burnout. Thus, planning for self-care necessarily includes some of the strategies listed. In addition, much can be done to work with the intrusive imagery and overarousal characteristic of vicarious trauma.

Yassen (1995) outlines an approach to individual self-care and prevention that includes physical, social, and professional approaches orchestrated into a personal plan. These strategies range from strenuous exercise and dietary control to meditations and trainings. Lists of coping strategies abound in professional as well as popular literature, but most focus upon "normal" stressors rather than the special stress of accumulated traumatic images and reminders of human suffering. Personal plans must address the extent of physiological overarousal and emotional distress or numbing. The effects of work upon family and other personal relationships must also be considered and addressed. The development of nonwork, non-trauma-related interests, particularly those providing an active outlet for personal expression and creativity, is important.

Munroe et al. (1995) point out that individual approaches are not enough. Since the problem is generated in part by the workplace, teams of professionals who deal with traumatized children need to address the workplace contribution to individuals' distress. Munroe et al. recommend incorporating the awareness of the depleting aspects of the work into the organization's attitudes toward and procedures for conducting business. This acknowledgment can do much to remove the isolating and disintegrative effects of compassion fatigue. Preventive measures can be incorporated into the workplace culture.

These strategies are all helpful and integral to the prevention of helper stress. Yet there remains a dimension not yet discussed. One of the least talked about areas in trauma work is the intensely personal level affected by the work. In reports of self-care attempts by trauma therapists (e.g., Arvay & Uhlemann, 1996; Wee, 1996 see Appendix I), one of the least utilized, but potentially most helpful and rewarding, strategies is personal therapy for the helper. The effect of the work upon one's view of oneself, others, and the world; the meaning of one's work and one's other interests; the course of one's relationships; and the effects of one's past life experiences upon the present are all areas that must be continually explored and integrated if one is to remain effective at helping others. To avoid confronting the deeper issues raised by the work is to miss the opportunity of a lifetime.

Investments in Helping

We help with our hearts. While we bring expertise to our encounters with those whom we work, it is in our relationships that the most good is done. The risk of working with others is great under the best of conditions, but increases dramatically if the relationship is not clear. Our personal investment in the helping relationship can obscure that clarity.

In the process of giving a covert operation assignment to Captain Willard, the commanding general in Francis Ford Coppola's film *Apocalypse Now* explains the behavior of Willard's target by reference to the darkness lying within all of us. "There is," he comments, "a conflict within every human heart between the rational and irrational, good and evil. And good does not always triumph. Sometimes the dark side overcomes what Lincoln called the 'better angels of our nature.'"

Sometimes we find ourselves drawn as if hypnotized toward the dark side of life as reflected in the lives of those whom we would help. Our attraction to our work sometimes leaves us questioning whether we are voyeurs. We get "hooked" by stories of violence, twisted sexuality, or destruction. Vicariously experiencing that which both draws and repels us, we are permitted to see the forbidden through our clients' eyes. We may experience discomfort and repulsion or we may even reject our clients but, like "rubberneckers" jamming traffic to savor an accident, we find ourselves straining to witness the evil of the world.

Psychoanalysts lay this compulsion at the feet of dark impulses toward destruction existing on a subconscious level, held in check only by the veneer of civilized restraint. Others see it as a recognition that human life—however controlled and sanitized we have attempted to make it—is, in reality, "nasty, brutish, and short." We are transfixed by misfortune like deer in the headlights of life.

Whatever the origin, we identify with the suffering of those we help. We inoculate ourselves against our coming horrors, and seek to take arms against those that have already ravaged us. Our moral compulsion to mitigate the pain of those we help gains energy from our own humanness, our own vulnerability. By soothing others' wounds, we calm our own. Yet there is more to our work then replaying our past. Our choice to mitigate others' pain is more than an investment in healing our own wounds.

The work of helping others has an archetypal dimension. We, like warriors of old, set sail toward trouble. We seize the opportunity to look into the jaws of life and death and hold them in our unblinking gaze. We grapple with the forces of despair. In so doing, we take on risks. We know we are likely to incur damage to our spirits by stepping into the arena of human suffering. But we do so in part because we sense a great prize for ourselves and for all others. If we can succeed in dealing effectively with human trauma, we can only do so by growing at the very points at which we are most limited. Our ability to do sustained and effective work with other human beings depends upon our ability to integrate and balance the light of compassion and empathy with the darkness in our own lives.

One psychologist who worked with rescuers following the Oklahoma City bombing reported her feelings about the work in a letter:

> I'm not sure why I was initially drawn to work with rescue personnel. It may have had something to do with my own needs to

rescue, or to be a part of something big and exciting. But lately it has become more and more special. It is a little like going to church, and the debriefing sessions are almost like prayer. We get closer to the heart of things, there.

There seems to be a special light surrounding many people who work in service to others. Whether the pain of that work is compensated by the growth of spirituality or central to it, personal evolution seems to be a part of the process.

HELPING AS ALCHEMY OF THE SPIRIT

In the middle ages, those seeking to understand the seeming chaos and suffering in the world looked for a key to transform the baser metals of the world into the most precious. The philosopher's stone was thought to be a chemical element that would enable a wonderful process to occur. It was not something to be valued in and of itself, like gold, but rather took its value from its usefulness. It would show the mutability of all manifestations of nature, and spell out the connectedness of humans to the cosmos.

We long for a substance that will transform the ordinary into the extraordinary. But drugs, alcohol, gambling, workaholism, and even wealth—all fall short of being the agents of transformation we seek. We long to turn the baser elements of our lives, and of humanity in general, into the higher form of existence for which we feel we are destined. We seek an authentic agent of transformation that will draw out and purify us, pulling us forth.

And what will it take to bring about such radical transformation? What sort of substance, agent, or content of experience will drive this process? And what sort of fire is necessary to purify our base metal?

What is the purpose—in our own lives—of our work with others? What did we seek in choosing lives of service rather than the more "normal" self-serving careers we might otherwise have pursued? We could have gone into sales, finance, or plastics. We might have done quite well in real estate or lab technology. Yet we chose a different path.

And however grand our intentions, our motives are always mixed, we being the humans we are. Some of our reasons we hold to the light of day, congratulating ourselves for our virtue, courage, and self-sacrifice. Others, some of which have already been discussed, are more obscure. We may need appreciation or crave others' needing us, or we may delight in the power implicit in our helping role. We might find validation for our fragile self-structure, or may even be drawn by a compulsion to view and embrace the darker sides of the human experience.

Yet, however mixed our motives, however unholy our desires, by taking on a life of service we nevertheless place ourselves on a developmental hotseat. By answering the call to help, a call that incites our baser as well as our higher motives, we are drawn forward.

Whether we are teachers, health care providers, social workers, or psychotherapists, service to others in need and pain provides a crucible. By finding the inner and outer resources to meet the demands of our work—demands so intrinsically challenging that we daily risk sliding backward into despair—we grow farther and more fully than would otherwise be possible. By facing and transforming the fires of our work, we may refine our very souls.

Conclusion

Working professionally with children who have been traumatized becomes very personal, whether as therapists, teachers, or in other capacities. This work calls into question our own childhood, traumatic, and existential human issues. When we become overinvested and overloaded, we are affected at very deep levels. Our sense of purpose, our capacity for sustained and intimate relationship, our personal integrity, and our experience of self can be impacted negatively. Like Pandora's box, the realities of childhood trauma release toxins into our adult lives that are not so easily put away.

Proactive and strategic stress management can help, but is often not enough. It is critical for professionals working in this field to look for more than palliative self-care measures, and to see the stress, eustress, and distress they experience as an inexorable call to personal growth and transformation.

Afterword

Whether the inevitable crises in our children's lives become traumatic depends in part upon the response of caring professionals. The first step in dealing with childhood crisis is prevention, starting with awareness of its frequency and manifestations. This knowledge includes the professional's awareness of his or her own history of personal crisis, and how that affects interpretation of and response to crisis in the lives of the children he or she serves. Thus prepared, the professional can begin to assess the needs of those children for prevention. As the last chapter indicated, children can be inoculated against the traumatic effects of crisis through a proactive prevention program.

The second step in dealing with crisis is intervention. Concerned, aware crisis intervention has several dimensions. As Chapter 3 points out, intervention on an individual level differs from intervention on a group or class level. Crisis intervention skills and procedures on both those levels can be preplanned and provided in advance, before crisis strikes. Additional dimensions to be considered are the effects of crisis upon the family and the need to work with the family in providing appropriate help for the child. Chapter 6 discussed the family's reaction and suggested ways to approach the family constructively. Getting appropriate help for the family often involves referral to outside mental health professionals, and Chapters 4, 5, and 6 discussed not only the therapeutic process, but also ways in which educators and therapists can work together to complement what each other can offer the child.

The third step in crisis management concerns those who serve the children. Airlines suggest to passengers that in the event of trouble, parents should first put on their own oxygen masks, and only then get oxygen to their children. It is a simple truth that an unconscious parent is of no use to a child in distress.

This book has provided the background necessary for accomplishing each of these three steps. Its intent has been to arm professionals with the information, perspectives, and strategies with which they can prevent the seemingly inevitable crises suffered by children from becoming unnecessary trauma. What this book cannot provide, however, is the planning, policy making, and skills acquisition necessary for implementation. That can be done only in the field. That is the charge for, and the professional obligation of, the reader.

Disaster Mental Health:
Impact on the Workers

David Wee, M.S.S.W. and Diane Myers, R.N., M.S.N.

Note: References cited are listed at the end of this appendix.

Mental health workers and people who work with adults and children in the wake of disasters and traumatic events often experience immense satisfaction with their work. The satisfaction may come from providing the consultation, intervention, and support that makes a critical difference in helping people begin the process of recovery, regain some feeling of safety, or return to normal routines. The rewards and satisfactions of disaster mental health work are also balanced with the secondary trauma of being exposed to the experiences of disaster and trauma survivors. Helpers may experience physical, emotional, behavioral, and cognitive reactions in the hours, days, and months following disaster crisis intervention. The literature describes some of the stresses and reactions of mental health workers engaged in long-term disaster recovery. Information provided by disaster mental health workers providing crisis counseling services to persons impacted by the Northridge earthquake in 1994 exhibited significantly higher stress responses than mental health workers not providing crisis counseling services.

The literature on the stresses for long-term recovery workers focuses primarily upon American Red Cross and FEMA workers. Myers (Hartsough & Myers, 1985) describes numerous stressors for disaster workers, of which two types, event stressors and occupational stressors, are the most prominent in long-term recovery efforts. Myers also identifies the typical phases involved in disaster work and the stressors inherent in each phase for the workers, including the "letdown" involved after long-term disaster assignments. Eby (1984) outlined some sources of stress for Red Cross workers involved in small, local disasters as well as those Red Cross workers who responded repeatedly to major disasters.

Stress reactions experienced by long-term disaster recovery workers fit characteristics of those of the cumulative stress category (Myers, 1995). The most common reactions include fatigue and depression; concentration, memory, and cognitive problems; irritability and interpersonal conflicts; anxiety, especially related to job tenure and to obligations at home that are "left undone"; feeling unappreciated; distancing from others and from the job; cynicism and negativity; use of derogatory labels; "sick" or gallows humor; blaming others; poor job performance; absences; physical complaints and illness; accident proneness; and alcohol and substance abuse.

Studies have examined the impact of disaster recovery work upon mental health staff providing postdisaster counseling. These studies recommend that this specialized group of disaster recovery workers pay special attention to their vulnerability to stress and posttrauma sequelae, lest they become "victims-by-proxy" (Bartone, et al., 1989; Berah, Jones, & Valent, 1984; Fredrick, 1987; Hodgkinson & Shepard, 1994; Raphael, et al., 1984; Winget & Umbenhauser, 1982; Mitchell, 1983). Other research suggests that workers continue to experience significant levels of symptomatology during their entire tenure of disaster support work. In their study of disaster crisis counselors, Hodgkinson & Shepard (1994) found significant levels of symptomatology twelve months into the disaster recovery work. Symptoms most frequently reported included cognitive difficulties, depression, and feelings of inadequacy and insecurity.

Figley, in his research and work on "compassion fatigue" (1995), or secondary traumatization of persons caring for victims of trauma, notes that nearly all of the hundreds of reports focusing on traumatized people exclude those who were traumatized indirectly or secondarily, although DSM-IV (APA, 1994) clearly indicates that mere knowledge of another's traumatic experience can be traumatizing. It would seem evident that mental health counselors listening to the experiences of victims of disaster would clearly be "at risk" for this secondary traumatization. Difficulty dealing with the pain of others may lead counselors to abandon their work with traumatized people (Figley, 1989). Despite current knowledge about the impact of trauma on the primary victims, little has been empirically researched or written about the "cost of caring" (Figley, 1982, 1989). It is vitally important to know how disaster mental health counselors are affected and, in many cases, traumatized as a result of their exposure to victims.

The Northridge Earthquake Crisis Counselor Study

The "Northridge Earthquake Reaction Questionnaire" was developed to measure the stress response of mental health workers providing crisis counseling services to earthquake victims ten months following the Northridge earthquake. The questionnaire was designed as a training tool to educate crisis counselors about the long-term psychological effects of the Northridge earthquake on the impacted population and on themselves as counselors. The Los Angeles County Department of Mental Health hired personnel to provide counseling services. The services were funded by the Federal Emergency Management Agency through the Center for Substance Abuse and Mental Health Services Administration, the Center for Mental Health Services, and the California Department of Mental Health. Questionnaires were distributed at five trainings for disaster crisis counselors, ten and eleven months following the Northridge earthquake. One training had participants who were mental health workers and not involved in the disaster crisis counseling program, who are used as a comparison group. Additional questionnaires were distributed using a "snowball methodology" to secure additional mental health worker respondents who were not involved in the disaster crisis counseling program. A total of 198 mental health workers completed the questionnaire.

The "Northridge Earthquake Reaction Questionnaire" asks for demographic information, information about the crisis counselor's disaster experiences, damage, progress toward physical recovery, empathy received from others, responses to the Frederick Reaction Index (Frederick, 1985), and general comments. The Frederick Reaction Index-A is a Posttraumatic Stress Disorder (PTSD) scale that has twenty-eight items and includes a 5-point scale from "None of the Time" to "Most of the Time." The items specify reactions based on the DSM-III. Scoring ranges from 0 to 4 for each item, with a total of 80 possible points. Some items are phrased in reverse order so that scoring is not always in the same direction. Degree of severity of PTSD ranges from "doubtful," when the score is less than 12, to "very severe," when the score is greater than 60.

Results

Demographically, the crisis counselors responding to the question-naire were female (n = 151); middle-aged (mean age 40.66 years); and ethnically diverse, with 59.1% (n = 118) Caucasian, 21.2% (n = 42) Latino, 11.1% (n = 22) African American, 3.0% (n = 6) Asian/Pacific Islander, and 5.1% (n = 10) other. The respondents were well educated, with 54.0% reporting earning a master's degree, 74.2% (n = 147) working disaster mental health workers, and 25.3% (n = 50) reporting other employment as mental health workers. The number of disasters experienced in respondents' lifetimes was a mean of 3.3 disasters with a range of 0 to 20 disasters.

Almost all of the mental health workers personally experienced the Northridge earthquake, with 66.2% (n = 131) experiencing damage or loss of property and 54.0% (n = 107) reporting that they feared they would die. The group of respondents with damage esti-mated that their progress in repairing damage from the earthquake averaged 56.1% recovered to normal. Of all respondents, 91.4% (n = 181) reported stress since the earthquake, with 79.3% (n = 157) reporting some level of stress-related problems now. When asked if they experienced stress-related problems since the earthquake, 51.5% (n = 102) of the respondents answered yes. The stress response to the Northridge earthquake as measured by the Frederick Reaction Index-A showed that 41.4% (n = 82) of the respondents had Frederick Reaction Index scores that placed them in the "Doubtful Degree of Disorder" for Posttraumatic Stress Disorder related to the earthquake. Of the residents having scores that put them in a mild to very severe "Degree of Disorder" group for Posttraumatic Stress Disorder, 30.8% (n = 61) had scores in the mild, 21.7% (n = 43) had scores in the moderate, 5.1% (n = 10) had scores in the severe, and 1.0% (n = 2) had scores in the very severe degree of disorder.

The disaster workers providing counseling to disaster survivors reported higher levels of distress as measured by the Frederick

Reaction Index-A than those of nondisaster workers. The mean Frederick Reaction Index scores for disaster workers was 18.37 and for nondisaster workers was 13.84. The difference in group means is statistically significant (p<.05). Examination and comparison of the disaster workers and nondisaster workers on demographic characteristics, disaster experience, disaster recovery, and empathy from others for the two groups resulted in no statistically significant differences between the groups (p<.05).

Discussion

The mental health workers in this sample were primary victims of the disaster, with the subgroup of disaster mental health workers showing evidence of secondary traumatization. The postdisaster stress response of mental health workers following the Northridge earthquake is identified with 58.6% of the sample reporting stress reactions in the mild to very severe degrees of Posttraumatic Stress Disorder. Providing mental health services to disaster victims during long-term recovery appears to be associated with increased levels of stress for the workers doing this work. The disaster worker group was significantly more distressed than were the nondisaster workers. These findings suggest that the primary and secondary traumatization of mental health workers providing disaster mental health services needs to be examined.

Additional considerations needing further study are the effects of predisaster stress reactions already present in the population, self-selection related to working in a disaster mental health program, and attending disaster mental health or stress management trainings. The intensity, duration, and nature of experiences of the disaster workers in their counseling of earthquake victims need to be examined. While further research is needed in this area, the findings of this study suggest that greater attention needs to be paid by mental health workers who are personally impacted by disasters such as earthquakes and who then go on to provide mental health services to earthquake victims and other victims of trauma. The impact of these two phenomena on workers' psychological health, family life, and professional careers must be better understood so that preventive approaches can be developed to mitigate negative effects.

References

American Psychiatric Association. (1994) *Diagnostic and Statistical Manual of the Mental Health Disorders*. 4th ed. Washington, D.C.: American Psychiatric Association.

Bartone, P., Ursano, R., Wright, K., & Ingraham, L. (1989) Impact of a military air disaster. *Journal of Nervous and Mental Disease*. 177, 317–328.

Berah, E., Jones, H., & Valent, P. (1984) The experience of a mental health team involved in the early phase of a disaster. *Australia and New Zealand Journal of Psychiatry*. 18, 354–358.

Eby, D. (1984) A disaster worker's response. *Role Stressors and Supports for Emergency Workers*. DHHS Publication No. ADM 85-1408. Rockville, Maryland: National Institute of Mental Health.

Figley, C. (1982) Traumatization and comfort: Close relationships may be hazardous to your health. Presented at Families and Close Relationships: Individuals in Social Interaction conference. Texas Tech University, Lubbock, Texas

Figley, C. (1989) *Helping Traumatized Families*. San Francisco: Jossey-Bass.

Figley, C. (1995) Compassion fatigue as a secondary traumatic stress disorder: An overview. *Compassion Fatigue*. New York: Brunner/Mazel.

Frederick, C. (1987) Psychic trauma in victims of crime and terrorism. *Cataclysms, Crises, and Catastrophes: Psychology in Action Master Lecture Series*. Washington, D.C.: American Psychological Association.

Frederick, C. (1985) Children traumatized by catastrophic situations. *Posttraumatic Stress Disorder in Children*. Washington, D.C.: American Psychological Association.

Hartsough, D., & Myers, D. (1985) Disaster work and mental health: Prevention and control of stress among workers. DHHS Publication No. ADM 85-1422. Rockville, Maryland: National Institute of Mental Health.

Hodgkinson, P., & Shepard, M. (1994) The impact of disaster support work. *Journal of Traumatic Stress.* 7, 587–600.

Mitchell, J. (1983) When disaster strikes . . . the critical incident stress debriefing process. *Journal of Emergency Medical Services.* 8, 36–39.

Myers, D. (1985) Helping the helpers: A training manual. *Disaster Work and Mental Health: Prevention and Control of Stress Among Workers.* DHHS Publication No. ADM 85-1422. Rockville, Maryland: National Institute of Mental Health.

Myers, D. (1995) Worker stress during long-term disaster recovery efforts. *Innovations in Disaster and Trauma Psychology, Volume One: Applications in Emergency Services and Disaster Response.* Baltimore: Chevron Publishing.

Raphael, B., Singh, B., Bradbury, B., & Lambert, F. (1984) Who helps the helpers? The effects of a disaster on the rescue workers. *Omega.* 14, 9–20.

Winget, C., & Umbenhauser, S. (1982) Disaster planning: The mental health worker as victim-by-proxy. *Journal of Health and Human Resources Administration.* 4, 363–373.

A Frequency Study Showing the Correlation Between Childhood Trauma and Maladaptive Adolescent Behavior

Up until now, the problems of understanding and managing children in crisis (e.g., children who have suffered loss, victimization, or pathogenic family systems) and adolescents with maladaptive behavior problems (e.g., drug and alcohol abuse, suicidal behavior, running away, serious school attendance problems) have been treated separately in empirical research. If the association between children's crisis experiences and subsequent behavior problems in adolescence could be established, the effective management of both types of situations could be enhanced.

In order to establish the association between childhood critical incidents (CCIs) and maladaptive adolescent behaviors (MABs), 203 adolescents were surveyed, using questionnaires developed in conjunction with an advisory group of 30 student peers. Also, 4 adolescents were trained as peer testing assistants to help administer the questionnaires in order to minimize reactive effects toward the testing situation. A causal-comparative design was utilized to test two hypotheses: that there would be a significant and positive correlation between CCIs and MABs, and, second, that certain parental responses to children during crisis would have a moderating effect upon maladaptive behavioral outcomes.

Higher frequencies of CCIs were found to be significantly associated with higher frequencies of MABs; $F(2, 189) = 25.87$, $p<.001$. Adolescents who had experienced the greatest number of critical incidents also engaged in the greatest number of maladaptive behaviors. Additionally, adolescents' reports of their parents' responses during the crises were analyzed regarding their correlation with subsequent behavior. Parental response patterns were found to have a differential effect, with three patterns positively correlated with higher rates of MABs and one pattern associated with lower rates of MABs.

One-way ANOVAs were performed to determine whether parental response indexes (generated by a factor analysis of response items) were associated with differential levels of MABs. Adolescents reporting high levels of MABs tended to report their mothers adopting "withholding" ($F[2, 185] = 6.5$, $p<.001$) or "inadequate" ($F[2, 185] = 12.80$, $p<.001$) response styles or their fathers adopting "reactive/escapist" ($F[2, 185] = 24.45$, $p<.001$) response styles. Conversely, students with low levels of MABs reported their fathers adopting "supportive" ($F[2, 185] = 2.98$, $p<.05$) response styles. An analogous positive effect, however, was not shown for mothers.

Data generated by this study indicate that childhood critical incidents may be strongly contributing factors to the development of maladaptive adolescent behavior. Further, this study indicates that parental response to the child during and shortly after the incident may significantly moderate the long-term effects of the crisis. Thus the present study sought to establish the general connection between antecedent events and subsequent maladaptive behaviors directly in addition to exploring the moderating effects of certain types of parental interventions.

Nature of the Study

The study used the methodology of causal-comparative research (Isaac, 1971). Adolescents' maladaptive behaviors were examined in terms of both childhood critical incidents and parental interventions. The purpose was to discover the effects of past events.

Sample Selection

The sample consisted of 203 adolescents from a relatively stable suburban community in Southern California. In order to reduce confounding variables, these were predominantly white, middle-class children, ages 15 to 17. Specifically, 133 subjects came from the community comprehensive high school, from five junior/senior–level English classes, including two advanced placement, three regular enrollment, and one lower-level placement. As all students must take English, this distribution was considered to result in a roughly representative sample of the student population at the school. Completing the sample were 70 continuation high school students of equivalent age from the same community. These students were included to ensure a sampling of chronic school attendance problems. (California operates special continuation high schools in each community for students seriously at risk of dropping out. These students characteristically have problems with attendance.)

These adolescents were queried as to their backgrounds, their history of critical incidents, the manner in which their parents or other significant adults responded to their crises, and their current behavior. Anonymous questionnaires were utilized for the reasons outlined below and were developed with the assistance of a panel of some 30 adolescents in order to maximize accessibility and relevance.

To minimize the reactive effects of perceived adult censure, male and female peer assistants were recruited to help administer the questionnaires and answer questions regarding item and procedural clarification. These experimental arrangements were adopted upon recommendation by the panel of peers, who were asked to comment on how the research could be done in a nonthreatening manner. It was felt that the above arrangements maximized the likelihood of sampling accurate information and minimized the possibility of reactive effects contaminating the data. The questionnaires were administered to whole classes to further minimize the pressure to withhold information, and names were not asked in order to guarantee anonymity.

Hypotheses

The following two hypotheses were tested by the study:

1. There will be a significant positive correlation between childhood critical incidents and the frequency of subsequent maladaptive adolescent behaviors as measured by self-reports (on the Critical Life Events Survey and Current Maladaptive Adolescent Behavior Inventory).

2. There will be a significant positive correlation between the frequency of negative parental/adult responses to childhood critical incidents and the frequency of the children's subsequent maladaptive adolescent behaviors as measured by self-reports (on the Parental/Adult Response to Crisis Checklist and Current Maladaptive Adolescent Behavior Inventory).

Definitions

Childhood critical incident. Any psychological trauma in childhood that overwhelms the individual's capacity to cope.

Parental/adult response. Those communicative interactions occurring during or after a child's critical incident that are (or are perceived by the child to be) in response to that incident.

Maladaptive adolescent behaviors. Behaviors detrimental to the well-being of the adolescent; for the purpose of this study, the following will be considered MABs:

1. alcohol or other substance use

2. attempted suicide or suicidal ideation

3. running away

4. serious school nonattendance

Posttraumatic stress response. Response to critical incident occurring after exposure, including acute reaction immediately following the incident and delayed response occurring months or even years following the event.

Loss. A class of critical incidents including death of parent or other loved ones.

Victimization. A class of critical incidents including assault, rape.

Pathogenic family structure. Family relationships involving disturbed patterns of communication, coercive power distribution, inadequate resources, or antisocial values. Critical incidents involving pathogenic family structure include incest, alcoholism, and parental fighting.

Assumptions

The following assumptions provided the basis for the procedures used in this study and the interpretation of results.

1. Adolescents, if provided reasonable assurance of anonymity to avoid stigma or other consequences and if under minimum peer or adult pressure, can and will disclose truthful sensitive information about prior events and current behavior. While this is assumed, the rationale for adopting the specific instruments utilized to elicit this information is presented in the Limitations section below, under "Reactive Effects of Experimental Arrangements."

2. Maladaptive adolescent behaviors can best be understood as delayed stress responses to childhood critical incidents. This explanatory model, developed to account for adult disorders resulting from combat or catastrophe, has recently become part of the psychological lexicon. This model, placed in a child developmental context, provides the operational connection between past experiences and current behavior.

Methodology

This section is devoted to the methodology utilized in the study. First, the methodology will be described, and then the research design will be outlined, including specification of variables and the research hypotheses. Next, a pilot study will be reported. This is followed by an explanation of the instrumentation, including construction of the questionnaires. Procedures followed in the study will then be described, and the analysis of the data will be outlined. The limitations of the study will then be analyzed and evaluated.

DESCRIPTION

This study utilizes a causal-comparative methodology (Isaac, 1971), establishing relationships among independent, moderating, and dependent variables by ex post facto correlation.

RESEARCH DESIGN

Questionnaires were utilized to gather self-reports of adolescents' background experiences and current behaviors from a sample of 203 adolescents (see Sample Selection, above, for details). The variables are formulated as follows:

Independent variables. Adolescents' self-reports of experiences during childhood that at the time overwhelmed their capacity to cope (childhood critical incidents), as indicated on a checksheet (the Critical Life Events Survey). Included are a wide range of such incidents (e.g., death of parent, sexual assault, divorce of parents, mental abuse) selected by a panel of 30 peers as being most critical. Space was provided for writing in repeats and events not listed. In addition, for each incident subjects indicated their age at the time, the severity of the incident, the degree to which they received support from their parents or other adults, and how stable the family was at the time. These latter factors can be treated as intervening variables (see below).

Intervening variables. Self-reports of the responses parents and other significant adults made to subjects during and after their critical incidents were collected on the Parental/Adult Response to Crisis Checklist. The same panel of peers was convened to discuss and determine a range of possible responses. The ten responses deemed most helpful and the ten responses deemed most hurtful by the panel were then randomized on the checklist, and subjects indicated separately how each parent and one other significant adult responded to them during their worst critical incidents.

Dependent variables. Maladaptive adolescent behaviors were sampled by self-report. MABs included serious school attendance problems, suicide ideation or attempts, drug and alcohol abuse, pregnancy, and running away. Serious school attendance was determined by enrollment at the continuation high school, as the predominant criterion for enrollment is a significant attendance problem at regular high school. Other maladaptive adolescent behaviors were sampled by self-reports on a checklist designed to maximize self-disclosure by being brief, anonymous, and matter-of-fact.

This study seeks to specify the relationships holding among these variables.

PILOT STUDY

The instruments utilized in this study (see next section) were pilot tested for adequacy of directions, clarity of questions and response procedures, and content concepts, as well as for administrative time. Subjects included those students who were initially used to construct the questionnaires. Through follow-up interviews, the instruments were evaluated and revisions made. The administrative procedure was formalized so that training of test administrators could begin.

INSTRUMENTATION

Researchers have generally supported self-reports as valid sources of data regarding sensitive issues (Gelles, 1978; Lourie, 1977). Adolescents, however, tend to either minimize or exaggerate their chemical use (Harris, 1980), so a data collection instrument that minimizes the interpersonal reaction effects of the testing situation was deemed necessary. Similarly, those exposed to victimization tend to underreport (Meizelman, 1978), so the same considerations applied regarding the need for anonymity in instrumentation.

The following instruments were utilized in the study:

1. Background and Current Status Questionnaire (BARC)

2. Current Maladaptive Adolescent Behavior Inventory (CMABI)

3. Critical Life Events Survey (CLES)

4. Parental/Adult Response to Crisis Checklist (PARC)

Copies of these four instruments appear at the end of this Appendix.

Due to its nature, this study required many data regarding previous experiences and current behavioral patterns. No existing tests that have been normed fit the requirements of this study. While some instruments concerning alcohol and drug use are available, they are far too long and cumbersome to be included in a test package without seriously compromising the student's ability to complete the testing. Instruments had to be designed, then, that could fit the demands of the test situation. Another requirement was that the tests had to be understandable to adolescents and sufficiently nonthreatening to encourage truthful responses. This section will detail the process by which these instruments were constructed. Considerations regarding validity of the instruments will be discussed in the section concerning threats to internal validity and in the section on methodological assumptions. Self-rating scales have been increasingly shown to be valid and reliable, and are currently widely used (Parker, Parker, Brody, & Schoenberg, 1982).

Constructing the Critical Life Events Survey. Adolescents are willing to discuss critical incidents—their own or those of others—when they feel comfortable about the context. They need reasonable assurance of confidentiality and a place where they will not have to make a public display of their misfortunes. But, perhaps more important, they need an organized format in which to present their experiences, which can be quite complex and confusing, and they need terminology available to them that is clear and unambiguous. For this reason a peer advisory group was formed of some 30 adolescents to help construct the questionnaire and determine language appropriate to it.

The group began by brainstorming the range of events that could befall children in the process of growing up and that would possibly be traumatic. Similar events were then consolidated, and extreme, fanciful, or wildly improbable events were eliminated from the list. The remaining items were rank ordered according to the group's perception of the severity of the event. Terminology was examined to ensure accessibility and clarity. Finally, 16 items were chosen as the most important. Several questions were formulated that could be answered with a yes or no, by using a Likert-type scale, or (in the case of age) directly with a numerical answer. These questions were then placed on a grid format so the respondent could first indicate whether a specific critical life event had occurred and then answer the various questions concerning that event.

Constructing the Parental/Adult Response to Crisis checklist. This same group of advisory peers was then asked to list, in their own words, all of the ways in which adults had responded to them when crises had occurred. Some 40 responses were recorded on a chalkboard so that all could see. Each item was considered for clarity, and a number were revised, broken down into components, or eliminated because of generality or profanity. The group was asked to favor medium-generality terms (such as "listened well") rather than terms that were too general to be meaningful (such as "helped me") or too specific for the test situation (such as "maintained good eye contact"). The resulting list was rank ordered (from the worst to the best possible responses), and the top 10 and bottom 10 were selected. The resulting list of 20 parental responses was scrambled and listed in random order. Next to each response was a place to be checked if the response was experienced. Columns for mother, father, and other adult were provided. Respondents could then check just how those adults had responded to them during their worst crises.

Constructing the Current Maladaptive Adolescent Behavior Inventory. The literature is mixed about the validity of self-reports in areas of maladaptive behavior, tending to support their use but indicating that subjects have a tendency to underreport in cases of sexual abuse and overreport in cases of drug use. On the other hand, for the purposes of sampling the general population, self-reports are the best available, and, keeping the caveats in mind, can be considered generally reliable. In order to obtain the most reliable self-reports possible, the adolescent peer group was again involved to help construct a nonthreatening questionnaire.

Upon the group's advice, it was decided to allow respondents to evaluate their own maladaptive patterns in the sense of determining if their drug use was "heavy," for instance, or whether their suicidal ideation was "occasional" rather than "frequent." Further, it was determined upon their advice to keep the number of questions to a minimum. Likert-type scale responses were adopted to allow frequency data to reflect the extent of involvement in the particular behavior.

Constructing the Background and Current Status questionnaire. Questions regarding parents' social/economic status and family structure were asked, as well as age and sex. With the exception of age, all responses required only checks in appropriate spaces.

PROCEDURES

The questionnaire packets were administered to subjects at their school classrooms by the experimenter and a group of four trained peer test administrators. The peers were trained during the pilot study and were available to answer questions, clarify terminology, and assist subjects in answering questionnaires when requested. The central function of the peer assistants was to circumvent possible fears of divulging sensitive material to adults. They were also trained to review questionnaires upon completion in a manner that did not disclose the content of the answers, in order to ensure as few missing answers and incomplete responses as possible. The questionnaires were administered to whole classes to minimize further the pressure to withhold information, and names were not asked in order to guarantee anonymity.

DATA ANALYSIS

Correlations between the variables were statistically determined; analyses of the hypotheses included intercorrelational matrices, factor analysis, and other analysis as appropriate. Each variable consisted of a set of items (e.g., MABs, the dependent variable, consisted of five items: drug and alcohol abuse, suicidal behaviors, and so on). The specific items as well as patterns of items were tested for correlation. Inferences were drawn from specific item relationships, according to the hypotheses.

LIMITATIONS

In order to assess the specific limitations of the study design, each possible source of invalidity as identified by Campbell and Stanley (1966) was explored and refuted (some of Campbell and Stanley's categories apply mainly to experimental or quasi-experimental designs and do not apply to this study).

Possible Threats to Internal Validity

Instrumentation. Aside from attendance at the continuation school (considered highly predictive of serious school attendance problems), the only instruments utilized in this study were the questionnaires. These remained constant across all groups being tested. One possible source of instrumentation invalidity was the procedure involving help in filling out portions of the questionnaire some students may have found confusing. The subject was able to choose either the tester or one of several student assistants to provide clarification. This was done to circumvent the inhibiting effects of either adult or peer or male or female interaction over sensitive information. The risk of contamination was controlled by the training of the assistants in how to clarify each question and how to project a warmly empathic but neutral position regarding content items. Missed responses were minimized by visual check by assistants, but subjects were first shown how to fold the questionnaire in such a way as to hide the content question from the assistant's view.

Another possible source of instrumentation invalidity concerns the reliability of the instrument itself. It was not known whether subjects would answer items concerning critical incidents the same way upon retest. This problem is compounded by the nature of the material being sampled. Obtaining a test-retest reliability coefficient would not be helpful in this case because of the contaminating reactive effects of testing. Pretest/posttest differences on retrospective self-reports regarding material of a highly sensitive nature are quite likely to differ, in that taking the test for the first time could well initiate a process of further recall within the subject. This has been termed the *preamble effect* by Cantril (1944) in his discussion of measurement as a change agent. At bottom, the issue of the adequacy of the instrument reduces to whether other methods (such as open-ended questions, personal interviews, or interviews with others) are likely to be better. It was determined that the value of anonymity as well as the structure and focus of the questionnaire offset the possible values of interviewer rapport or a more open-ended questionnaire. Further, interviewing others or researching records presented practical difficulties due to the sample size needed and would not reflect the subjects.

Differential selection of subjects. Because this design was constructed to sample background factors among differing groups, preexisting differences were controlled by stratification, not avoidance. In analyzing data, control groups for each background difference or each behavioral difference were formed from within the sample.

Thus subjects in this study were used as their own controls. Taken to an extreme, groups of subjects could be selected according to the maladaptive behavior pattern they exhibited to ensure diversity. What makes that unattractive is the need to sample a wide range of adolescents and avoid the possible contaminating effects of statistical regression. Using conventional wisdom as a heuristic, then, it was determined that a representative sample of regular high school students (approximately 2/3 of the sample) combined with an adequate number of continuation students (approximately 1/3 of the sample, who ensured an adequate sampling of maladaptive behaviors) provided sufficient diversity and an approximation of representativeness. As the purpose of the sampling was to explore background differences in relation to current behavior (as opposed to determining relative frequencies of current behavior), this approximate representativeness was deemed to provide adequate protection against threats to internal validity due to selection bias.

As to the extent to which the sample adequately represents the population studied, it must be made clear that the sample is nonrandom but stratified, and generalizations are limited to the populations studied. Stratification measures include parameters to maximize representation. As English classes are required of all comprehensive high school students, all students funnel through them. This presented a unique opportunity to access a stratified sample. The ten or so courses offered varied according to level (advanced, regular, remedial), and classes were sampled proportionately. This provided a roughly representative sample (n = 133) of all students in the school. The continuation school student sample included all those present on the day of testing, a total of 70 students.

Possible Threats to External Validity

Interaction effects of selection bias. The population sample includes fifteen 18-year-old adolescents from a predominantly Anglo, fairly stable, suburban middle-class community in Southern California. The first question is, assuming the subjects sampled to be representative of that population, to what extent are the results generalizable to a larger population? It must be answered that populations differing in significant ways (in terms of ethnic and socio-economic class, inner city or rural, and so on) are likely to produce different results. Specifically, mean values of frequency of both background incidents and current behaviors could differ significantly as could the nature of each. Less obvious but more important, cultural and ethnic variables influencing family patterns of response toward children's crises could be expected to influence postcrisis functioning differentially. Indeed, that differential effect is one hypothesis the study sets out to establish. Among different groups, specific parental responses could differ in both frequency and meaning. Consequently, results of the study must be considered only tentatively generalizable, particularly among the parent response variables. Further, among diverse populations, the results may be of more heuristic than descriptive usefulness.

Reactive effects of experimental arrangements. Of the several possible methods of sampling the data, the format of anonymous questionnaires was adopted on the following basis. Information about critical events in childhood involves evoking unpleasant memories and associations. Often subjects are unwilling to disclose such sensitive information publicly, because of fears of stigma, embarrassment, and rejection. To talk about an event with another person somehow raises a new issue of the meaning of the event and the adequacy with which one dealt with it then and now. Further, descriptions of current behavior frequently amount to admissions of guilt (legal or moral) and raise fears of social or legal consequences as well as personal rejection by the interviewer. For these reasons, an anonymous questionnaire was chosen as most likely to elicit accurate information by minimizing reactions of nondisclosure to the social pressure of interviewers. Second, scaled responses as well as checklists were constructed to assist subjects in organizing and presenting their experiences. This was deemed necessary because of the inhibiting effects upon memory and expression of painful or embarrassing experiences. Finally, in order to minimize the reactive effects of perceived adult censure, both male and female peer assistants helped administer the questionnaire and were available to answer questions regarding item and procedural clarification. These experimental arrangements were adopted upon recommendation by a panel of peers who were asked to comment on how the research could be done in a nonthreatening manner. It was felt that the above arrangements maximized the likelihood of sampling accurate information and minimized the possibility of reactive effects contaminating the data.

• • •

On the basis of the above considerations, it was concluded that the study design remains sound, and the results generalizable within the limits discussed in the section above on the interaction effects of selection bias.

This study sought to investigate the relationship between psychologically traumatic events in childhood (childhood critical incidents) and subsequent maladaptive behavior in adolescence. This ambitious project could perhaps be best pursued with a large sampling representing diverse regional and ethnic populations and studied longitudinally. Unobtrusive observers could record all critical incidents befalling the population, assess the involved family and support system dynamics surrounding each child at the time of the incident, and follow each child into adolescence to assess his or her behavior further. Several difficulties are inherent in such an approach, however. First, it would take 15 to 18 years to complete the project. Second, a prohibitively large research team would be required. Third, and more important, observations and cross-validations do not capture what is essentially a highly personal and subjective event. Often traumas are aggravated by the responses of those surrounding the victim; consequently the interaction itself is suspect, as is the appraisal of the event by family or outside observers. Finally, any such presence of observers and testers would contaminate the situation with possible reactive effects.

Memory is notoriously subject to distortion, exaggeration, and selective amnesia. This makes the subject's recall of childhood events a tenuous database from which to draw generalizations. However, due to the considerations noted above regarding outside observers, and due to the same vulnerability on the part of family or other involved persons, combined with the inherent subjectivity of trauma, the subjects themselves appeared to present the best possible source of information regarding their own critical incidents.

Thus this study approached the subjects themselves, specifically, a population of Southern California, predominantly Anglo, middle-class adolescents. These adolescents were queried as to their backgrounds, their history of critical incidents, the manner in which their parents or other significant adults responded to their crises, and their current behavior. Anonymous questionnaires were utilized for reasons outlined above and were developed with the assistance of a panel of some 30 adolescents in order to maximize accessibility and relevance.

Results

This research study investigated the relationship between children's background of critical incidents and subsequent maladaptive behavior. Specifically, two questions were addressed:

1. Are childhood critical incidents associated with maladaptive adolescent behavior?

2. In what way does parents' manner of responding to their children's critical incidents affect subsequent maladaptive behavior during adolescence?

DESCRIPTION OF THE SAMPLE

This section consists of three parts. First, the various characteristics of the research sample will be described, including student demographics, family demographics, and students' past experiences and current behavior. Second, a description of the scale construction used in testing the hypotheses is offered. Construction of the critical incidents scale and maladaptive adolescent behaviors scale, as well as the parental response index, is described, and reliability of the scales reported. Third, the various relationships found among the data that bear upon the research questions will be presented.

Student demographics. Students surveyed ranged in age from 14 to 19 years, with 17-year-olds constituting 53% of the sample. Table A.1 indicates frequencies and percentages of age groups represented. Subjects were nearly evenly distributed by sex: 105 were male (52%) and 98 were female (48%). A total of 75% were Anglo; the remaining 25% were divided nearly evenly among African Americans, Hispanics, and Asians.

The sample was compared on the basis of family composition, education, and occupation. In terms of composition, 56% reported living with both parents, 27% with a single parent, and 17% with a parent or stepparent.

Finally, the students were compared as to what sorts of maladaptive behaviors they had engaged in. Each of these was reported in the form of frequency, ranging from the extremes of "none" to "often" in appropriate terms.

Table A.1.
Ages of the Students Participating in This Study

Age	Students from regular school		Students from continuation school	
	n	*%*	*n*	*%*
14	3	2.2	2	2.9
15	1	0.8		
16	23	17.3	32	45.7
17	71	53.3	23	32.9
18	30	22.6	12	17.1
19	5	3.8	1	1.4
Total	133	100.0	70	100.0
$\overline{X}$	17.05		16.66	

SCALE CONSTRUCTION

Scales for each variable were constructed to allow analysis of data provided by the study in order to test the hypotheses. The construction of these scales is described below and reliability data provided.

Constructing the Critical Incidents Scale. A simple scale for critical incidents was constructed. This was summative, a simple count of the types of incidents experienced (not their quality or intensity). Table A.2 indicates the percentage of the sample experiencing each type of incident. The most frequently experienced event was the death of someone close, which was experienced by 57% of the sample. The mean frequency of events was 2.66, with 12% experiencing no incident on the list and 11% reporting 6 to (a maximum of) 10 events. The experiences of the sample are summarized in Table A.2.

Table A.2. Frequencies for Critical Incidents

Event	Students experiencing event	
	n	*%*
Death of parent	11	5
Death of someone close	115	57
Frequent moves	84	41
Physical/mental abuse	31	15
Sexual assault	16	08
Serious accident	33	16
Child molestation	6	3
Pressure by gangs	12	6
Foster placement	12	6
Mental hospital/group home	16	8
Parental rejection	28	1
School failure by sixth grade	8	4
Divorce/stepparent conflict	69	34
Parental fighting	84	41
Family alcoholism	39	19
Incest	1	

NOTE: The total sample size was 203. Of this number, 24 experienced none of the critical life events included in this study.

Constructing the Maladaptive Behaviors Scale. Two methods of constructing the maladaptive behaviors scale were considered. The first was a simple count of the behaviors engaged in by the students, each behavior weighted by the intensity of the experience. Students could engage in from 0 to 6 behaviors. Frequencies were as follows: 33% of the sample engaged in 0–1 behavior, while 30% engaged in 4 or more. When these frequencies are weighted by intensity of experience, reliability for the resulting scale (measured by Cronbach's alpha) was .75. This scale provided a numerical value that directly represented behaviors in the world for comparison purposes. In other words, groups of students could be compared using this scale without the confusion introduced by an elaborate weighting system.

From a clinical perspective, however, this scale lacks sensitivity to the important differences between types of maladaptive behavior.

There is a qualitative difference between an occasional beer and one attempt at suicide. In order to increase the variability of the scale by incorporating clinical judgments of the relative importance of the different behaviors, an attempt was made at devising a weighted scale. This weighting scheme ranked behaviors in terms of clinical seriousness or importance.

After consultation with two other judges, the following scheme was employed for the purposes of weighting. In cases of runaways, one time was added to frequency count if any of the times exceeded one night. The usage level of cocaine was computed at 1.5 times marijuana or alcohol. As suicide attempts were considered the most serious on the list, attempts were multiplied by two and an extra point was added for frequent thoughts. This attempt at weighting is arbitrary, but it appears to be an improvement over no weighting system at all.

Frequencies of maladaptive behaviors in the sample utilizing this weighted scale are presented in Table A.3. Cronbach's alpha for this scale remains .75, providing a reliable scale that reflects the relative seriousness of the behavior.

Constructing the Parental Response Index. Prior to the study, a group of 20 students was asked to generate a list of the ways parents might respond to their children's crises. The resulting list of 35 responses was ranked from most to least helpful, as judged by the students. The best and worst responses were then randomized and incorporated into a checklist.

In the current study, students were asked to check off those responses that their parents actually adopted during their (the students') crises. Students indicated how their mothers responded to their crisis and how their fathers responded to their crisis. A principal components factor analysis was performed on each set of parent data to see whether particular parental responses coalesced into identifiable modes or styles of response. The factor loadings for mothers' and fathers' responses are given in Table A.4 and A.5, respectively. These tables present the correlations of particular responses with the factors (modes of response), as well as the reliability of the scales suggested by the factors. The mothers' modes of reacting to their children's crises are shown in Table A.4. On the

TABLE A.3. Number of MABs Experienced by Students

Number of MABs	Students from regular school		Students from continuation school	
	n	*%*	*n*	*%*
0	49	39.8		
1	53	39.8	5	7.1
2	21	15.8	13	18.6
3	7	5.3	11	15.78
4	3	2.3	18	25.7
5			19	27.1
6			4	5.7

basis of an informal content analysis of the factor loadings, factors were named for the apparent emotional set underlying them. Factor 1 consisted of items suggesting warmth, acceptance, and accessibility and is consequently named "supportive." Factor 2 consisted of items suggesting a focus upon the parent's own reactions rather than upon those of the child. Thus Factor 2 was named "withholding." Factor 3 consisted of items suggesting an inability to deal with the child or the situation in an effective manner and is named "incompetent." Cronbach's alpha for these scales is .88, .75, and .62, respectively. The relatively low reliability of scale 3 is perhaps explained by the fact that the mothers' largely negative responses were split between Factors 2 and 3, leaving only three items in Factor 3. The resulting three styles of children's crisis management will be associated with adolescent behavioral outcomes in the next section.

The fathers' modes of reacting to their children's crises are shown in Table A.5. Two factors were derived from the fathers' responses and named in the same manner as those of the mothers. While content items in Factor 1 differed slightly, the apparent underlying emotional set appears to be clearly the same, so Factor 1 was also labeled "supportive." Factor 2 consisted of a content item reflecting an apparently mixed emotional set including elements of overreaction and escapism; thus it was termed "reactive/escapist." Cronbach's alpha for these scales is .91 and .79.

Table A.4. Mothers' Responses to Crisis

Variables	Factor loadings: three factors		
	1	*2*	*3*
	Supportive	*Witholding*	*Incompetent*
Expressed worry	.52		
Allowed me to talk	.66		
Showed warmth, acceptance	.69		
Gave reasonable assurance	.70		
Listened well	.67		
Respected privacy	.57		
Came through in past	.62		
Showed patience	.70		
Showed understanding	.68		
Made helpful suggestions	.67		
Was there when needed	.70		
Focused on self		.74	
Denied seriousness		.76	
Shrugged off my feelings		.64	
Concerned about how it affected self		.56	
Unable to cope			.71
Told me not to talk about it			.55
Made false assurances			.73
Eigenvalue	6.73	2.21	1.24
Percentage variance explained	34	11	6
Reliability Cronbach's alpha	.88	.75	.62

RELATIONSHIPS FOUND AMONG THE DATA

The scales described in the previous section were devised in order to test the hypotheses of the study. This section describes that testing and reports the extent to which the data support those hypotheses. Hypothesis 1 reads as follows:

Table A.5. Fathers' Response to Crisis

Variables	Factor loadings: two factors	
	1 Supportive	2 Reactive/escapist
Was there when needed	.80	
Made helpful suggestions	.77	
Came through	.77	
Showed warmth	.74	
Showed understanding	.73	
Showed patience	.73	
Listened well	.71	
Gave reassurance	.70	
Allowed me to talk	.70	
Made assumptions		.71
Blamed me		.69
Shrugged off my feelings		.67
Concerned with self		.67
Focused on self		.67
Made false assurances		.58
Didn't want to talk		.56
Eigenvalue	6.70	2.87
Percentage variance explained	33.3	14.3
Reliability Cronbach's alpha	.91	.80

Hypothesis 1. There will be a significant positive correlation between childhood critical incidents and the frequency of maladaptive adolescent behaviors as measured by self-reports (on the Critical Life Events Survey and Current Maladaptive Adolescent Behavior Inventory).

Thus this hypothesis concerned the relationship between the critical incidents scale and the maladaptive behaviors scale. To determine this relationship, two questions were asked. The first concerned whether the students who were engaging in maladaptive behaviors were the same students who had experienced many critical incidents.

To explore this relationship, the critical incidents summative scale was divided into a trichotomy, creating three groups of students roughly equal in number. The first group had experienced few critical incidents (0–1 events); this group constituted 33% of the sample. The second group, constituting 37% of the sample, had experienced a moderate number of critical incidents (2–3). The third group had experienced many events (4–10) and made up 30% of the sample.

These three groups were then compared as to whether they differed on their weighted maladaptive behaviors scale scores. A one-way analysis of variance was performed on the weighted maladaptive behaviors scale scores of the three groups. There was indeed a difference between groups, $F [2, 185] = 25.87$, $p<.001$.

The second question asked relative to Hypothesis 1 had to do with whether the relationship between childhood critical incidents and maladaptive adolescent behaviors was linear. That is, were MAB scale score levels related positively to CCI scale levels? To answer this question, a correlation analysis was conducted. Individual MAB items making up the composite scale were correlated with childhood critical incident scores. Individual correlation coefficients are reported in Table A.6.

On the basis of these results, it seems clear that adolescents' maladaptive behaviors are positively and significantly related to the number of critical events they have experienced.

Hypothesis 2. There will be a significant positive correlation between the frequency of negative parental/adult responses to children's critical incidents and the frequency of the children's subsequent maladaptive adolescent behaviors as measured by self-reports (on the Parental/Adult Response to Crisis Checklist and the Current Maladaptive Adolescent Behavior Inventory).

This hypothesis concerns the relationships between the parental response scales and the maladaptive behaviors scale.

In investigating the manner in which parents responded to their children's crises, we focused upon what the differences are between parents' responses to crises for children who behave maladaptively and for those who do not.

To explore this relationship, the maladaptive behaviors scale was divided into a trichotomy. This created three groups of subjects on the basis of the (weighted) frequency of their maladaptive behaviors:

Table A.6. Correlation of Maladaptive Adolescent Behaviors with Childhood Critical Incidents

MAB	Correlation
Running away	r (202) = .37
Alcohol use	r (197) = .28
Marijuana use	r (196) = .35
Cocaine use	r (184) = .32
Suicide attempts	r (201) = .21
School attendance problems	r (203) = .39

1. few (0–1) maladaptive behaviors: 47% of the sample

2. moderate (2–3) maladaptive behaviors: 22% of the sample

3. many (4–6) maladaptive behaviors: 31% of the sample

The question asked was whether these groups differed in the degree to which their parents' responses to crises could be characterized as being:

for mothers

1. supportive
2. withholding
3. incompetent

for fathers

1. supportive
2. reactive/escapist

These response styles were derived from the factor analysis of the parent/adult responses as discussed above.

A one-way ANOVA, in which the between-groups factor was the level of maladaptive behavior experienced, was performed on the mothers' supportive response index to investigate this relationship. This analysis did not produce a group difference, indicating that mothers responding supportively did not significantly alter the outcome of the critical incident, at least in terms of maladaptive adolescent behaviors.

To investigate the possibility that students experiencing differing levels of maladaptive behavior differed in terms of their mothers' withholding responses, a one-way ANOVA was performed on the mothers' withholding index. This analysis revealed a strong group effect (F[2, 185] = 6.5, p<.001), with students in the high MAB group reporting more withholding responses among their mothers than those in the low MAB group.

Similar analyses were performed on the remaining three indices (mothers' inadequate index, fathers' supportive index, and fathers' reactive/escapist index). Strong group effects were found between students with high levels of maladaptive behaviors and both mothers' inadequate index (F[2, 185] = 12.80, p<.001) and fathers' reactive/escapist index (F[2, 185] = 24.45, p<.001). In addition, a significant effect was discovered between students with low levels of maladaptive behaviors and the fathers' supportive index (F[2, 185] = 2.98, p<.05). Students in the low MAB group reported a greater incidence of supportive responses from their fathers in reaction to crises than did students in the high MAB group.

The results of these analyses support the second hypothesis, namely, that parental response following children's critical incidents affects MABs. These findings indicate that mothers can have a significant negative effect by adopting withholding or inadequate response styles in the face of their children's critical incidents. Similarly, fathers can have a negative effect by adopting a reactive/escapist style. Fathers, however, can exert a positive effect by adopting a supportive style. However, no such positive effect was shown for mothers' supportive responses.

Discussion

Data generated by the study supported both of the hypotheses. Hypothesis 1—that childhood critical incidents would correlate positively with subsequent maladaptive adolescent behaviors—was supported. This finding supports similar results of Harris's (1980) study of dropouts. It also amplifies those studies mentioned in the literature reviewed in Chapter 2 of this volume, of both specific CCIs and specific MABs. Literature concerning specific CCIs (e.g., Briere & Runtz, 1985; Klagsbrun & Davis, 1977) indicated that they could, separately, be considered antecedents to a range of subsequent MABs. Further, literature cited studying antecedents to specific MABs showed each of those behaviors to follow a range of antecedent CCIs (e.g., Anderson, 1981; Nilson, 1981; Robins et al., 1977). This study confirmed that a general relationship between CCIs and MABs exists.

Because so many confounding variables exist in determining the cause of maladaptive behavior, it would be unfounded to attribute causal agency to CCIs for subsequent MABs. However, there is no evidence to suggest that CCIs stand as necessary and sufficient conditions for MABs to occur. Indeed, part of this study concerned with assessing the effects of parents' responses to their children's crises indicated that various factors can mitigate the effects of CCIs. It can be safely stated, however, that CCIs are strongly contributing factors to the development of maladaptive adolescent behavior.

Hypothesis 2 was also supported, namely, that certain parental responses to children's crises are associated with subsequent maladaptive adolescent behavior; mothers' "withdrawal" and "incompetent" responses and fathers' "reactive/escapist" responses. Of considerable interest in this study is the definition of parental response styles that are predictive of outcomes in terms of MAB development. These will be summarized below. Those responses associated with positive outcomes for fathers (fathers' "supportive" index) are listed in the Results section (as are the rest of the profiles). Interestingly, the corresponding factor for mothers (mothers' "supportive" index), which consisted of responses nearly identical to those of fathers (differing slightly in ranking of items) did not correspond with positive (low MAB) outcome. Mothers, it seems, cannot do anything right, at least according to adolescents.

Upon further reflection, it may be that this discrepancy indicates a culturally biased sex-role expectation. It stands to reason— due to culturally evolved expectations—that mothers are expected to be warm, supportive, and empathic, and that fathers are not; no one expects fathers to come through in a crisis, and everyone expects mothers to. Because of this bias, if a mother does not come through (withdraws or proves inadequate in terms of responsibilities), it is considered a serious breach; if she does come through, it is considered only as it should be. Similarly, if a father fails to respond with all of the positive virtues, it is par for the course, but if he manages to rise to the occasion, it is an event of some consequence. This somewhat cynical interpretation seems to make sense of an otherwise puzzling discrepancy. Further research on this issue might investigate children's role expectations regarding mothers' and fathers' behavior.

Similarly, while mothers seem to suffer by having two response profiles that result in compounding the effects of trauma, fathers have only one. This again makes a certain sense if one assumes that mothers are expected to be there emotionally for their children and men are not. Reversing the profiles for a moment, men might be expected to withdraw or be inadequate in terms of emotional response, but it is only when they initially overreact and then remove themselves emotionally that traumas are compounded. Mothers' initial overreactions may be expected, however.

The results of this study suggest several ways in which parents can respond positively to their children's crises and several responses they should avoid. In general, following a crisis, parents should allow children to talk about the incident and its ramifications, showing patience and understanding and using listening techniques that convey to the child that they did, in fact, hear what was said. Parents can offer suggestions and assurances, but not to the extent that they are experienced as impositions or as denying the importance of the event or its attendant feelings.

It is important for fathers not to initially overreact and then avoid the situation. It is equally important for mothers not to withdraw emotionally from the event or become focused upon themselves, and it is important for them to maintain composure and not to "fall apart."

It is the contention of this author that the most useful explanatory construct available to make sense of the relationship between CCIs and MABs is that of Posttraumatic Stress Disorder. This construct is explored with particular emphasis upon the manner in which posttraumatic stress interacts with normal development and the evolution of symptomatology among children and adolescents in Chapter 2 of this volume. Chapter 3 elaborates on the implications of adult response styles for the child in crisis.

Current Maladaptive Adolescent Behavior Inventory (CMABI)

1. Some students have *run away* from home. How often have you?

   Never ____ Once ____ 2–3 times ____ More than 3 ____

   How long at a time?

   1 Night ____ 2–3 Nights ____ Longer ____

2. *Alcohol* and/or *Drugs:* If alcohol or drug use is something you have experienced, please check appropriate squares below to indicate usage:

	Never	Tried Once	Several Times	Occasional Use	Frequent Use	Heavy Use
Alcohol	[ ]	[ ]	[ ]	[ ]	[ ]	[ ]
Pot	[ ]	[ ]	[ ]	[ ]	[ ]	[ ]
Cocaine	[ ]	[ ]	[ ]	[ ]	[ ]	[ ]
Other	[ ]	[ ]	[ ]	[ ]	[ ]	[ ]

3. At some time in their lives some people have wished they could just go to sleep and never wake up. Some people think about actually killing themselves.

   Have you wished you were dead?

   Never ____ Once or twice ____ Occasionally ____ Frequently ____

   Have you thought about killing yourself?

   Never ____ Once or twice ____ Occasionally ____ Frequently ____

   Have you ever tried?

   Never ____ Once ____ More than once ____

4. For Women Only:

   Have you ever been pregnant? Yes ____ No ____

   How many times?

   Once____ Twice____ Three or more times____

The next page asks you to list *Critical Life Events* you have experienced. Those are events so powerful that coping is difficult. At the end of the page you will have a chance to list repeat events or those not listed.

Take your time, and ask questions if you get confused. You will find that it really will be easier and faster than it first appears.

Thanks!!

Critical Life Event

Directions: If any of the following events happened to you, check YES, note your questions. THANKS!

	Did the event happen to you?	How old were you at the time?	How much did it affect you? 1–just a little 2–a little more 3–a lot 4–very seriously 5–devastating
EVENT	*circle*	*write in*	*circle*
1. Death of a parent	Y / N	( )	1 2 3 4 5
2. Death of someone close	Y / N	( )	1 2 3 4 5
3. Frequent moves/school changes	Y / N	( )	1 2 3 4 5
4. Physical or mental abuse	Y / N	( )	1 2 3 4 5
5. Sexual assault/rape	Y / N	( )	1 2 3 4 5
6. Serious accident or natural disaster	Y / N	( )	1 2 3 4 5
7. Child molestation	Y / N	( )	1 2 3 4 5
8. Pressure by gangs	Y / N	( )	1 2 3 4 5
9. Foster placement or abandonment	Y / N	( )	1 2 3 4 5
10. Commitment to mental hospital or group home	Y / N	( )	1 2 3 4 5
11. Rejection by parents	Y / N	( )	1 2 3 4 5
12. School failure by 6th grade	Y / N	( )	1 2 3 4 5
13. Divorce and/or stepparent conflict	Y / N	( )	1 2 3 4 5
14. Parental fighting	Y / N	( )	1 2 3 4 5
15. Alcoholism in the family	Y / N	( )	1 2 3 4 5
16. Incest	Y / N	( )	1 2 3 4 5
Were any of these events repeated?			
17. (fill in)	Y / N	( )	1 2 3 4 5
18.	Y / N	( )	1 2 3 4 5
Any other really bad things not listed above?			
19.	Y / N	( )	1 2 3 4 5
20.	Y / N	( )	1 2 3 4 5

Survey (CLES) (Confidential)

age when it happened, and CIRCLE the appropriate number on the rest of the

How did your Mom respond to you at the time? 1–not supportive 2–just a little 3–so-so 4–fairly supportive 5–very supportive	*How did your Dad respond to you at the time?* (use same answering system as for Mom)	*What about adults (such as relatives or teachers)?*	*How stable was your family at the time?* 1–very unstable/ insecure 2–unstable/ insecure 3–so-so 4–fairly stable/ secure 5–very stable/ secure
circle	*circle*	*circle*	*circle*
1 2 3 4 5	1 2 3 4 5	1 2 3 4 5	1 2 3 4 5
1 2 3 4 5	1 2 3 4 5	1 2 3 4 5	1 2 3 4 5
1 2 3 4 5	1 2 3 4 5	1 2 3 4 5	1 2 3 4 5
1 2 3 4 5	1 2 3 4 5	1 2 3 4 5	1 2 3 4 5
1 2 3 4 5	1 2 3 4 5	1 2 3 4 5	1 2 3 4 5
1 2 3 4 5	1 2 3 4 5	1 2 3 4 5	1 2 3 4 5
1 2 3 4 5	1 2 3 4 5	1 2 3 4 5	1 2 3 4 5
1 2 3 4 5	1 2 3 4 5	1 2 3 4 5	1 2 3 4 5
1 2 3 4 5	1 2 3 4 5	1 2 3 4 5	1 2 3 4 5
1 2 3 4 5	1 2 3 4 5	1 2 3 4 5	1 2 3 4 5
1 2 3 4 5	1 2 3 4 5	1 2 3 4 5	1 2 3 4 5
1 2 3 4 5	1 2 3 4 5	1 2 3 4 5	1 2 3 4 5
1 2 3 4 5	1 2 3 4 5	1 2 3 4 5	1 2 3 4 5
1 2 3 4 5	1 2 3 4 5	1 2 3 4 5	1 2 3 4 5
1 2 3 4 5	1 2 3 4 5	1 2 3 4 5	1 2 3 4 5

If so, fill in the one or two most important, and answer as before.

1 2 3 4 5	1 2 3 4 5	1 2 3 4 5	1 2 3 4 5
1 2 3 4 5	1 2 3 4 5	1 2 3 4 5	1 2 3 4 5

If so, fill in the one or two most important below.

1 2 3 4 5	1 2 3 4 5	1 2 3 4 5	1 2 3 4 5
1 2 3 4 5	1 2 3 4 5	1 2 3 4 5	1 2 3 4 5

Parental/Adult Response to Crisis Checklist (PARC)

On this page you are asked to describe how parents or other significant adults responded to you during your crisis, or during the weeks or months afterwards.

Place a *check* after the things they *did* do for the most part. Leave the things they did not do *blank*. (If they did different things in different situations, check what they did after the most *serious* incident.)

ADULT RESPONSE	Mother	Father	Other important adults
1. Expressed worry	_____	_____	_____
2. Were unable to cope (couldn't meet responsibilities)	_____	_____	_____
3. Made assumptions or jumped to conclusions too quickly	_____	_____	_____
4. Allowed me to talk	_____	_____	_____
5. Showed warmth, acceptance	_____	_____	_____
6. Focused on themselves, not me	_____	_____	_____
7. Denied the seriousness of the incident	_____	_____	_____
8. Shrugged off my feelings	_____	_____	_____
9. Gave reasonable reassurance	_____	_____	_____
10. Listened well	_____	_____	_____
11. Respected my privacy	_____	_____	_____
12. Concerned about what it meant to them, not me	_____	_____	_____
13. Told me not to talk about it (don't be a crybaby)	_____	_____	_____
14. Had come through for me in the past	_____	_____	_____
15. Made false assurances (unrealistic promises)	_____	_____	_____
16. Showed more patience	_____	_____	_____
17. Blamed me	_____	_____	_____
18. Let me know they understood by what they did and said	_____	_____	_____
19. Made helpful suggestions, but didn't push	_____	_____	_____
20. Reliable: they were there when I needed them	_____	_____	_____

APPENDIX III

Resources

A large number of local public agencies and organizations provide information and services relating to children in crisis. This appendix lists possible starting points for those seeking help in this area, starting with the following institutions or agencies that are close at hand.

- *Schools and school districts* frequently have extensive resources that are not widely known. Start with school psychologists and resource specialists, and explore for hidden human and material resources at home first.

- *County and state departments of education, mental health, and social services* frequently provide free or low-cost services, including consultation. Consultants from these agencies are usually well trained and willing to assist through individual conferencing, staff training, or networking local talent. Often one person will specialize in crisis-related services, and that fact will be known to others in the office. A phone call to anyone in that office is usually the best way to get in touch with the right person.

- *Private mental health agencies* are often good resources, as are special groups such as Parents United, Alcoholics Anonymous, Narcotics Anonymous, and others. Private agencies will often provide free or inexpensive consultation in exchange for community goodwill. Ask others on your staff for referral. Also, be clear with them that your understanding is that the service is gratis, and that they do not expect to be paid.

In addition, a number of private national organizations offer literature, materials, and services that can be of great assistance. Many of the most helpful are listed below:

American Academy of Pediatrics
141 Northwest Point Boulevard
Elk Grove Village, IL 60007

(800) 433-9016
(312) 228-5005

American Bar Association
National Legal Resource Center
for Child Advocacy and Protection
40 15th Street NW   (202) 662-1000
Washington, DC 20005

Children's Rights Project
404 Park Avenue S, 11th Floor   (212) 683-2210
New York, NY 10016

American Humane Association
American Association for Protecting Children
9725 East Hampden Avenue   (303) 792-9900
Denver, CO 80231

American Medical Association
Health and Human Behavior Department
515 North State Street   (312) 464-4818
Chicago, IL 60610

American Psychological Association
750 First Street NE   (202)336-5500
Washington, DC 20002

American Public Welfare Association
810 First Street NE, Suite 500   (202) 682-0100
Washington, DC 20002

Big Brothers/Big Sisters of America
230 North 13th Street   (215) 567-7000
Philadelphia, PA 19107

Boys Club of America
Government Relations Office   (301) 251-6676
600 Jefferson Plaza #203
Rockville, MD 20852

Centers for Disease Control and Prevention
National HIV and AIDS Hotline   (800) 342-2437
                           Spanish (800) 344-7432

**C. Henry Kempe Center for Prevention
and Treatment of Child Abuse and Neglect**
1205 Oneida Street   (303) 321-3963
Denver, CO 80220

Child Find, Inc.
P.O. Box 277   (914) 255-1848
New Paltz, NY 12561

Child Help USA   (800) 422-4453

Child Welfare League of America
440 First Street NW, Suite 310   (202) 638-2952
Washington, DC 20001

Families Anonymous, Inc.
P.O. Box 3475   (818) 989-7841
Culver City, CA 90231-3475

Family Services America
11700 West Lake Park Drive   (414) 359-2111
Park Place
Milwaukee, WI 53224

Missing Children Hotline
300 Orchard City Drive, Suite 151   (800) 235-3535
Campbell, CA 95008

National Alcohol and Drug Abuse Hotline   (800) 252-6565

National Association of Social Workers
3070 Presidential Drive #226   (770) 234-0567
Atlanta, GA 30314

National Black Child Development Institute
1023 15th Street NW   (202) 387-1281
Washington, DC 20005

**National Center for Child Abuse and Neglect (NCCAN);
Children's Bureau, Administration for Children, Youth and
Families; Office of Human Development Services;
Department of Health and Human Services**
P.O. Box 1182   (202) 879-4839
Washington, DC 20013

National Center for Missing and Exploited Children;
Education, Prevention and Public Awareness Division
2101 Wilson Boulevard #550 (202) 634-9821
Arlington, VA 22201 (800) 843-5678

National Council of Jewish Women
Children and Youth Priority, Program Department
53 West 23rd Street (212) 645-4048
New York, NY 10010

National Council of Juvenile and Family Court Judges
P.O. Box 8970 (702)784-6012
Reno, NV 89507

National Council on Child Abuse and Family Violence
1155 Connecticut Avenue NW, Suite 400 (800) 222-2000
Washington, DC 20036 (202) 429-6695

National Education Association
Human and Civil Rights Unit
1201 16th Street NW (202) 822-7711
Washington DC 20036

National Exchange Club Foundation
for Prevention of Child Abuse
3050 Central Avenue (419) 535-3232
Toledo, OH 43606

National Child Abuse Hotline: Childhelp, U.S.A.
P.O. Box 630 (800) 4-A-CHILD
Hollywood, CA 90028

National Committee for the Prevention of Child Abuse
(NCPCA)
332 South Michigan Avenue, Suite 1600 (312)663-3520
Chicago, IL 60604

Parents United/Daughters and Sons United/
Adults Molested as Children United
615 15th Street (209) 572-3446
Modesto, CA 95354

Save the Children
National Office   (203) 226-7271
54 Wilton Road
Westport, CT 06880

National Runaway Hotline   (800) 231-6946

National Runaway Switchboard   (800) 621-4000

SCAN (Stop Child Abuse and Neglect) Associates
1400 West Markham   (501) 372-7226
Little Rock, AR 72201

Volunteers of America
340 West 85th Street   (212) 873-2600
New York, NY 10024

Youth Crisis Hot Line   (800) HIT HOME

Bibliography

Abbott, M. W., & Gregson, A. M. (1981). Cognitive dysfunction in the predication of relapse in alcoholics. *Journal of Studies in Alcoholics, 41*(3), 230–243.

Abelson, H. I., Fishburn, P. M., & Cisin, I. (1977). *National survey on drug abuse.* Washington, DC: National Institute on Drug Abuse, U.S. Department of Health, Education and Welfare.

Aguilera, D. C., & Messick, J. M. (1982). *Crisis intervention: Therapy for psychological emergencies.* St. Louis: C. V. Mosby.

Alline, V. (1947). *Play therapy.* New York: Ballantine.

American Probation and Parole Association (1992). *Identifying and intervening with drug-involved youth.* Lexington, KY.

American Psychiatric Association. (1980). *Diagnostic and statistical manual* (3rd ed.). Washington, DC: American Psychiatric Association.

American Psychiatric Association. (1987). *Diagnostic and statistical manual* (3rd ed., rev.). Washington, DC: American Psychiatric Association.

American Psychiatric Association. (1994). *Diagnostic and statistical manual* (4th ed.). Washington, DC: American Psychiatric Association.

Anderson, D. (1981). Self-destructive behavior in children and adolescents. In C. F. Wells & I. R. Stuart (Eds.), *Self-destructive behavior in children and adolescents.* New York: Van Nostrand Reinhold.

Arroyo, W., & Eth, S. (1985). Children traumatized by Central American warfare. In S. Eth & R. S. Pynoos (Eds.), *Post-traumatic stress disorder in children.* Washington, DC: American Psychiatric Press.

Arvay, M., & Uhlemann, M. (1996). Counsellor stress in the field of trauma: A preliminary study. *Canadian Journal of Counselling/Revue Canadienne de Counseling* (2).

Bard, M., & Sangrey, D. (1979). *The crime victim's book.* New York: Basic Books.

Barnes, G. E. (1979). Solvent abuse: A review. *International Journal of the Addictions, 14,* 1–26.

Benedek, E. (1985). Children and psychic trauma: A brief review of contemporary thinking. In S. Eth & R. S. Pynoos (Eds.), *Post-traumatic stress disorder in children.* Washington, DC: American Psychiatric Press.

Birchnell, J. (1969). The possible consequence of early parental death. *British Journal of Medical Psychiatry, 42,* 1–12.

Black, C. (1979). Children of alcoholics. *Alcohol Health and Research World, 4,* 23–27.

Bloom, B. L., Asher, S. J., & White, S. W. (1978). Marital disruption as a stressor. *Psychological Bulletin, 85,* 867–894.

Bowen, M. (1978). *Family therapy in clinical practice.* New York: Jason Aronson.

Bowlby, J. (1961). The Adolf Meyer Lecture: Childhood mourning and its implications for psychiatry. *American Journal of Psychiatry, 118,* 481–498.

Bowlby, J. (1973). *Attachment and loss: Separation, anxiety and anger.* New York: Basic Books.

Bremner, J., et al. (1995). MRI-based measures of hippocampal volume in patients with PTSD. *American Journal of Psychiatry, 152,* 973–981.

Bremner, J., Davis, M., Southwick, S., Krystal, J., Chrney, D. (1994). In R. Pynoos (Ed.) *Post-traumatic stress disorder: A clinical review.* Lutherville, MD: Sidran Books.

Brenner, T., Huizinga, D., & Elliott, D. S. (1978). *The social psychology of runaways.* Lexington, MA: Lexington Books.

Brewer, D., et al. (1995). Preventing serious, violent, and chronic juvenile offending; A review of evaluations of selected strategies in childhood, adolescence, and the community. *Guide for implementing the comprehensive strategy for serious, violent, and chronic juvenile offenders.* Washington, DC: Office of Juvenile Justice and Delinquency Prevention, U.S. Department of Justice.

Briere, J. (1984). *The effects of childhood sexual abuse on later psychological functioning: Defining a post-sexual-abuse syndrome.* Paper presented at the Third National Conference on Sexual Victimization of Children, Washington, DC.

Briere, J., & Runtz, M. (1985). *Symptomatology associated with prior sexual abuse in a non-clinical sample.* Paper presented at the annual meeting of the American Psychological Association, Los Angeles.

Briere, J., Runtz, M., & Lightfoot, A. (1978). *Suicidality in former sexual abuse victims.* Paper presented at the meetings of the American Association of Suicidology, Toronto.

Bryant, R., & Harvey, A. (1996). Initial posttraumatic stress responses following motor vehicle accidents. *Journal of Traumatic Stress, 9* (2).

Burgess, A., & Holstrom, L. (1974). Rape trauma syndrome. *American Journal of Psychiatry, 131,* 981–986.

Cameron, C. (1994). Women confronting their abusers: Issues, decisions, outcome. *Journal of Child Sexual Abuse, 3* (1), 7–35.

Cameron, C. (1996). Comparing amnesic and non-amnesic survivors of childhood sexual abuse: A longitudinal study. In K. Pezdek & W. Banks (Eds.), *The Recovered Memory/False Memory Debate.* New York: Academic Press.

Campbell, D. T., & Stanley, J. C. (1966). *Experimental and quasi-experimental designs for research.* Chicago: Rand McNally.

Cantril, H. (1944). *Gauging public opinion.* Princeton, NJ: Princeton University Press.

Carlson, J. G., Chemtob, C. M., Rusnak, K.., Hedlund, N. L., & Mureaoka, M. Y. (in press). Eye movement desensitization and reprocessing for combat related posttraumatic stress disorder. *Journal of Traumatic Stress.*

Chafetz, M. E., Blane, H. T., & Hill, M. J. (1971). Children of alcoholics: Observations in a child guidance clinic. *Quarterly Journal of Alcohol, 32,* 687–689.

Chemtob, C. M. (1996). *Eye movement desensitization and reprocessing (EMDR) treatment for children with treatment resistant disaster related distress.* Paper presented at the International Society for Traumatic Stress Studies, San Francisco.

Cocco, N., & Sharpe, L. (1993). An auditory variant of eye movement desensitization in the case of childhood posttraumatic stress disorder. *Journal of Behavior Therapy and Experimental Psychiatry, 24,* 373–377.

Cohn, L. (1996). Conversation and written communication with author.

Cohn, L. (1993). Psychotherapy and the new eye movement desensitization and reprocessing (EMDR) method: An integrated approach. In E. Dishup (Ed.), *California art therapy trends.* Chicago: Magnolia Street.

Coleman, F. W., & Coleman, W. S. (1984). Helping siblings and other peers cope with dying. In H. Wass & C. A. Corr (Eds.), *Childhood and death.* Washington, DC: Hemisphere.

Coleman, J. C., Butcher, J. N., & Carson, R. L. (1980). *Abnormal psychology and modern life.* Glenville, IL: Scott Foresman.

Courtois, C. (1979). Characteristics of a volunteer sample of adult women who experienced incest in childhood or adolescence. *Dissertation Abstracts International, 40,* 2194A–3195A.

Courtois, C. (1992). The memory retrieval process in incest survivor therapy. *Journal of Child Sexual Abuse, 1* (1), 15–31.

Creamer, M., Burgess, P., & Pattison, P. (1992). Reaction to trauma: A cognitive processing model. *Journal Of Abnormal Psychology, 20* (1), 452–459.

Danieli, Y. (1994). Countertransference, trauma and training. In J. Wilson & J. Lindy, *Countertransference in the treatment of PTSD*. New York: The Guilford Press.

Davidson, J., & Swartz, M. (1985). A diagnostic and family study of posttraumatic stress disorder. *American Journal of Psychiatry, 142* (1).

Davidson, J., & Van der Kolk, B. (1996). The psychopharmacological treatment of posttraumatic stress disorder. In B. Van der Kolk, A. McFarlane, & L. Weisaeth, (Eds.) *Traumatic stress: The effects of overwhelming experience on mind, body, and society*. New York: The Guilford Press.

Deaton, W., & Johnson, K. (1991). *Living with my family*. Alameda, CA: Hunter House Publishers.

Deaton, W., & Johnson, K. (1991). *No more hurt*. Alameda, CA: Hunter House Publishers.

Deaton, W., & Johnson, K. (1993). *My own thoughts and feelings (for young girls/boys)*. Alameda, CA: Hunter House Publishers.

Deaton, W., & Johnson, K. (1993). *My own thoughts and feelings on stopping the hurt*. Alameda, CA: Hunter House Publishers.

Deaton, W., & Johnson, K. (1994). *Drinking and drugs in my family*. Alameda, CA: Hunter House Publishers.

Deaton, W., & Johnson, K. (1994). *A separation in my family*. Alameda, CA: Hunter House Publishers.

Deaton, W., & Johnson, K. (1994). *Someone I love died*. Alameda, CA: Hunter House Publishers.

Donaldson, M. A., & Gardner, R. (1985). Diagnosis and treatment of traumatic stress among women after childhood incest. In C. R. Figley (Ed.), *Trauma and its wake*. New York: Brunner/Mazel.

Donnelly, D., & Murray, E. (1991). Emotional changes in written essays and therapy interviews. *Journal of Social Clinical Psychology. 10*, 334–350.

Dunton, R. (1996). Conversation and written communication with author.

Earle, E. (1979). The psychological effects of mutilating surgery in children and adolescents. *Psychoanalytic Study of the Child, 34,* 527–546.

Elkind, D. (1981). *The hurried child: Growing up too fast, too soon.* Reading, MA: Addison-Wesley.

Emery, V., Emery, P., Shama, D., Quiana, N., & Jassani, A. (1991). Predisposing variables in PTSD patients. *Journal of Traumatic Stress, 4* (3).

Erickson, E. (1950). *Identity and the life cycle.* New York: International Universities Press.

Erickson, E. (1968). *Identity, youth and crisis.* New York: Norton.

Erickson, E., & Rossi, E. (1976/1980). Two level communication and the microdynamics of trance and suggestion. In E. Rossi (Ed.), *The collected papers of Milton Erickson on hypnosis. Vol. I. The nature of hypnosis and suggestion.* New York: Irvington.

Eth, S., & Pynoos, R. S. (1985a). Developmental perspective on psychic trauma in childhood. In C. R. Figley (Ed.), *Trauma and its wake.* New York: Brunner/Mazel.

Eth, S., & Pynoos, R. S. (Eds.) (1985b). *Post-traumatic stress disorder in children.* Washington, DC: American Psychiatric Press.

Eth, S., & Pynoos, R. S. (1985c). Children traumatized by witnessing acts of personal violence: Homicide, rape, or suicide behavior. In S. Eth & R. S. Pynoos (Eds.), *Post-traumatic stress disorder in children.* Washington, DC: American Psychiatric Press.

Eth, S., & Pynoos, R. S. (1985d). Interaction of trauma and grief in childhood. In S. Eth & R. S. Pynoos (Eds.), *Post-traumatic stress disorder in children.* Washington, DC: American Psychiatric Press.

Eth, S., Randolf, E., & Brown, J. (1988). Post-traumatic stress disorder. In J. Howell (Ed.), *Modern perspectives in the psychiatry of the neuroses.* New York: Brunner/Mazel.

Federal Bureau of Investigation. (1994). *Uniform Crime Report, 1993.* Washington, DC: U.S. Department of Justice.

Figley, C. R. (1985). From victim to survivor: Social responsibility in the wake of catastrophe. In C. R. Figley (Ed.), *Trauma and its wake*. New York: Brunner/Mazel.

Figley, C. R. (1995). Compassion fatigue as secondary traumatic stress disorder: An overview. In C. R. Figley, *Compassion fatigue: Coping with secondary traumatic stress disorder in those who treat the traumatized*. New York: Brunner/Mazel.

Fine, E., Yudin, L. W., Holmes, J., & Hinemann, S. (1975). *Behavioral disorders in children with parental alcoholism*. Paper presented at the annual meeting of the National Council on Alcoholism, Milwaukee, WI.

Fossey, R. (1996). *School dropout rates: Are we sure they are going down?* Paper presented at the annual meeting of the Southwest Educational Research Association, New Orleans, LA.

Frears, L. H., & Schneider, J. M. (1981). Exploring loss and grief within a holistic framework. *Personnel and Guidance Journal, 59* (2), 341–345.

Fredrick, C. J. (1985a). An introduction and overview of youth suicide. In M. Peck, N. Farberow, & R. Litman (Eds.), *Youth suicide*. New York: Springer.

Fredrick, C. J. (1985b). Children traumatized by catastrophic situations. In S. Eth & R. S. Pynoos (Eds.), *Post-traumatic stress disorder in children*. Washington, DC: American Psychiatric Press.

Freud, S. (1917/1966). *Introductory lectures in psychoanalysis*. (J. Strachey, Ed. and Trans.) New York: Norton.

Freud, S. (1920). Beyond the pleasure principle. In J. Strachey (Ed.), *The standard edition of the complete psychological works of Sigmund Freud* (Vol. 18). London: Hogarth.

Freud, S. (1926). Inhibitions, symptoms and anxiety. In J. Strachey (Ed.), *The standard edition of the complete psychological works of Sigmund Freud* (Vol. 18). London: Hogarth.

Freud, S. (1939). Moses and monotheism. In J. Strachey (Ed.), *The standard edition of the complete psychological works of Sigmund Freud* (Vol. 23). London: Hogarth.

Furman, E. (1984). Children's patterns in mourning the death of a loved one. In H. Wass & C. A. Corr (Eds.), *Childhood and death*. Washington, DC: Hemisphere.

Gardner, R. (1976). *Psychotherapy with children of divorce*. New York: Jason Aronson.

Garmezy, N., & Rutter, M. (Eds.) (1983). *Stress, coping, and development in children*. New York: McGraw-Hill.

Gelles, R. (1978). Methods for studying sensitive family topics. *American Journal of Orthopsychiatry, 48*, 408–424.

Glang, G. (1996). Conversation and written communication with author.

Golan, N. (1981). *Passing through transitions*. New York: Free Press.

Green, A. (1985). Post-traumatic symptoms of incest victims. In S. Eth & R. S. Pynoos (Eds.), *Post-traumatic stress disorder in children*. Washington, DC: American Psychiatric Press.

Greenwald, R. (1994). Applying eye movement desensitization and reprocessing (EMDR) to the treatment of traumatized children: Five case studies. *Anxiety Disorders Practice Journal, 1*.

Gregory, I. (1965). Ante-retrospective data concerning childhood loss of a parent: Delinquents and high school drop-outs. *Archives of General Psychiatry, 13*, 99–109.

Gumser, R. J., Myrich, R., & Holdin, W. (1971). A study of play process in counseling. *Elementary School Guidance and Counseling, 5*, 256–263.

Harber, K., & Pennebaker, J. (1992). Overcoming traumatic memories. In S. Christianson (Ed.), *The handbook of emotion and memory: Research and theory*. Hillsdale, NJ: Lawrence Erlbaum.

Harris, L. J. H. (1980). *Middle-class high school drop-outs: Incidents of physical abuse, incest, sexual assault, loss, symptomatic behaviors, and emotional disturbance*. Unpublished doctoral dissertation, University of Minnesota.

Havinghurst, R. J. (1972). *Developmental tasks and education*. New York: McKay.

Hawkins, J., & Catalano, R. (1995). *Risk focused intervention: Using the social development strategy.* Seattle: Developmental Research and Programs.

Headington, B. J. (1981). Understanding a core experience: Loss. *Personnel and Guidance Journal, 59* (2), 338–341.

Heatherington, E. M., Cox, M., & Cox, R. (1978). *Family interaction and the social and cognitive development of children following divorce.* Washington, DC: Institute of Pediatric Service.

Hendlin, H. (1985). Suicide among the young: Psychodynamics and demography. In M. Peck, N. Farberow, & R. Litman (Eds.), *Youth suicide.* New York: Springer.

Herman, J. (1981). *Father-daughter incest.* Cambridge: Harvard University Press.

Herman, J. (1992). *Trauma and recovery: The aftermath of violence—from domestic abuse to political terror.* New York: Basic Books.

Hindemann, M. (1976). Children of alcoholic parents. *Alcohol Health and Research World, 1,* 2–6.

Horowitz, M. (1976). *Stress response syndrome.* New York: Jason Aronson.

Horowitz, M. (1991). *Person schemas and maladaptive interpersonal patterns.* Chicago: University of Chicago Press.

Horowitz, M., & Reidbord, S. (1992). Memory, emotion, and response to trauma. In S. Christianson (Ed.), *The handbook of emotion and memory: Research and theory.* Hillsdale, NJ: Lawrence Erlbaum Associates.

Horowitz, M., & Solomon, G. F. (1975). Delayed stress response syndrome in Vietnam veterans. *Journal of Social Issues, 31,* 67–80.

Horowitz, M., & Solomon, G. F. (1978). Delayed stress response in Vietnam veterans. In C. R. Figley (Ed.), *Stress disorders among Vietnam veterans.* New York: Brunner/Mazel.

Howell, J. (1994). *Gangs.* Washington, DC: Office of Juvenile Justice and Delinquency, April Fact Sheet.

Huizinga, et al. (1994). *Urban delinquency and substance abuse.* Washington, DC: Office of Juvenile Justice and Delinquency Prevention, U.S. Department of Justice.

Institute of Medicine. (1994). *Reducing risks for mental disorders: Frontiers for preventive intervention research.* Washington, DC: National Academy Press.

Isaac, S. (1971). *Handbook in research and evaluation.* San Diego: Edits.

Janoff-Buhlman, R. (1989). Assumptive worlds and the stress of traumatic events: Applications of the schema construct. *Social Cognition, 7* (2), 113–136.

Jaremko, M. (1983). Stress inoculation training for social anxiety. In D. Meichelbaum & M. Jaremko (Eds.), *Stress reduction and prevention.* New York: Plenum.

Johnson, K. (1985). Family sculpture in the interpersonal relations classroom. *Journal of Continuation Education, 7,* 7–11.

Johnson, K. (1987). *Classroom crisis: A readi-reference guide.* Claremont, CA: Turnpoint.

Johnson, K. (1993). *School crisis management.* Alameda, CA: Hunter House Publishers.

Justice, B., & Duncan, D. F. (1976). Running away: An epidemic problem of adolescence. *Adolescence, 1,* 365–371.

Kalff, D. (1991) Introduction to sandplay therapy. *Journal of Sandtray Therapy (1)* 1. (published originally in 1978 as Eine kurze einfürung in die sandspeil therapie. *Praxis Der Psychotherapie, 23.*)

Kaplan, H. S. (1979). *Disorders of sexual desire and other new concepts and techniques in sex therapy.* New York: Brunner/Mazel.

Khan, M. M. R. (1963). The concept of cumulative trauma. *Psychoanalytic Study of the Child, 18,* 286–306.

Klagsbrun, F., & Davis, D. E. (1977). Substance abuse and family interaction. *Family Process, 16,* 149–163.

Knell, S. (1995). *Cognitive/behavioral play therapy.* Northvale, NJ: Jason Aronson.

Kopp, S. (1971). *Guru: Metaphors from a psychotherapist.* Palo Alto, CA: Science and Behavior Books.

Kramer, E. (1971). *Art as therapy with children.* New York: Schocken.

Krugman, S. (1987). Trauma in the family: Perspectives on the intergenerational transmission of violence. In Bessel A. Van der Kolk (Ed.), *Psychological trauma.* Washington, DC: American Psychiatric Press.

Krystal, H. (1968). Trauma and effects. *Psychoanalytic Study of the Child, 33,* 81–96.

Krystal, J., Kosten, T., Southwick, S., Mason, J., Perry, B., & Giller, E. (1989). Neurobiological aspects of PTSD: Review of clinical and preclinical studies. *Behavior Therapy, 20.*

Kübler-Ross, E. (1969). *On death and dying.* New York: Macmillan.

Langer, T. S., & Michael, S. T. (1963). *Life stress and mental health.* New York: Free Press.

Lerner, M. (1970). The desire for justice and reactions to victims: Social psychological studies of some antecedents and consequences. In J. Macauley & L. Berkowitz (Eds.), *Altruism and helping behavior.* New York: Academic Press.

Lichter, S. O., Rapien, E. B., Seibert, F. M., & Sklansky, M. A. (1962). *The drop-outs: A treatment study of intellectually capable students who drop out of high school.* New York: Free Press.

Lidz, T., Fleck, S., & Cornelison, A. R. (1965). *Schizophrenia and the family.* New York: International University Press.

Lifton, R. (1979). *The broken connection.* New York: Simon & Schuster.

Lindemann, E. (1944). Symptomatology and management of acute grief. *American Journal of Psychiatry, 101,* 141–146.

Litman, R. E. (1976). Beyond crisis intervention. In E. Schneidman (Ed.), *Suicide: Contemporary developments.* New York: Grune & Stratton.

Loftus, E., Garry, M., & Feldman, J. (1994). Forgetting sexual trauma: What does it mean when 38% forget? *Journal of Consulting and Clinical Psychology, 62* (6), 1177–1181.

Lourie, I. S. (1977). The phenomenon of the abused adolescent: A clinical study. *Victimology, 2,* 268–276.

Lovett, J. (1996). Conversation and written communication with author.

Lovett, J. (in press) *Small Wonders.*

Lowenfield, M. (1979). *The world technique.* London: George Allen and Unwin.

Lowenthal, M. F., & Chiriboga, D. (1973). Social stress and adaptation: Toward a life-course perspective. In C. Eisdorfer & M. P. Lawton (Eds.), *The psychology of adult development and aging.* Washington, DC: American Psychological Association.

Lustig, N., & Zeitlin, M. (1985). Bipolar affective disorder: A delinquent variable. In M. Peck, N. Farberow, & R. Litman (Eds.), *Youth suicide.* New York: Springer.

McCann, I., & Pearlman, L. (1990). Vicarious traumatization: A framework for understanding the psychological effects of working with victims. *Journal of Traumatic Stress, 3* (1).

McIntosh, J. (1996). *Suicide state data page.* Washington, DC: American Association of Suicidology, March 21, 1996.

Meichenbaum, D. (1983). *Stress reduction and prevention.* New York: Plenum.

Meichenbaum, D. (1985). *Stress inoculation training.* New York: Pergamon Press.

Meizelman, K. (1978). *Incest: A psychological study of causes and effects with treatment recommendations.* San Francisco: Jossey-Bass.

Mendel, R. (1995). Prevention or pork: A hard-headed look at youth oriented anti-crime programs. Washington, DC: American Youth Policy Forum.

Middleton, W., Raphael, B., Martinek, N., & Misso, V. (1993). Concepts of normal bereavement: A response. In M. Stroebe, W. Stroebe, & R. Hansson (Eds.), *Bereavement: A sourcebook of research and intervention.* New York: Cambridge University Press.

Millman, R. B., Khuri, E. T., & Hammond, D. (1981). Perspectives on drug use and abuse. In C. F. Wells & I. R. Stuart (Eds.), *Self-destructive behavior in children and adolescents.* New York: Van Nostrand Reinhold.

Mills, J., & Crowley, R. (1986). Positive effects of cartoon images. *Telemedia, 1* (2).

Mitchell, J. (1983). When disaster strikes: The critical incident stress debriefing process. *Journal of Emergency Medical Services, 8,* 36–39.

Mitchell, R., & Friedman, H. (1994). *Sandplay: Past, present, and future.* New York: Routledge.

Monk, G., Winslade, J., Crocket, K., & Epston, D. (1996). *Narrative therapy in practice: The archeology of hope.* San Francisco: Jossey-Bass.

Munroe, J., Shay, J., Fisher, L., Makary, C., Rapperport., & Zimering, R. (1995). Preventing compassion fatigue: A team treatment model. In C. R. Figley (Ed.), *Compassion fatigue: Coping with secondary traumatic stress disorder in those who treat the traumatized.* New York: Brunner/Mazel.

Murphy, L., & Moriety, A. (1976). *Vulnerability, coping, and growth.* New Haven: Yale University Press.

Murray, E., & Segal, D. (1994). Emotional processing in vocal and written expression of feelings about traumatic experiences. *Journal of Traumatic Stress. 7,* (3).

Murray, E., et al. (1989). Emotional expression in written essays and psychotherapy. *Journal of Social Clinical Psychology. 8,* 414–429.

Myrich, R., & Holdin, W. (1971). A study of play process in counseling. *Elementary School Guidance and Counseling, 5,* 256–263.

National Center of Educational Statistics. (1994). Characteristics of the 100 largest public elementary and secondary school districts in the U.S. 1991–1992. Washington, DC: Author.

National Center for Health Statistics. (1966). Advance report of final mortality statistics, 1993. *NCHC Monthly Vital Statistics Report, 44* (7, supp.)

Neidengard, T., & Yaliscove, D. (1981). Juvenile alcoholism and alcohol abuse. In C. F. Wells & I. R. Stuart (Eds.), *Self-destructive behavior in children and adolescents.* New York: Van Nostrand Reinhold.

Newman, C. J. (1976). Children of disaster: Clinical observations at Buffalo Creek. *American Journal of Psychiatry, 133,* 306–312.

Nilson, P. (1981). Psychological profiles of runaway children and adolescents. In C. F. Wells & I. R. Stuart (Eds.), *Self-destructive behavior in children and adolescents.* New York: Van Nostrand Reinhold.

Nir, Y. (1985). Post-traumatic stress disorder in children with cancer. In S. Eth & R. S. Pynoos (Eds.), *Post-traumatic stress disorder in children.* Washington, DC: American Psychiatric Press.

Norem-Hebeison, A., & Hedin, D. (1981). Influences on adolescent problem behavior. In U.S. Department of Health Services (Ed.), *Adolescent peer pressure.* Washington, DC: U.S. Department of Health Services.

Office of Juvenile Justice and Delinquency Prevention (1995). *Delinquency prevention works.* Washington, DC.

Office of National Drug Control Policy (1996). *Juveniles and drugs.* Rockville, MD: National Clearinghouse for Alcohol and Drug Information.

Ornitz, E., & Pynoos, R. (1989). Startle modulation in children with post-traumatic stress disorder. *American Journal of Psychiatry, 147,* 866–870.

Parker, E., Parker, D., Brody, J., & Schoenberg, R. (1982). Cognitive patterns of premature aging in male social drinkers. *Alcoholism: Clinical & Experimental Research, 6* (1), 46–52.

Parks, C. (1965). Bereavement and mental illness. *British Journal of Medical Psychology, 38,* 388–397.

Parson, E., (1994). Inner-city children of trauma: Urban violence traumatic stress response syndrome (U-VTS) and therapists' responses. In J. Wilson & J. Lindy, *Countertransference in the treatment of PTSD.* New York: The Guilford Press.

Pearlman, L., & Saakvitne, K. (1995). Treating therapists with vicarious traumatization and secondary traumatic stress disorders. In C. R. Figley (Ed.), *Compassion fatigue: Coping with secondary traumatic stress disorder in those who treat the traumatized.* New York: Brunner/Mazel.

Peck, M. (1984). Youth suicide. In H. Wass & C. A. Corr (Eds.), *Childhood and death.* Washington, DC: Hemisphere.

Pellicer, X. (1993). Eye movement desensitization treatment of a child's nightmares: A case report. *Journal of Behavior Therapy and Experimental Psychiatry, 24,* 73–75.

Pennebaker, J. (1985). Traumatic experience and psychosomatic disease: Exploring the roles of behavior inhibition, obsession, and confiding. *Canadian Psychology, 26,* 82–95.

Pennebaker, J., & Beal, S. (1986). Confronting a traumatic event: Toward an understanding of inhibition and disease. *Journal of Abnormal Psychology, 95,* 274–281.

Pennebaker, J., et al. (1988). Disclosures of trauma and immune function. *Journal of Consulting and Clinical Psychology, 56,* 239–245.

Penner, C. (1996). Conversation and written communication with author.

Pfeffer, C. R. (1984). Death preoccupations and suicidal behavior in children. In H. Wass & C. A. Corr (Eds.), *Childhood and death.* Washington, DC: Hemisphere.

Plass, P., & Hotaling, G. (1995). The intergenerational transmission of running away: Childhood experiences of the parents of runaways. *Journal of Youth and Adolescence, 24* (3).

Puffer, M., Greenwald, R., & Elrod, D. E. (in press). A single session EMDR study with twenty traumatized children and adolescents. *Traumatology.*

Pynoos, R. (1990). Posttraumatic stress disorder in children and adolescents. In B. Garfinkel, G. Carlson, & E. Weller (Eds.), *Psychiatric disorders in children and adolescents.* Philadelphia: W. B. Saunders.

Pynoos, R., & Eth, S. (1984). Child as witness to homicide. *Journal of Social Issues, 40,* 87–108.

Pynoos, R., Nader, K., & March, J. (1991). Posttraumatic stress disorder. In J. Weiner (Ed.), *Textbook of child and adolescent psychiatry.* Washington, DC: American Psychiatric Press.

Pynoos, R., Steinberg, A., & Goenjian, A. (1996). Traumatic stress in childhood and adolescence: Recent developments and applications. In B. Van der Kolk, A. McFarlane, & L. Weisaeth (Eds.), *Traumatic stress: The effects of overwhelming experience on mind, body, and society.* New York: The Guilford Press.

Raphael, B., Wilson, J., Meldrum, L., & McFarlane, A. (1996). Acute preventive measures. In B. Van der Kolk, A. McFarlane, & L. Weisaeth (Eds.), *Traumatic Stress.* New York: The Guilford Press.

Reider, C., & Cicchetti, D. (1989). Organizational perspective on cognitive control functioning and cognitive-affective balance in maltreated children. *Developmental Psychology, 25* (3), 389–393.

Resick, P., & Schnicke, M. (1992). Cognitive processing therapy for sexual assault victims. *Journal of Consulting and Clinical Psychology, 60,* 748–756.

Richman, J. (1981). Family treatment of suicidal children and adolescents. In C. F. Wells & I. R. Stuart (Eds.), *Self-destructive behavior in children and adolescents.* New York: Van Nostrand Reinhold.

Robins, L. N., Davis, D. H., & Wish, E. (1977). Detecting predictors of rare events. In J. S. Strauss, et al. (Eds.), *The origins and course of psychopathology*. New York: Plenum.

Rowan, A., & Foy, D. (1993). Posttraumatic stress disorder in child sexual abuse: A literature review. *Journal of Traumatic Stress, 6.*

Rudd, L. (1981). Pregnancies and abortions. In C. F. Wells & I. R. Stuart (Eds.), *Self-destructive behavior in children and adolescents.* New York: Van Nostrand Reinhold.

Russell, D. H. (1981). On running away. In C. F. Wells & I. R. Stuart (Eds.), *Self-destructive behavior in children and adolescents.* New York: Van Nostrand Reinhold.

Saarni, C., & Azara, V. (1981). Anxiety (developmental). In R. Woody (Ed.), *Encyclopedia of clinical assessment* (Vol. 2). San Francisco: Jossey-Bass.

Satir, V. (1967). *Conjoint family therapy.* Palo Alto, CA: Science and Behavior Books.

Scheck, M. M., et al. (in press) Brief pyschological intervention with traumatized young women: Efficacy of eye movement desensitization and reprocessing. *Journal of Traumatic Stress.*

Schukit, M. A., Morrissey, E. R., Lewis, N. J., & Buck, W. T. (1977). Adolescent problem drinkers. In F. A. Seixus (Ed.), *Currents in alcoholism* (Vol. 2). New York: Grune & Stratton.

Scroi, S. M. (Ed.). (1976). *Handbook of clinical intervention in child sexual abuse.* Lexington, MA: Lexington Books.

Scurfield, R. M. (1985). Post-traumatic stress assessment and treatment: Overview and formulations. In C. R. Figley (Ed.), *Trauma and its wake.* New York: Brunner/Mazel.

Sedlak, A., Mohadjer, L., & Hudock, V. (1990). *Nismart household survey methodology.* Rockville, MD: Westat.

Seligman, M. E., & Garber, J. (1980). *Human helplessness.* New York: Academic Press.

Shaffer, D., & Fisher, P. (1981). Suicide in children and young adolescents. In C. F. Wells & I. R. Stuart (Eds.), *Self-destructive behavior in children and adolescents*. New York: Van Nostrand Reinhold.

Shapiro, F. (1996). Conversation and written communication with author.

Shapiro, F., & Forrest, M. S. (1997). *EMDR: The breakthrough therapy for overcoming anxiety, stress, and trauma*. New York: Basic Books.

Shapiro, F. (1995). *Eye movement desensitization and reprocessing: Basic principles, protocols, and procedures*. New York: Basic Books.

Shuchter, S., & Zisook, S. (1993). The course of normal grief. In M. Stroebe, et al. (Eds.) *Handbook of bereavement*. Cambridge: Cambridge University Press.

Siegler, M., Osmond, H., & Newell, S. (1968). Models of alcoholism. *Quarterly Journal of Studies of Alcoholism, 29,* 571–597.

Symonds, M. (1976). The rape victim: Psychological patterns of response. *American Journal of Psychoanalysis, 5*(1), 27–34.

Teicher, J. D. (1979). Suicide and suicide attempts. In J. D. Hoshpitz (Ed.), *Basic handbook of child psychiatry* (Vol. 2). New York: Basic Books.

Terr, L. C. (1979). The children of Chowchilla: A study of psychic trauma. *Psychoanalytic Study of the Child, 34,* 547–623.

Terr, L. C. (1981). Psychic trauma in children. *American Journal of Psychiatry, 138,* 14–19.

Terr, L. C. (1985). Children traumatized in small groups. In S. Eth & R. S. Pynoos (Eds.), *Post-traumatic stress disorder in children*. Washington, DC: American Psychiatric Press.

Terr, L. (1990). *Too scared to cry: Psychic trauma in childhood*. New York: Basic Books.

Terr, L. (1994). *Unchained memories: True stories of traumatic memories, lost and found*. New York: Basic Books.

Thornberry, T., et al. (1995). The prevention of serious delinquency and violence: Implications from the Program of Research of the Causes and Correlates of Delinquency. In J. Howell, et al. (Eds.), *Sourcebook on serious, violent, and chronic juvenile offenders.* Thousand Oaks, CA: Sage Publications.

Thorneburg, H. D. (1975). Attitudinal determinants in holding dropouts in school. *Journal of Education Research, 68,* 181–185.

Tinker, R. (1996). Conversation and written communication with author.

Trimble, M. R. (1981). *Post-traumatic neurosis.* Chichester, U.K.: John Wiley.

Trimble, M. R. (1985). Post-traumatic stress disorder: History of a concept. In C. R. Figley (Ed.), *Trauma and its wake.* New York: Brunner/Mazel.

Tsai, M., Feldman-Summers, S., & Edgar, M. (1979). Child molestation: Variables related to differential impacts on psychosexual functioning in adult women. *Journal of Abnormal Psychology, 80,* 407–417.

Tuckman, J., & Connon, H. E. (1962). Attempted suicide in adolescents. *American Journal of Psychiatry, 119,* 228–232.

Van Houten, T., & Golenbiewski, G. (1978). *Adolescent life stress as a predictor of alcohol abuse and/or runaway behavior.* Washington, DC: National Youth Alternatives Project.

Van der Kolk, B., & Fisler, R. (1995). Dissociation and the fragmentary nature of traumatic memories: Review and experimental confirmation. *Journal of Traumatic Stress, 8,* 505–525.

Van der Kolk, B. (1996). The body keeps score: Approaches to the psychobiology of posttraumatic stress disorder. In B. Van der Kolk, A. McFarlane, & L. Weisaeth (Eds.), *Traumatic stress: The effects of overwhelming experience on mind, body, and society.* New York: The Guilford Press.

Van der Kolk, B. (1996). The complexity of adaptation to trauma: Self-regulation, stimulus discrimination, and characterological development. In B. Van der Kolk, A. McFarlane, & L. Weisaeth (Eds.), *Traumatic stress: The effects of overwhelming experience on mind, body, and society.* New York: The Guilford Press.

Walker, D. (1975). *Runaway youth: An annotated bibliography and literature overview.* Washington, DC: U.S. Department of Health, Education and Welfare.

Wallerstein, J. S., & Kelly, J. B. (1974). The effects of parental divorce: The adolescent experience. In E. J. Anthony & C. Koupernik (Eds.), *The child in his family: Children at psychiatric risk.* New York: John Wiley.

Wass, H. (1984). Concepts of death: A developmental perspective. In H. Wass & C. A. Corr (Eds.), *Childhood and death.* Washington, DC: Hemisphere.

Wass, H., & Cason, L. (1984). Fears and anxieties about death. In H. Wass & C. A. Corr (Eds.), *Childhood and death.* Washington, DC: Hemisphere.

Wegscheider, S. (1981). *Another chance: Hope and health for the alcoholic family.* Palo Alto, CA: Science and Behavior Books.

White, M., & Epston, D. (1991). *Narrative means to therapeutic ends.* New York: Norton.

Williams, L. (1994). Recall of childhood trauma: A prospective study of women's memories of childhood sexual abuse. *Journal of Consulting and Clinical Psychology, 62* (6), 1167–1176.

Wilson, J. (1951). The treatment of attitudinal pathosis by bibliotherapy: A case study. *Journal of Clinical Psychology, 7,* 345–351.

Wilson, J., & Lindy, J. (1995). Empathic strain and countertransference. In J. Wilson, & J. Lindy. *Countertransference in the treatment of PTSD.* New York: The Guilford Press.

Wilson, J. P. (1978). *Identity, ideology and crisis: The Vietnam veteran in transition* (2 vols.). Washington, DC: Disabled American Veterans.

Wolkind, S. N., & Rutter, M. (1973). Children who have been "in care": An epidemiological study. *Journal of Psychological Psychiatry, 14,* 97–105.

Wright, K. N., & Wright, K. E. (1995). *Family life, delinquency and crime: A policymaker's guide.* Washington, DC: Office of Juvenile Justice and Delinquency Prevention.

Yassen, J. (1995). Preventing secondary traumatic stress disorder. In C. R. Figley (Ed.), *Compassion fatigue: Coping with secondary traumatic stress disorder in those who treat the traumatized.* New York: Brunner/Mazel.

Zlotnick, C., Zariski, M., Shea, M. T., Costello, C., Begin, A., Pearlstein, T., & Simpson, E. (1996). Long-term sequelae of sexual abuse: Support for a complex posttraumatic stress disorder. *Journal of Traumatic Stress, 9* (2), 195–206.

Index

A

abuse, sexual, 1; effects of, 14–16; incest, 12; professional stress and, 238–240
abuse, substance, 4, 35–39
accidents, 12, 13, 16
acting out, adolescent, 26, 72
Acute Stress Disorder, 46, 48–49, 56–57
acute stress response, 84, 104
adolescents, and alcohol abuse, 35–39; and crises, 4, 27; and drug addiction, 38; and family mediation, 156–158; and maladaptive behaviors, 26–42, 77–78; and PTSD, 62, 72–73; at-risk, 33; and running away, 4, 30–32; and substance abuse, 35–39; and suicide, 27–29; and therapy, 152–158
adult trauma, effect on family, 183–184
Adults Molested as Children United, 298
"aging, advanced," 72, 74–75
alcohol abuse, adolescent, 35–39
alcoholic families, 24–25; roles in, 24
American Academy of Pediatrics, 295
American Association for Protecting Children, 296
American Bar Association, 296
American Humane Association, 296

American Medical Association, Health and Human Behavior Department, 296
American Psychological Association, 296
American Public Welfare Association, 296
anger, 16, 76–77; displaced, 72–73
anxiety, 15, 16; children's methods of limiting, 133; developmental, 74
art therapies, 113–114, 127, 142–146; and EMDR, 169–173
assertive communication, 215
assessment, of traumatized children, 124–127
attachment theory, 20
attachment, anxious, 69
attention deficit hyperactivity disorder (ADHD), 177–178
autonomous symptoms, 15

B

behavior, and PTSD, 61, 68–73; signs, for referral, 103; symptoms, trauma, 47, 48
behavioral therapies, 146–147
benzodiazepines, 150
bereavement (see also grief), models, 17, 19
beta adrenergic blockers, 150
bibliotherapy, 135–136

D

E

F

GROW: GROWTH AND RECOVERY OUTREACH WORKBOOKS
by Wendy Deaton, MFCC, with Kendall Johnson, Ph.D.

A creative, child-friendly program designed for use with elementary school children, filled with original exercises to foster healing, self-understanding, and optimal growth.

These popular workbooks are designed for those helping children who have experienced general or specific trauma. Each has friendly artwork and plenty of space in which to write and draw. With one-on-one support and feedback, the child works through the exercises in the book, which are balanced between writing and drawing, thinking and feeling. Exercises follow a therapeutic sequence: creating an alliance, debriefing trauma, exploring reactions, teaching coping strategies, integrating the experience.

Each workbook comes with a removable four-page guide containing explanations of each activity. The explanations are cross-referenced to *Trauma in the Lives of Children*.

WORKBOOKS FOR CHILDREN 9–12:

I Am a Survivor — for children who have survived a natural disaster such as a flood, tornado, hurricane, fire, or earthquake.

I Saw it Happen — for children who have witnessed a traumatic event such as a shooting at school, a frightening accident, or other violence.

No More Hurt — provides a safe place for children who have been physically or sexually abused to explore and share their feelings.

Living with My Family — helps children traumatized by domestic violence and family fights to identify and express their fears.

Someone I Love Died — for children who have lost a loved one and are dealing with grief, loss, and helplessness.

A Separation in My Family — for working with children whose parents are separating or have already separated or divorced.

Drinking and Drugs in My Family — for children who have family members who engage in regular alcohol or substance abuse.

WORKBOOKS FOR CHILDREN 6–10:

My Own Thoughts and Feelings (for Girls) or My Own Thoughts and Feelings (for Boys) — for exploring early symptoms of depression, low self-esteem, family conflict, and maladjustment.

My Own Thoughts and Feelings on Stopping the Hurt — helps communication with young children who may have suffered physical or sexual abuse.

All single workbooks: $9.95 ... 10-pack: $70.00

Workbook Library (one of each workbook–10 total) Special: $75.00

For bulk discounts and additional ordering information, please call Hunter House

To order or for our FREE catalog or call (800) 266-5592

MAKING THE PEACE: A 15-Session Violence Prevention Curriculum for Young People

by Paul Kivel and Allan Creighton, with the Oakland Men's Project

This is a highly respected violence prevention curriculum for youth group leaders and educators. The ready-to-use exercises, roleplays, and discussion guidelines show students how to explore the roots of violence in the community and their lives; deal with dating violence, fights, suicide, guns, and sexual harassment; and develop practical techniques for stopping violence. The Oakland Men's Project is a multicultural non-profit organization dedicated to violence prevention and to building alliances across lines of gender, race, sexual orientation, and age.

192 pages ... 15 b/w photos ... 35 reproducible handouts ... Paperback $24.95

DAYS OF RESPECT: Organizing a School-Wide Violence Prevention Program *by* Ralph Cantor, with Paul Kivel, Allan Creighton, and the Oakland Men's Project

A unique, collaborative program that empowers students to create a climate of respect and tolerance in their school. The Days of Respect program, developed by an experienced teacher and the Oakland Men's Project, speaks directly to young people's immediate need for participation and respect. It brings students, teachers, administrators, parents, and members of the community together to create a school-wide event on the theme of violence prevention.

64 pages ... 6 b/w photos ... 21 reproducible handouts ... Paperback $14.95

MAKING ALLIES, MAKING FRIENDS: A Curriculum for Making the Peace in Middle School

by Hugh Vasquez, M. Nell Myhand, Allan Creighton, and the Todos Institute ... *Coming OCTOBER 2002*

This new curriculum for students in grades 6 through 9 integrates with the Making the Peace program but also stands on its own. More than 30 innovative classroom sessions address diversity and violence issues that middle schoolers face, and can be adapted to many different school environments. Some of the themes are: *What respect is; Who am I / Who are my people?; Safety;* and more.

This timely and carefully crafted work will be a valuable resource for middle-school personnel and teachers of violence prevention, youth development, conflict resolution, social studies, art, and theater.

224 pages. ... 15 b/w photos ... 48 reproducible handouts ... Paperback $29.95

HELPING TEENS STOP VIOLENCE: A Practical Guide for Counselors, Educators, and Parents
by Allan Creighton with Paul Kivel

Today's teenagers live in a violent world. They can be subjected to violence at home, at school, and in society. For the past several years, the Oakland Men's Project (OMP) and Battered Women's Alternatives (BWA) have conducted seminars and workshops with teens and adults around the country, weaving issues of gender, race, age, and sexual orientation into frank discussions about male violence and its roots. This book by the founders of OMP and BWA provides guidelines on how to help teenagers help themselves out of the cycle of abuse and reduce the violence in the world around them.

168 pages ... 16 b&w photos ... Paperback $14.95 ... Spiral bound $17.95

I CAN MAKE MY WORLD A SAFFER PLACE: A Kid's Book about Stopping Violence *by* Paul Kivel • Illustrations and games by Nancy Gorrell

This book for kids ages 6–11 shows what children can do to find alternatives to violence in their lives. Kivel explains public danger (gangs, fights, and drug-related violence) and private danger (sexual assault and domestic violence) and gives suggestions for staying safe. Simple text and activities such as mazes and word searches encourage young readers to think about and promote peace. Activism is discussed, using examples such as Cesar Chavez and Julia Butterfly. The multicultural drawings by Nancy Gorrell are playful and engaging, guiding the reader, reinforcing the text, and making difficult ideas easier to understand.

96 pages ... 90 illus ... Paperback $11.95

SCHOOL CRISIS MANAGEMENT: A Hands-on Guide to Training Crisis Response Teams *by* Kendall Johnson, Ph.D. ... Revised Second Edition

This guide helps schools develop crisis contingency plans and train school crisis response teams, while providing detailed strategies and specific procedures for managing any emergency that may hit a school. More than 100 full-page charts clarify each area of discussion and may be reproduced as overheads or copied for training sessions.

The second edition includes a chapter to help administrators create systematic plans as well as sidebars by national experts discussing specific incidents and issues from the Columbine High School shooting to computer-based threat assessment programs.

248 pages ... 4 illus. ... 106 reproducible overhead masters
Paperback $24.95 ... Spiral bound $29.95

ORDER FORM

10% DISCOUNT on orders of $50 or more —
20% DISCOUNT on orders of $150 or more —
30% DISCOUNT on orders of $500 or more —
On cost of books for fully prepaid orders

NAME

ADDRESS

CITY/STATE   ZIP/POSTCODE

PHONE   COUNTRY (outside of U.S.)

TITLE	QTY	PRICE	TOTAL
Trauma in the Lives of Children (paper)		@ $ 19.95	
School Crisis Management (paper)		@ $ 24.95	

Prices subject to change without notice

Please list other titles below:

		@ $	
		@ $	
		@ $	
		@ $	
		@ $	
		@ $	
		@ $	

Check here to receive our book catalog ☐   *FREE*

Shipping Costs		
By Priority Mail: first book $4.50, each additional book $1.00	TOTAL	
	Less discount @____%	( )
By UPS and to Canada: first book $5.50, each additional book $1.50	TOTAL COST OF BOOKS	
	Calif. residents add sales tax	
For rush orders and other countries call us at (510) 865-5282	Shipping & handling	
	TOTAL ENCLOSED	
	Please pay in U.S. funds only	

☐ Check ☐ Money Order ☐ Visa ☐ MasterCard ☐ Discover

Card # _____ Exp. date _____

Signature _____

Complete and mail to:
Hunter House Inc., Publishers
PO Box 2914, Alameda CA 94501-0914
Website: www.hunterhouse.com
Orders: (800) 266-5592 or email: ordering@hunterhouse.com
Phone (510) 865-5282 Fax (510) 865-4295

TLC2-R3 9/2002